Howson's Choice

by

Simon Warr and Michael Gold

Howson's Choice

Published by Bronwyn Editions 2011

Photo's courtesy of Simon Warr and Michael Gold
www.howsonschoice.com

Website courtesy of
www.bartram.net

Printed by Lightning Source UK 2011

"Hobson's Choice"

This well-known phrase entered the language as a result of a 17th century horse trader by the name of Thomas Hobson, of Cambridge, England. If you wished to purchase one of his horses, you were taken to the stables and offered the one nearest the stable door. If you declined, then you were refused custom. In other words, you were given no choice at all.

The most celebrated application of Hobson's choice in the 20th century was Henry Ford's offer of the Model-T Ford in "any colour you like, so long as it's black".

Introduction

Howson's Choice was inspired by a real event, a scandal that made headline news during the 1990s. The headmaster of a famous public school was exposed for consorting with a call girl. He had purported to be the school gardener and had risked inviting the prostitute on to the school premises. However, she was not to be misled, recognising her host as, by a strange coincidence, the distinguished man who had been Guest of Honour at her convent school the previous year.

Unsurprisingly, the prostitute sought to profit from the discovery and the resulting exposure of this salacious tale of the 'beak and the tart' was one of those tabloid stories so beloved by the British public.

Although this scandal was the inspiration for the forthcoming pages, it is important to note that the characters and events portrayed within are completely fictional. The main public school at the heart of the tale bears no relationship whatsoever to any real school.

The events which take place in 'Howson's Choice' are rather more explosive than those which occurred in the original real life scenario.

Sir Oswald Mosley was a British aristocrat, who defected from the Labour Party and founded the British Union of Fascists in the 1930s. They were nicknamed the 'Blackshirts' because of the quasi-military uniform they wore. Mosley had strong personal links with Hitler and the Nazis and the Blackshirts had many violent clashes with the Jewish community in London.

Acknowledgements

The authors would like to thank Bernie Morris for her endless enthusiasm, editing and encouragement.
www.bronwynwrite.vpweb.co.uk

We would also like to thank the very many friends who have read the manuscript and offered helpful suggestions.

The Prologue
SINGING FROM A DIFFERENT HYMN SHEET
'You shall judge a man by his foes as well as by his friends.'
J. Conrad

The exodus from chapel at the prestigious public school, Cranford College, took on a ceremonial atmosphere after the annual Carol Service. Tradition dictated that the Headmaster was the first to leave, his wife following just behind. As usual on this occasion, the entire Board of Governors was present. The tall, bronzed and be-gowned Headmaster and his elegant wife were followed by the President, Sir Marcus Silver, Bishop of the diocese, David Montgomery, complete with mitre, in all his purple finery. Next in line was the Guest of Honour, Vice Chancellor of the University of Oxford, Professor John Forest, in academic robes, followed by the old Cranfordian Chair of Governors, bewigged and robed, Lord Justice of Appeal, Anthony Harris.

Various dignitaries followed, including Major General Chetwin-Jones in full military dress, more senior academics, the Chairman of a National Bank, and then the Head Boy; in their turn, the senior staff, followed by junior staff and then pupils, each group of whom was led out by their respective Head of House.

Today there was something unusual, something that was incompatible with the dignified procession. The low beat of rap music permeated from somewhere: a less sartorially elegant figure was also moving on the driveway, but this individual was walking in the opposite direction, towards the emerging procession. The figure was that of a tall, bearded, Afro-Caribbean, dressed in t-shirt and jeans. *He* was not moving in an orderly fashion but, iPod in hand, was ambling in the casual manner of a street person.

Seeing him, the Headmaster turned and gestured to his deputy, who was a few places behind in the procession. The cadaverous figure of Nathan Worsthorne overtook the intervening slow-

7

moving Governors and, when he reached the Head's side, the latter whispered something to him, nodding in the direction of the interloper. The Deputy headed towards him and, so he could not be heard by anyone other than the unwanted guest, he quietly suggested that he might be kind enough to accompany him towards the main gate. He was not expecting to be told to

'Fuck off, man!'

The formidable disciplinarian Worsthorne was described by colleagues as a one hundred yarder, the nomenclature deriving from his legendary ability to amend any pupil's behaviour within a hundred yard radius. The Worst (his nickname) was not accustomed to Anglo-Saxon dismissals. Indeed, any member of staff who was unfortunate enough to be on the receiving end of the Deputy's wrath would not be likely to forget the encounter until the full onset of Alzheimer's disease. The Worst's diatribes were invariably punctuated by a well chosen Latin phrase, delivered like a judgement of doom. If he wanted to be really frightening, he would quote Ancient Greek. This sent shivers down the spine of the targeted pupil, being a signal that the matter was being taken very seriously indeed. Worsthorne, who had a Double First in Ancient History, was highly respected for his acerbic, witty and brilliant lessons, even though the faint smell of whisky could often be detected on his breath. In fact, no one could recall whether Worsthorne had actually ever punished a pupil. His friends knew that the brilliant classicist and historian was, in fact, an extremely kind man, well disposed towards his pupils, who tended to become his life-long friends. He was known to be an atheist and somewhat to the left of Lenin and the only occasions he attended Chapel were on Speech Day and at the Carol Service; nevertheless, he was the nearest thing Cranford had to represent the wrath of God! He had spent many fruitless years trying to have his views published, under a nom-de-plume, on what he believed to be the fraudulent nature of the origin of Christianity.

The Headmaster did not hear the impolite response endured by his deputy, but beads of sweat appeared on his forehead as he realised that something unpleasant, something possibly dangerous and, at the very least, extremely embarrassing was about to happen. It was imperative that he appear unfazed by the situation: he had no choice, he had to brazen things out. The intruder, muscular arms heavily tattooed, face pock-marked and ravaged, continued to approach. The Deputy persisted with his remonstrations: but these were ignored. The Major General stepped forward in front of the Head, gripping the handle of his ceremonial sword and barked at the approaching figure, requesting him to halt in his tracks. The Afro-Caribbean was sufficiently awestruck by the approaching group of representatives of the British establishment that he restrained himself from the utterance of any further street expletives. Maybe he fleetingly imagined that with the Army, the Judiciary and the Church, all well represented, that this might well be an occasion to exercise restraint, something which was alien to his usual mode of behaviour. However, he was not to be deterred from his simple purpose: he sidestepped the now apoplectic Major General, whispered something in the Headmaster's ear, and then ran off back down the front drive. The Head faltered momentarily. Few could see his face but it briefly turned, as that musical combo, *Procol Harum*, would have described it, a whiter shade of pale. Within seconds, his Deputy was back at his side, his wife quietly asking him for an explanation of the incident: his unconvincing rejoinder was, 'Oh... nothing'.

The procession continued but with a quiet undercurrent of shocked whispering.

The British upper middle classes are quite secure and confident in the sacrosanct nature of their rituals: they do not expect to be disturbed in their displays of self-confident grandeur. The Head quickly recovered his composure and, whenever various concerned parties made mention of the incident, he responded by saying that

he didn't hear what had been whispered to him and he was as bemused by the odd encounter as everyone else. There was much speculation, some of it humorous, including the suggestion that the intruder was in fact a newly appointed governor, designed to meet ethnic minority representational criteria. Another suggested that the interloper was a candidate for the post of Assistant Director of Music, who had mistaken the time of his interview.
There were others who suggested that the visitor had simply been delivering the Head's daily supply of cocaine.

In fact, the major response to the incident provided a field day for all the wags and wits in the community. The reaction of the Head to the incident was devoid of any such levity: he had, in fact, heard exactly what had been said, and there was certainly no laughter in *his* eyes.

Chapter One
TOO GOOD TO BE TRUE
'The pursuit of perfection is always linked to some important deficiency.'
B. Grasset

Things are rarely exactly as they seem. Is there one perfect human being on this planet? There are a few, maybe, who are ostensibly so. They are particularly clever, remarkably fine-looking, naturally entertaining, extremely quick-witted or maybe outstandingly accomplished musicians or athletes. Many go on to earn vast quantities, marry partners of equivalent charm and beauty and, of course, spawn seemingly perfect offspring. Such characters often find their way into the educational world and there are few environments capable of welcoming and utilising such talent better than the classical English Public School. Of course, such a career does not generally lead to great wealth, but it can provide immense social status and personal power. But such communities are like pressure cookers: peace, tranquillity and sunshine await in July and August but the intensity of life in the heat of a boarding school can sometimes stretch the seemingly immaculate individual to such an extent that cracks appear, sometimes a conduit to unfortunate consequences.

Joseph Howson seemed to possess all the above attributes: he appeared to have been born with a spoon of the highest quality silver firmly embedded in his mouth. It was quickly apparent to those around him that he had been furnished with a particularly keen intellect. He also possessed medium-pace swing bowling skills, the likes of which his prep school masters had never seen during their plethora of years at St John's. He was not only a remarkable young cricketer but the grace with which he propelled a javelin was a joy to behold in itself. He cut an impressive figure around the school with his rangy gait, his shock of blond hair and a tan more typical of the Mediterranean than Maidstone, where his adoptive family raised him. He never said a word out of place and not only effortlessly avoided the prep school minefield of detentions and other petty sanctions but never even attracted a mild reprimand from any of the stentorian martinets who populated the Victorian buildings and green fields of St John's. Indeed, in his final year, he was the unanimous choice for Head Boy and some thought that, at the age of thirteen, he exercised a level of skill in the administration of good order and discipline which ought to have been the envy of one or two members of staff. The more discerning might have detected an unusual streak of quiet ruthlessness in his determination to ensure that his will prevailed.

It came as no surprise to anyone when the Common Entrance Examination and various competitions led to an award of the top scholarship to one of the great English Public Schools. Highdown Abbey had been founded by a medieval monk. Situated in the Hardy area of Wessex, motto "Deum Servare" (to serve the Lord), the school was set in 500 acres: the focus of the school was its impressive central building, restored and extended from the original Abbey. Joseph was allocated to the oldest boarding house, situated within this main building, known as Abbey House, reserved primarily for scholars. The Housemaster was by tradition the Headmaster, who was still entitled the Abbot, after long-standing tradition. The school had long since abandoned its strict Roman Catholic origins, which was, perhaps, why Henry VIII spared dissolving this particular institution. Nevertheless, it certainly practised a high church version of Anglicanism, which bordered on the Roman Catholic. In practice the House was run by a Deputy, as the Headmaster of a modern public school is laden with too many responsibilities to deal with the daily and nightly detritus generated by energetic and occasionally wayward young men.

* * *

Joseph continued to develop along expected lines. He was as respected and as popular as any of the roguish jack-the-lads, mainly because of his intellectual and sporting prowess and his general clubability, so important when living among peers in a boarding school. However, he was never to be found at the end of the orchard, enjoying a furtive cigarette, in the disused Abbey Tower, which had traditionally also been used for illicit drinking parties. On one occasion an overzealous Deputy had organised a raid, discovering many of his prefects and senior pupils engaged in the consumption of rather lethal mixtures of cider and vodka. He also discovered a very fat book, which had the names, dates and signatures of miscreants stretching back over many decades. When parents were summoned to the school to collect their errant offspring for a weekend's rustication in disgrace, there was a certain amount of embarrassment, as many of the distinguished and wealthy alumni who had arrived to collect their offspring had also been signatories to the book during their own time at the Abbey. However, it will not surprise the reader to learn that the signature of one Joseph Howson was absent from this particular tome!

During the term before Joseph's final year, the Abbot held the traditional staff meeting to discuss the appointment of Head Boy. The meeting was unusually brief as the proposed choice was unanimously unopposed, although the Head of Classical Studies, a deep and thoughtful man, with a Double First from Cambridge, did remark that Howson was too good to be true. However, this could hardly disqualify him, although it was a legend which would be ascribed to Howson later in his life.

Following the inevitable array of A-level distinctions, Joseph was awarded the top scholarship to read History at Trinity College, Oxford. He didn't take it up immediately but applied to do a year's voluntary work in Ethiopia, where he taught English in an impoverished village and earned himself the first mark of excellence at work from his highly impressed employers.

At Trinity he was very popular and his mid-week soirées became the talk of the town, his modest rooms hosting the most intelligent men of his year and the most beautiful women, many of whom rivalled the men in intellectual acumen. It was indeed at one of these Oxford social high points that he met a slender brunette of remarkable beauty and femininity, by the name of Marie-Christine Hervé, herself an Oxford student, at St Hilda's, situated a couple of hundred metres down the road from Trinity. She was the daughter of one of the Directors of the French rail network, SNCF. This French 'princess', brought up in a *Château* in the Loire Valley, was studying for a diploma in education. There were many at those gatherings who were so over-awed by her aristocratic, demure beauty that the normally confident and voluble became tongue-tied and self-conscious when introduced to her. However, Joseph, with his fluent French and grand charm, was in no way intimidated and, indeed, swept the girl off her proverbial feet.

Their courtship was brief. When Joseph Howson set his mind on something or on someone, he would home in like an eagle: champagne and strawberries on Magdalen lawn, punting down the Isis, languid romantic dinners at Oxford's finest restaurants, symphony concerts at the Sheldonian, theatre trips, and picnics by the river; all were the catalytic backdrops to the romance. Howson's technique did not include clumsy, premature attempts at physical seduction: indeed, other than placing a masterful arm around the girl's shoulder and a respectful French kiss on each cheek, at the end of a date, Howson refrained from intimate contact until Marie's expression one day in a motorboat made it clear that she was more than ready for something a little more passionate. The resulting clinch unleashed a mutual demonstration of such intensity that vows of eternal betrothal followed immediately. Marie's strict Catholic upbringing was such that it would have been unthinkable for her to engage in explicitly sexual activity before marriage and Howson was far too sophisticated even to hint at such unseemly conduct. That is not to say that Howson himself was without experience in such matters: there were many willing blue-stockings, who had frequented his Oxford parties. To describe his predilection for the pleasures of the flesh as a fault would be a trifle unfair. He had never needed to initiate these encounters and he was, after all, a very fit and healthy young man and he certainly never made promises he had no intention of keeping: he could never have been accused of dishonourable conduct. Suffice to say, the non-smoking, light-social-drinking young man, with no apparent vices, was certainly willing to avail himself of the irresistible pleasures which were thrust at him on that particular afternoon on the Isis.

The hot passion unleashed under the July sunshine led to the inevitable outcome of immediate marriage plans. Indeed, Marie-Christine's parents had to interrupt a Mediterranean cruise, flying back from Bodrum, in Turkey, barely half way through their voyage, for the wedding. Joseph and his virgin bride were married in the Trinity Chapel and a number of high-ranking individuals attended, including the Master, who had taken a keen interest in his young protégé. Even the Abbot of Highdown was present. At the celebration in the Fellows' garden, many remarked that they had never attended a wedding of two such beautiful and brilliant young people and both sets of parents glowed with pride and pleasure as the warm congratulations flowed along with the vintage Krug champagne, ordered for the occasion by Monsieur Hervé.

Chapter Two
BRAVE NEW SCHOOL

'Gladstone founded the great tradition, in public to speak the language of the highest and strictest principle, and in private to pursue and possess every sort of woman.'

Peter Wright

No one was surprised when Oxford University awarded Joseph Howson a First Class degree *summa cum laude*. Joseph's tutors encouraged him to reside for an extra three years to work on a thesis; he completed a brilliant study into Gladstone's lifelong obsession with ladies of the night. Many predicted that Gladstone, when he was a young man, would become Archbishop of Canterbury and that his contemporary, Manning, would end up as Prime Minister. In a sense these predictions were correct, except that the ultimate roles were reversed. Nevertheless, Gladstone was a deeply religious man, with many missions in life. Like many subsequent national leaders, he was obsessed with solving the Irish problem. However, he also had a personal mission to rescue fallen women. There has always been much speculation as to whether his fascination for the company of ladies of the night was fuelled by something other than moral or religious fervour.

Working diligently to complete his thesis, Joseph did not merely study the routine historical records in the libraries, he also sought out the company of London prostitutes, searching for one or two who may have been descendants of those who had known Gladstone. There was certainly some street folklore to be found. He failed to provide a definitive solution to the most interesting question but certainly unearthed some circumstantial evidence which supported the view that Gladstone's interests went well beyond the detached and the academic. Joseph was awarded his D.Phil. after only two years. Life is full of strange coincidences and, as our tale unfolds, the reader may perceive some irony, in the light of much later events.

In the meantime Marie-Christine had managed to secure a teaching post at a local public school, St Edwin's, where she was admired for the attractiveness of both her accent and her shapely legs.

It was 1985 and Dr Joseph Howson had the world at his feet. His adoptive father Michael, who ran The Mitre pub, deep in the heart of the Kent countryside, with his wife Margaret, encouraged his son to enter the world of politics, an area in which Joseph had displayed a keen interest. He had been an active figure in many of the great Oxford Union debates, being largely responsible for persuading his audience to support a motion condemning Margaret Thatcher for her conduct of the Falklands War. He drew brilliantly on many historical facts to illustrate his theme that the conduct of the Argentineans, while certainly unlawful, did not constitute an adequate *casus belli*. Some felt that he was over-apologetic for Galtieri's fascist junta but others admired him for his courage in presenting an unpopular view. He had also written many controversial and erudite articles for the student magazine 'Isis', which he had also edited for a year during his D.Phil. studies. Despite uninterrupted success in the safe, cloistered environment to which he had become accustomed and in which he had found much personal fulfilment, Joseph Howson's mind soon began turning to the next challenge and it was only natural that the former Head Boy of a preparatory school, having made it as Head Boy of a major public school, would ultimately aspire to the highest of all boarding school offices, Headmaster. For now he was looking forward to securing his first teaching post, but even at the genesis of his career a voice inside was telling him that he would one day have his hands on the ultimate prize.

After lengthy discussions with Marie-Christine, they decided to seek a double appointment at the same boarding school, perhaps as a housemaster and wife team, one or both of them teaching in the classroom. As luck would have it (Joseph enjoyed more than his fair share), St Catherine's School, in Tricester, Oxfordshire, had advertised for a young, energetic, well-qualified couple to run their day house. St Catherine's, which was a respectable but minor girls' academic public school, was bowled over by the impressive pair and felt that the tall, handsome, sporting young Oxford D.Phil. and his beautiful, aristocratic, French wife would make an excellent impression on parents, while inspiring the pupils towards high achievement and good behaviour. Both written and telephone references were strongly supportive and the Abbot of Highdown informed the Headmistress of St Catherine's that Joseph was a real catch and that she would be well advised to make an immediate appointment.

So, in September 1986, the Howsons made their way the short distance down the A40 to take up their posts at St Catherine's, a small GMIS of some 250 bright teenage girls. Marie-Christine proved to be an excellent classroom teacher and role model and, although she was much impersonated for the extravagant use of her arms and her wonderful French accent, the pupils adored her. For his part, Joseph taught History with great inspiration, insight and wit. He would bring the great characters of history alive and would always have a fund of anecdotes about the lesser-known personal eccentricities of many of the major players on the historical stage. Certainly, older pupils would not be spared details of the sexual peccadilloes of the great and famous. His classroom audiences were particularly fascinated by his insights into the mind of Gladstone and a favourite party-piece would be his production of a recording of Gladstone's awesome voice, which Howson had gone to a lot of trouble to obtain.

19

As a housemaster, Howson had an effective way of dealing with some of the more temperamental teenage girls, with a blend of firmness, charm and empathy, which was unusual within the teaching profession. Inevitably, Marie-Christine had rather a lot of competition from some of the older pupils for the attention of her husband. Indeed, there was more than one love-struck sixth former with a crush on Joseph, but the immaculate professional never gave the slightest sign that he could be seduced by any of the beautiful young nymphettes, whose imagination he had aroused. School dances were a particularly fertile ground for pupil attempts at close physical contact but, although Joseph would freely dance with his pupils, he never allowed anything more than hand-contact and never permitted himself to dance more than once with any particular pupil, at no time discriminating between the sylph-like beauties and the bespectacled plump and plain.

After three years the Howsons were offered a significant promotion. The headmistress had been forced to remove the housemistress and housemaster of the sixth form boarding house, amidst whispers about a liaison between the housemaster and one of the pupils. Suffice to say that morale was low and there was an urgent need to restore confidence, both amongst pupils and parents. Joseph and Marie-Christine came to the rescue with their customary verve and enthusiasm. Within a matter of weeks, the incident had been largely forgotten and School House was restored to a happy buzz of purposeful activity and achievement. The pupils put on an impressive production of Wilde's *The Importance of Being Earnest* to great acclaim. Joseph's production and directorial skills and Marie's talents of advising on line-delivery and of costume design ensured a pièce de thèâtre of the highest quality.

After some four years in this post, it was a considerable disappointment, but no surprise, to the headmistress that Joseph was appointed as a housemaster at the prestigious Wellingborough College (at the tender age of thirty-two). This career advance was remarkable on two counts: the first was that Wellingborough had never before appointed a housemaster who was not home-grown, as it were; the school's governing body's standing orders required all such posts to be advertised, which led to a charade of interviews of unsuspecting applicants, but, invariably, the post had already been earmarked for a favoured colleague within the Wellingborough common room. Secondly, thirty-two was a particularly tender age for someone to secure a housemastership in an HMC school. The fact was that the High Master (as he was titled at Wellingborough) was so impressed by the CV of the young Howson, not to mention the opportunity of acquiring the services of Marie-Christine, that he apologised to the internal hopeful and strongly hinted that he would, in all probability, be offered the next vacancy. The Headmistress of St Catherine's wrote a superlative reference, which reflected on Howson's charisma and natural classroom technique and his refusal to allow any pupils to fall short of the required standard. His record of professionalism and success in the pastoral care of the pupils was also highlighted. Here was a man who contributed on the sports field, directed plays and played a vigorous part in most areas of school life. There was also mention of Marie-Christine and how she was adored by pupils, parents and colleagues. Both were also commended for their unflagging loyalty and their consistent willingness to take on any responsibility or task requested of them. The Headmistress said that she wrote with a heavy heart because she did not want to lose the Howsons but recognised that it would be wrong of her to stand in the way of their advancement. Marie-Christine was offered a full salary for acting as house matron, with a part-time teaching timetable. Their careers were well and truly underway.

Running a house, as those who work in a boarding school refer to it, is one of the most challenging responsibilities of a boarding school teacher's career. Some even say that the day-to-day pressure of such a role can match, or even exceed, that endured by a Head. You may think you have finally put fifty or so pupils to bed by 11 p.m., only to discover there is often life after death, and it is the housemaster who is often up until the early hours 'fire-fighting', while the Head enjoys a full night's sleep and only has to pick up the pieces the following morning. The housemaster is not merely *in loco parentis* but carries heavy administrative responsibilities, including the oversight of every child's academic progress. All classroom escapades and dilatory work efforts tend to be laid at the overburdened housemaster's door. Dealing with poor behaviour outside the classroom (most houses will often have three or four pupils who, between them, take up more time and energy than the rest put together) is usually the sole responsibility of the housemaster. He must sit with his charges at the chapel service on Sundays; he would be expected to be on the rugby field touchline, cheering on his house team whenever it played. A conscientious housemaster would make up the usual audience of about four staff members listening to a lunchtime recital of a grade two violin examination piece (in such circumstance being tone deaf can be a positive advantage). In short, the role is that of a parent – and more – to over four dozen teenagers. For all this, the housemaster is fortunate to have a reduced teaching timetable, maybe twenty-six forty minute periods per week, instead of the usual thirty-four, nothing like sufficient compensation for the additional workload. Housemasters at Wellingborough would normally have two or three assistants but their role was mainly confined to providing the housemaster with a couple of evenings off each week. There was not normally any significant delegation, as housemasters preferred to keep personal control of their charges and indeed they were expected so to do.

Howson matched the challenge with the energy, enthusiasm and determination, which had been part of his make-up since his prep school days. His best work in the house (and in the class) was with the recalcitrant and those with learning difficulties. He also found time to act as a cricket coach to Wellingborough's second eleven and as specialist bowling adviser to the firsts. It was generally agreed that Howson's contribution to school bowling (he spent many hours with them at both the indoor and outdoor nets) was largely responsible for Wellingborough's triumph in all inter-school matches during his very first year. Although Wellingborough was a renowned school, such was the economy and attitude of the country in the early nineties, that fewer and fewer parents were sending their offspring away to school, so these establishments were obliged to be less and less selective. Howson's attitude was that any teacher can deal with bright, motivated pupils but it is the slower, the less robust and the unmotivated who provide the real challenge, a challenge he relished from the moment he started his career.

Under Howson's predecessor, James Evans, Hawke House had been in gradual decline, as the final years of his tenure had been dominated by his failing marriage and his mind was, inevitably, elsewhere. Standards in the boarding house had gradually slipped and by the time Howson arrived, things had become ragged and most worrying was the presence of quite a serious bullying problem. However, with Howson ensconced, things went from strength to strength within a very short space of time. In fact, so remarkable was the turnaround, that at the end of his first year, Hawke House won the much sought-after Queen's Banner, awarded to the top house (of eleven) for the most success in work, sport, music, drama, behaviour and smartness of appearance. Indeed, it was the first time the house had won the award since 1942, when it was presided over by a legendary master, the eponymous Harry Hawke, who was killed, unfortunately, by a direct hit from a WW2 bomb before fighting had ceased.

So, at the very tender age of thirty-three, Howson had already made a name for himself in one of the country's top public schools.

During his third year in Hawke, Howson wrote a thesis entitled "A critical analysis of boarding education with particular reference to the provision of pastoral care", a work which became the definitive document used by the Boarding Schools' Association and other such esteemed educational bodies.

During Howson's fourth year, he sought a bigger challenge: a minor public school in Lancashire, St James's, was in serious economic trouble. Numbers had fallen from a healthy 400 to a worrying 250. The local bank was still owed a hefty £1,000,000 for a loan towards the building of a new Art Block and was threatening to pull the proverbial fiscal plug. A rather aloof, ageing Head had been left in post for far too long. Discipline among the pupils (and staff!) had declined markedly and the governors were desperate. Wellingborough's Head, Dr James Wilson, had rung his friend, Cambridge contemporary Jeremy March, Chairman of Governors at St James's, and had strongly recommended the *young Turk*, Howson. So it was that Dr and Mrs Howson assumed their first Headship in the leafy, undulating environs of the Ribble Valley in September 1997.

It was without doubt the biggest challenge hitherto for Howson; he realised, early during his tenure, that the average age of the staff was far too high (forty-nine to be precise), so he set about an immediate cull of teachers, whom the Chairman of Governors described as "past their sell-by date". What was surprising to those around him was Howson's extraordinary ability to end a teacher's career without apparent disquiet. One such unfortunate was Mr Anthony Jefferson, who had spent his entire teaching career, spanning forty-one years, at St James'; what he lacked in organisational skills and sartorial taste (he never had a wife to advise him), he more than made up for in his enthusiasm and dedication to the pupils in his care. Colleagues would often tell him that the expertise he showed in running the Model Railway club seemed to suggest that he would make a much better job of running the national rail network than the present incumbents. Howson had him pensioned off by the end of his first term. It was only on account of Marie-Christine's firm insistence that her husband instructed the school catering staff to provide a leaving buffet for poor old Jefferson. Joseph Howson was not one for dwelling on the past; indeed in his mind, the bumbling egg-head was part of the reason why St James' was in its present parlous state. Jefferson was a teacher who had been content to hide in the school, away from the demands of the real world – household bills, mortgages, travel costs, rising crime, the burden of having to cook for oneself and launder one's own clothes. There was no place for these rather pathetic, ageing bachelor-types in the Brave New School, run by the efficient Dr Joseph Howson.

As well as stringent staff cuts and the elongation of working hours for those remaining, Howson announced what to the staff was the unthinkable. As from the following September, girls would be introduced into the school in every year group. As he made his announcement in a staff meeting during January of his first year, Richard Harris-Letwin (teacher of Geography and under-fourteen tennis coach) let out an involuntary gasp, stood up and exited the Common Room in high dudgeon. He was subsequently told by Howson that, as he was evidently opposed to the co-education initiative, he was best advised to seek alternative employment with immediate effect. Harris-Letwin was the eighth teacher to leave during Howson's first year, out of an original full-time academic staff of only thirty. Common Room spirits were low but pupil numbers, under the super-salesmanship of Joseph Howson, manifested a resurgence. Within three years, the good Doctor presided over a school with a much more efficient structure, improved examination results and a staff of sycophants, very wary of offering any criticism at all. Half the bank loan had been repaid and Howson had already employed a PR firm to raise much needed funds from the local community, parents and past pupils, confidently stating that the remaining outstanding loan would be repaid within the year and that no further advances were likely to be needed.

Dr Howson was certainly in control.

Chapter Three
LA CRÈME DE LA CRÈME

'Our errors are not such awfully solemn things: a certain
lightness of heart seems healthier than an excessive
nervousness on their behalf.'
W. James

Since 1886, the famous public school, Cranford College, had spawned a number of pupils who had gone on to fame and fortune – esteemed politicians, high court judges, television executives, film stars, musicians, sportsmen, military commanders or captains of industry, to mention just some examples. Most of the staff were Oxbridge educated and a number had authored major textbooks in their chosen speciality. Traditionally the school employed Olympic and national sports professionals, an artist in residence, a concert pianist in residence, even visiting chess and bridge experts. The school did not merely boast impressive academic results, but provided an environment in which almost any talent could bloom: leadership via the Combined Cadet Force, an active theatrical society and an outstanding school choir, rarely rivalled outside the specialist music schools. The school's debating society was modelled on the Oxford Union and many a public speaker first learned his craft at Cranford. Entry at Cranford was based upon its own entrance examination process. There were a large number of scholarships available and outstanding candidates could obtain up to 100% of funding, subject to means testing. The result was that Cranford's intake was highly impressive.

After fifteen years, Sir Gordon Chadwick was retiring as Headmaster and, as is usual in top public schools when replacements are being considered, particularly successful heads of smaller schools are approached, before the crème de la crème is finally selected. Joseph Howson's reputation was well known and was certainly considered high quality 'crème'. Nevertheless, the young Head was certainly surprised when he received a telephone call from a well known firm of educational agents. The call was brief and to the point. He was given the news of the impending retirement of Chadwick and then was asked if he would be interested in being considered for the forthcoming vacancy. Howson's response was that, although he was very happy at St James', he was always ready to consider a fresh challenge.

Howson was even more intrigued when, later the same day, he received another call. With his fortieth birthday imminent, Joseph Howson was invited to London to dine at the home of the Rt. Hon. Sir Marcus Silver, the Honorary President of Cranford College. Cranford was an unusual foundation: the school was governed by a Board, which elected its own Chairman. However, the Governors traditionally invited a public figure as the college's President. This had often been a member of the Royal Family. The President was more of a figurehead and non-executive: he could attend Governors' meetings but without a vote. However, the present incumbent was particularly influential on account of his respected educational expertise.

Howson drove his S class Mercedes nervously into Princes Gate Mews, in the salubrious South Kensington area of London, and parked in front of Silver's three-storied residence.

'Thank you for coming,' was Silver's introductory remark, as Joseph Howson entered a spacious hall.

'It is good to meet you, Sir Marcus, I have heard so much about you.'

Indeed, anyone of any standing in the educational world knew who Sir Marcus Silver was – a retired Headmaster himself, he was now Chief Education Advisor to the Home Office and sat on the management board of the Times Educational Supplement. He played polo with Mark Phillips, estranged husband of Princess Anne, and regularly featured in the Nigel Dempster, latterly

Richard Kay, column in the Daily Mail. He was a large man, with a personality to match his size. He was renowned for his wit and eloquence and was one of the most popular after-dinner speakers on the London circuit. His wife, Rosemary, a former debutante and one of the most beautiful women of her generation, led an unusually nervous and humbled Howson into an elegantly furnished lounge.

'May I get you a drink?' she asked with exquisite charm.

'Gin and tonic, thank you.'

'I'm afraid it is rather too chilly to sit on the terrace, quite an autumnal feel to the air,' she added.

'Quite,' interrupted Sir Marcus, 'Did you know that young rookie, Flintoff, hit another century today? He has so much strength, such courage, he never knows when he's beaten; sort of qualities we're looking for in the new man at Cranford when Gordon leaves next year. Having spoken to a number of interested parties, it seems that your name ranks high on their lists.'

Sir Marcus always came speedily to the point, on this particular occasion even before his dutiful wife had time to return with the pre-prandials.

Joseph was well aware of the reason why he had been invited, without Marie-Christine, chez Silver – he was being given the proverbial once-over by Sir Marcus, prior to the forthcoming interviews, which would probably take place before the end of the calendar year.

'I am flattered to be considered, Sir Marcus.'

'Of course, some consider you to be too young – we've never appointed anyone so young and I, for one, am certainly unsure about a candidate barely a quadragenarian.'

'If you're good enough, you're old enough,' Joseph quickly retorted.

'The question is – are you good enough?' snapped Sir Marcus.

'If I were afforded this opportunity, Sir Marcus, I should devote my immediate life to ensuring the present high standards at

Cranford were maintained and, indeed, improved upon, where possible.'

'You wouldn't find it easy; there are a lot of chaps who've been at Cranford for decades. They know the place inside out and they won't take kindly to being led by someone young enough, in a number of cases, to be their son. We're languishing in seventeenth place at present in the league tables of academic success,' barked Sir Marcus. 'We feel that Chadwick has taken his eye off the ball, lately. I daresay his thoughts have begun to wander towards the villa he has recently purchased in the south of France; La Collobrière is the name of the village, I seem to recall.'

'Anyway,' continued Sir Marcus, as his elegant wife handed him a schooner of dry pale sherry, 'we want someone who will rekindle the school's fortunes and place it back at the top of the academic tree, where it belongs in the shortest time possible. Have you the ability to lead our efforts?'

'I feel my record speaks for itself. My whole life has been devoted to the pursuit of personal excellence; I am committed to promoting the same on every front around me. I believe that I can inspire men and women, as well as children; my time at St James' has proven this. I can engender confidence within the parent body. My wife, Marie-Christine, has excellent complementary strengths. Although I may have to encourage some early retirements and recruit some outstanding younger staff, I feel my own academic credentials will command the respect of the best Oxford and Cambridge graduates. I also have the business expertise to launch successful appeals for financing improved facilities, wherever needed. I will take Cranford into the 21st Century as a beacon of outstanding educational excellence: as well as the academic, sport, music, art, drama, indeed, any area which enriches the lives of the pupils, will not be neglected. I will need time to put Cranford into the lead again, of course. However long it may take, I will do all in my power to give you what you want, providing I am afforded unqualified support.'

Sir Marcus was temporarily taken aback by Howson's confidence and evident single-mindedness.

'I am impressed by your self-assurance but it is easier said than done. We are not talking about some minor boarding school here, cosseted in the leafy lanes of Lancashire. This is the big time; the Headmaster of Cranford is known nationally, will have his opinions quoted in both the broadsheets and the tabloids, will be invited to comment on national TV and radio on the latest educational initiatives – and I can tell you there is a plethora of these each year – his private life may well be intruded upon. He will be under constant day-to-day pressure in and outside school. There'll be no going home early to see the family each evening – you have, I know, devoted yourself to the schools at which you have worked, but even as a Head at St James', you had something of a holiday to recharge your batteries; at Cranford, particularly in the early years, the pressure will be unrelenting. It is my duty to ensure that the man we choose is not going to suffer a nervous breakdown or do something imprudent – I do not need to spell out that to which I refer.'

'Dinner is served,' announced Mrs Silver, as Sir Marcus fixed Howson with a penetrating glare.

In many ways, Joseph Howson was relieved that the lady of the house was to be present at dinner: this was not only because Rosemary Silver possessed intellectual acumen of the highest order, nor was it only because Rosemary, although in her fifties, was still an exceptionally beautiful woman (almost certainly assisted by the ubiquitous Botox), Howson's relief was mostly due to the likely relaxation of the Gestapo–like interrogation at the hands of her husband.

Dinner turned out to be a feast: Sir Marcus showed quite a Fallstaffian side with the enthusiasm in which he attacked a starter of fried *foie gras d'oie* with peaches, followed by a second starter of a terrine of salmon and prawns. The main course was *maigret de canard* with sauté potatoes and lightly cooked *haricots verts*. A fine Bordeaux wine was selected to complement the savoury courses. However, Rosemary really came into her own when she produced a selection of desserts, which included an exquisite *crème brûlée*, a raspberry pavlova, a lemon mousse and a chocolate gâteau. A bottle of fine Muscat was produced to accompany this course. Last, but by no means least, came a selection of fine cheeses, washed down by a generous supply of calvados.

Many topics were touched upon, but fortunately very little appertained directly to the Headmastership of Cranford. Silver deliberately wanted to change tack and put Howson at his ease. He felt that far more would be revealed about the nature of the man under consideration by touching on a variety of topics. Obviously, Howson was very capable of providing impressive responses to direct questions. He demonstrated an array of personal qualities: wit, charm and culture flowed with apparently effortless ease and Sir Marcus had no doubt that Joseph Howson would be a great hit with the parent body.

Rosemary Silver took a particular interest in Marie-Christine's upbringing in Tours, a picturesque town in the 'Jardin de la France'.

'We, too, adore sojourns in the Loire Valley,' she purred, 'we normally reside in Poitiers; such beautiful countryside. Do you speak French, Dr Howson?'

'Couramment,' came the reply, 'bien entendu j'ai beaucoup d'occasions de le pratiquer, étant donné que ma femme est française.'

With that, the two pursued a lengthy conversation in French, discussing such matters as the French Government's reluctance to participate in hostilities in Iraq, and 'la loi BB', a French law which forbids journalists from publishing matters appertaining to an individual's private life, a ruling which both Howson and Mrs Silver fully supported.

As the final cut of Stilton was digested, Sir Marcus and Howson repaired to a lounge, which the latter thought would not be out of place at the Ideal Home Exhibition. Sir Marcus did not give any indication to Howson that the head-hunting agency employed by Cranford had placed Joseph Howson comfortably at the top of the list. There were not too many successful headmasters with Howson's academic standing and, although he had not published anything other than the odd article since his university days, it was well known that, had he chosen that particular academic direction, he would have been an outstanding historian. The Governors were seeking a man who not merely had an exceptional record as a Headmaster, but also someone with serious academic credibility. It was the agency which had advised Cranford to relax their age requirements.

As Howson took a seat on one of a brace of buffalo-hide sofas, Sir Marcus leant against a mantelpiece of Regency elegance, lit some St Bruno flake, sipped his *digestif* and threw at Howson the comment, 'I feel your appointment to the Headmastership at Cranford would be a risk.'

Joseph lowered his eyes; he had attended many interviews in his life, formal and informal, both as a student and also during his professional life. In none had he experienced such a feeling of insecurity. He found Sir Marcus inscrutable – what *did* he think about this 'colt', purporting to be a potential Cranford Head Man? Was Howson deluding himself? Had he himself confirmed what Sir Marcus thought prior to his arrival this evening? Ought he to have shaved his healthy locks, artificially flecked his blond hair with grey, grown a moustache, all in an effort to look more mature?

'Maybe a risk in your eyes, Sir Marcus, but I have spent many hours researching Cranford during the past few days and I could not be more confident of the fact that I know what it is looking for in terms of energy and enthusiasm. I feel also that I have the proven expertise, after three years of a successful Headship under my belt, and have the required academic weight. I would certainly strive day and night to fulfil my obligation to restore Cranford's reputation as England's premier public school.'

Mrs Silver slipped into the room as unobtrusively as possible, but the air was so tense that both men's attention was immediately distracted.

'Coffee, gentlemen?'

She exited almost as soon as she had deposited the tray. There was a pause as both men sipped their rich Columbian coffee. Sir Marcus broke the silence.

'Of course you appreciate that the question of your appointment is not actually my decision. All I am to do now is report my impressions to the Governing Body.'

Both finished their coffee as they moved on to lighter matters, such as the state of the youth of Britain, with their propensity towards binge drinking and their ever-increasing use of soft drugs. Eventually Sir Marcus put his hands behind his head and leant back in his armchair and Howson took this to mean it was time to depart.

'Thank you for coming this evening, Joseph. It was interesting to meet you. I hope I may see you again but, either way, I wish you the best of luck.'

Sir Marcus gave Joseph a very strong handshake, which the latter did his best to match.

After thanking Rosemary Silver for the excellent hospitality and, all pleasantries having been completed, Joseph Howson left to undertake the short journey to a local hotel in Knightsbridge, where he was enjoying a brief sojourn with Marie-Christine, his Mercedes windscreen battling against heavy, driving rain. Howson felt elated at having negotiated Sir Marcus's once-over without serious mishap. However, as he negotiated the heavy traffic on the Brompton Road, he turned over in his mind what had been said during the evening and found it impossible to gauge Sir Marcus's true feelings. Did he really think that this comparatively youthful pretender was the right man to run his beloved school? Was Silver simply softening him up for the forthcoming formal interviews? He parked in the hotel's underground facility and sat for a while, staring through the wet windscreen. Howson had certainly begun to doubt himself for the first time in his life.

Chapter Four
THE MAN OF THE MOMENT
'To reign is worth ambition, even if it's in hell: better to reign in hell than to serve in heaven.'
J. Milton

It was not long before Joseph Howson was called officially for the first round of interviews in the grandiose, oak-panelled conference room at Cranford. Chairman of Governors, High Court Judge, Anthony Harris, was flanked by four people on either side. President, Sir Marcus, was sitting immediately next to him on his left. Introductions were made and the interview was brief. Howson had to answer a small number of basic questions, mostly based upon reference to his *Curriculum Vitae*. Sir Marcus played no part in this process, indeed didn't seem to show any interest in the proceedings. The Governors were all stony-faced and inscrutable and, apart from the natural urbane charm of the Judge, there was nothing to give any pointer as to the impression Howson had made. The Governors were seeing a number of candidates during this first round and he was informed that he would know whether he was to make the shortlist within three working days.

It was Marie-Christine who took the call from the Clerk to the Governors at lunchtime two days later.
'This is Julian Scholey. May I speak to Dr Howson?'
Joseph almost snatched the receiver from his wife's grasp.
'Joseph Howson speaking.' His pulse was racing.
'My name is Julian Scholey. I am Clerk to the Governors of Cranford College. I am pleased to inform you that you have been shortlisted for the Headship of Cranford. Can you be available at the College for 1p.m, a week on Wednesday?'

Howson found much difficulty relaxing during the Tuesday evening prior. This was to be by far the sternest test of his professional life; success would bring him status and respect, for which he had striven since leaving school. The possibility of becoming Head of one of Britain's most prestigious public schools before reaching his fortieth birthday made the prize that much sweeter. He had convinced himself that the only stumbling block was indeed this matter of his relative youth.

The day of reckoning finally arrived. Howson darkened the doors of Cranford, immaculately attired as usual. A rather glum porter-type ushered him through to a forbidding, spacious drawing room. It had a very high, artistically-decorated, ceiling. Howson was greeted by a tall, spare, well-spoken individual, who introduced himself as Nathan Worsthorne, Deputy Head. There were another three candidates already seated. Worsthorne handed him a single A4 sheet of paper, which provided Howson with a four-hour programme, involving a tour of the school to be conducted by Worsthorne himself, a series of short meetings with senior staff, including the current Headmaster, the Chaplain, the Bursar, the Head of Science and the Senior Housemaster, and finally an interview with the Governors. One of Howson's great strengths was also a handicap. He was an extremely handsome, youthful, athletic-looking man, who could have passed easily for no more than thirty-five years of age. He had an almost James Bond type of appearance and style, and would not have looked out of place as a film star in the casinos of the *Cote d'Azur*. Howson's combination of man about town sophistication, combined with intellectual power of professorial quality, was a potent combination. He also looked as if he could sprint a hundred yards without running out of breath and indeed, in that respect, the reality would have been as convincing as the impression. He would certainly cut an imposing figure with the pupils. However, although he possessed a worldly type of gravitas, he did not come across as the elder patrician-type, usually associated with the position of a Head of a traditional Public School. Certainly, one or two bushy eyebrows were raised by a couple of the other candidates, who were of the more conventional breed.

A recurring theme during the interview process had been the issue of Howson's ability to exert leadership and authority over the many older staff at Cranford. Quite a few were themselves highly qualified, strong characters, who were no pushovers. It may be said that of the typical staff complement of a major public school, half of them think they could do a better job than the appointed Head. The other half *know* that they could!

Howson noted that deputy Worsthorne had been allocated almost exclusively to him. Apart from about an hour in which Howson was left alone with the Bursar, followed by the Chaplain, the attentive Worsthorne remained by Howson's side throughout. He did not question Howson directly but mainly encouraged *him* to ask questions and when Howson asked Worsthorne why Cranford's academic performance had slipped, the answer was full and frank.

Worsthorne explained that the incumbent Head had been in post for some fifteen years and that, in his view, the management had become somewhat complacent. Discipline had become too relaxed and some colleagues were not pulling their weight. Cranford had also lost a few of its thirty to forty-year-old top classroom performers, possibly due to their opportunities for internal advancement being held back by older staff, who had no intention of moving on.

'Do you think a number of the present staff have outstayed their welcome?' enquired Howson.

Worsthorne did not mince his words.

'What we need here is a clearout – i.e. a few early retirements.'

The Deputy's frankness gave Howson a sense that his candidature was being taken very seriously and this temporarily lifted his confidence.

'My track record clearly shows that I do not tolerate fools and lightweights and you can be assured that, in the event of my appointment, I'll take a long, hard look at staff effectiveness and act accordingly.'

'I've heard you've done a splendid job at your present school – we need more of the same here.'

Worsthorne's response was enthusiastic and it became increasingly clear to Howson that he was a man of outstanding intellect and perspicacity, who recognised Howson as a man of similar pedigree.

As the time approached for the crucial interview with the Governors, Howson felt a lot more confident than he had on the evening of his gruelling soirée with Sir Marcus.

At 4p.m, Howson was deposited outside the hall where he had originally met Worsthorne. A combination of the previous fitful night and that afternoon on his feet had drained quite a lot of his energy. The interview had been scheduled for precisely 4 p.m. Howson waited for about twenty minutes, which felt like one of the longest such periods in his life. As is said to happen to a drowning man, Howson's entire life seemed to run through his mind in that short period. Since the age of about fifteen, he had waited for a moment like this. He knew that he was a man of destiny and that his time would come. Was this really his time or had he made a mistake? Had he put a foot wrong somewhere along the line? If they wanted him, why were they keeping him waiting so long? Howson was not a man possessed of great patience. When the door finally opened, and the slight figure of clerk Julian Scholey appeared, Howson immediately arose to his feet.

'The Governors are terribly sorry to have kept you waiting. Please come through.'

As Howson entered, he was surprised to see that the Governors present were all on their feet behind their chairs. As he approached the long table, Judge Harris addressed him,

'Dr Howson, we are sorry for the delay. Sir Marcus would like to say a few words.'

Sir Marcus Silver cleared his throat.

'First and foremost, I thank you for being so forbearing as the recipient of so many of our questions. Everyone who has met you has been most impressed. The Chairman has asked me to inform you of the unanimous decision of the Governing Body to invite you to accept the position of Headmaster of Cranford College.'

Howson was not expecting this. He was psyched up for a final, main interview. He was a like a gladiator, prepared for the greatest battle of his life, adrenalin coursing through his veins. In a flash he realised that the other candidates had been invited mainly so that the Governors could make a second choice in the event that he himself declined the post. Howson had sufficient experience to realise that interviews were often mere formalities. On this occasion the Governors had switched from buyers to sellers: they had already decided to 'buy' Howson; now they wanted to 'sell' Cranford to him.

Howson did not waste any time in responding.

'Gentlemen, I am most honoured and I have great pleasure in accepting your offer and you have my immediate pledge that I will work unceasingly and tirelessly on Cranford's behalf.'

Judge Harris nodded to the Bursar, who immediately opened the great doors of the Hall. Flunkeys appeared with trays of drinks and canapés and within no time the whole process rapidly turned into a very polite, but markedly social, occasion. During the course of the various exchanges, Judge Harris took Howson aside.

'I would be very grateful if you could arrange to visit us at your earliest convenience to discuss details and, of course, we would be very honoured if you would bring your wife along too. Could you manage this coming Saturday? Perhaps you would both join us for lunch? We will arrange to show you the Headmaster's residence and Mrs Howson will have an opportunity to discuss any special requirements she may have.'

After words of mutual admiration had been indulged in, goodbyes ensued and Howson was escorted to his parked car by Anthony Harris. In spite of his nervous exhaustion, Howson felt a definite spring in his step. He was really the man of the moment. The great and the good of Cranford were looking to him to lead their hallowed institution back to the unrivalled forefront of the league tables. He did not intend to disappoint them. As soon as he was on his own, he rang his wife.

'Hi, darling.'

'How did it go?'

'You will not be surprised to learn that your husband has been offered the job and he's accepted it and you, *ma chérie*, had better watch out because the new Headmaster of Cranford College may well want to have 'un petit mot avec toi ce soir', (a long established code between the Howsons for an encounter which, in fact, would involve very few words indeed).

There was a short silence followed by a stream of rapid-fire superlatives in French from wife to husband and vice versa. Joseph Howson knew he could, this night, look forward to a private celebration of a very passionate and carnal nature.

Chapter Five
COLDITZ

'Whoever in discussion adduces authority uses not intellect
but rather memory.'
E. McCurdy

On September 9th 2000, Joseph Howson donned his D.Phil. gown and hood, straightened his tie, picked up his mortar board and made his way down the cloister connecting the main school building to 'Big School', which was the rather strange nomenclature for the Assembly Hall.

In true Cranford tradition, as he approached the hall doors, the Head of School (i.e. the head pupil) shouted: 'The Head Man!' and the entire body of the school, both pupils and staff alike, rose to their feet.

Howson made his way down the central aisle of the hall and felt himself pierced by a multitude of eyes on both sides. Apart from the click of the Headmaster's heels, there was absolute silence. He climbed the steps to the stage, his senior staff ready and waiting for the traditional nod of the HM's head. It duly came, they sat down and the eight hundred pupils followed suit.

After the preliminaries of introducing himself, Howson wasted no time before delivering a speech, almost reminiscent of war-time Churchill; his text was the assembled company's duty to recapture the high standards set by preceding generations:

'... Excellence in effort, in manners, in kindness and consideration to others; likewise, excellence in the classroom and on the sports field, as well as excellence in chapel and in the corps ...' He reminded them of the four virtues upon which Cranford's reputation was built – *wisdom, justice, fortitude and temperance.* Every single pupil was told that, collectively and individually, they carried the responsibility for Cranford's reputation as one of the greatest pre-university educational institutions in the world. They should all wake up and go to sleep proud to be Cranfordians. Whatever their talents, they were expected to develop them to the full: the sporty must endeavour to find peak fitness, the musicians must diligently practise, the artists must lovingly complete their projects, the aspiring actors must deliver their lines with aplomb; every pupil should take pride in his preparation ('prep' being the term normally used in boarding schools for homework). Shirts would be tucked in; ties would be worn properly, close to the collar. Bad language in public would not be tolerated. After lessons were complete, although there would be relaxation in the dress code, even casual wear had to be worn neatly. The dropping of litter would be categorised as minor vandalism. (Howson had met the day before with his staff and he had made it clear that he would be demanding high standards and that he expected all the staff to be active in enforcing his requirements. Indeed, he demanded that the staff show their support by nodding their heads positively). Howson informed the school that all his teaching staff would react uniformly to any breach of these standards – of this they should be in no doubt.

Such criteria had always been in the rule book at Cranford but things had become ragged. Some of the staff did not consider it their job to comment on slovenly dress, bad language or poor behaviour. Howson was determined to shake up this complacent attitude, and the staff were in no doubt that the new Head would react to any failure on their part to meet his requirements.

Howson continued his assault on the gathered assembly: he talked about team efforts and that he himself would brook no slackers, no quibblers; it was the community which counted and if any individual thought it prudent to upset the status quo, then they would be afforded a strong warning via rustication in the first instance, expulsion in the second. No individual would be allowed to bring the name and reputation of this great English public school into disrepute.

With his speech concluded, Howson turned on his heels and exited stage right. As he did so, the Head of School nearly forgot to utter his traditional directive for the school to stand. James Enever, the son of an Ambassador in the Netherlands, the latter himself an alumnus of Cranford, finally spluttered,

'All rise for the Head Man.'

Howson departed, the school remaining in a guard-like position, almost fearful to move.

Such was the tone of Joseph Howson's opening days at Cranford. He felt it his duty to be ubiquitous during this period, touring the various classrooms and boarding houses, speaking to as many members of the community as possible. It was in the course of one of his perambulations, during a morning break, that he happened to notice a pupil purposely dropping the wrapping from a chocolate bar onto the main quad grass. He was not the only witness to this routine act of schoolboy slovenliness, as the incident had been clearly seen by a young bachelor member of staff, Paul Hughes, a newly appointed teacher of Modern Languages; he was walking a matter of yards from the offending miscreant, but simply continued on his way without reacting. Howson moved in and ordered the boy to go and stand outside his study. Howson then called to Hughes and, without engaging in any pleasantries, discreetly asked the young master if he had noticed what the boy had done. Hughes admitted witnessing the infringement and immediately apologised for not reacting. Howson asked Hughes to accompany him for a short walk.

'Paul, may I respectfully ask why you failed to follow my very clear instructions to all staff?'

'I am sorry, Headmaster. To be honest, it's very difficult to react to every small thing the boys do wrong. I've only just started here. They don't know me yet.'

'Well, if you're unfailing in your reactions to their misconduct, they will get to know you pretty quickly, won't they?'

'I suppose so, Headmaster. But I don't want to get that sort of reputation. The boys will resent me and play me up in lessons.'

'On the contrary: they will respect you and will be most unlikely to risk playing you up. You are not here to win a popularity contest; you are here to enforce Cranford's high standards. For that purpose, you carry my full authority and I expect you to exert it. If any pupil shows you disrespect, they are showing me disrespect and that will not be tolerated. I do not want to witness such a dereliction of professional duty from you again – is this clear?'

After gulping, Hughes nodded.

With that, Howson sent the embarrassed and now red-faced, young teacher on his way. The Head had not finished with this issue. His next step was to send for Worsthorne and he informed his Deputy that there was to be an emergency meeting of all staff before lunch in the common room. Meanwhile he returned to his study and asked the offending litterbug to step inside.

The boy was surprised when Howson addressed him by name. The new Head had acquired a passport-sized photograph of every boy in the school and had been at pains to memorise as many names as possible.

'Mr Harry Jones, I believe. You have the distinction of being the first pupil I have had cause to deal with over a disciplinary matter.'

'I'm really sorry, Sir,' said Jones, visibly shaking.

'I'm sure you know that you have to answer for your shabby conduct. Do you behave similarly in your mother's garden?'

'No, Sir.'

'Then why are you prepared to use the lawns of Cranford as a dustbin?'

'I don't know, Sir, just habit. Everyone does, Sir.'

'The cowboys in the wild west all used to spit on the floor of the saloons, so I suppose that was OK?'

'No, Sir, it wasn't.'

'Jones, you're on a suspended sentence; if there's a next time, you'll be punished twice. Don't be so thoughtless again. Now hurry to your next lesson.'

A thoroughly humbled fourteen-year-old was not expecting such an anti-climax.

'Thank you so much, Sir. I'm really sorry. I promise I won't ever do it again.'

Jones couldn't get out of the Head's study quickly enough.

Worsthorne had to work hard to ensure that all members of staff were informed of the emergency meeting. As colleagues entered, the dutiful deputy ticked each of their names off on a list, so he could ensure all were present. After the last breathless colleague had arrived, Howson made his entry.

'Ladies and gentlemen, I know you are all very busy, so I will be brief. I have called you together to express my disappointment that one of you present failed to react at break-time today when a pupil contravened my litter regulations.'

Paul Hughes felt as if he would like to sink through the common room floor.

'I am not accustomed to wasting my breath. I want all of you to know that I mean what I say, down to the finest detail. Anyone who does not wish to comply with my standards is free to seek employment at another school.'

After a lengthy pause, one member of staff raised his hand.

'Yes, Benjamin?'

It was Benjamin Fine, late scholar of Balliol College, Oxford, now highly-respected Housemaster of Sternberg House.

'Dr Howson, I am sure that we all agree with your good intentions but Cranford is not Colditz: relations between staff and pupils are important to us here. Young staff need time to settle in. We can't all go round like SS Officers, reacting to every infringement with *force majeure*. I am sure that we can achieve your aims without the zero-tolerant rigour that you are demanding.'

'This is not a debating society. I have no intention of consulting my staff over every matter and I strongly object to your Nazi comparison – it was flippant, unnecessary and downright rude. When I do wish to seek your opinions, I will let you all know and, on those occasions, I will value any input but, as it happens, not on this fundamental code of conduct. The Governors have appointed me to restore Cranford's former impeccable standards. I do not intend to do so in a half-hearted manner.'

'Fair enough, Headmaster, point taken. I'm sure we'll all do our best to support you; it's just the tone you use is not what we're used to.'

Howson glared ahead, manifestly irked by the fact that Fine seemed determined to have the final word.

'Mr Fine, I care little about what you're used to and neither should you if you wish to remain at Cranford. I have nothing further to say on the matter.'

He then thanked the staff for assembling at such short notice and departed. There were a few moments of stunned silence. This was a completely different style from that to which they were accustomed. Chadwick's meetings had always been relaxed and staff had always been free to express their views on all matters: no longer, it seemed.

What's more, everyone knew that Benjamin Fine's proverbial card had been marked, including Fine himself.

Chapter Six
THE PARTING OF THE RED SEA
'Wherever there is a man who exercises authority, there is a man who resists authority.'
O. Wilde

Inevitably, disciplinary issues continued to come Howson's way, right from the first week. The most serious was a tradition which had built up at the school of Upper Sixth-formers – those in their final year – taking themselves off into the local town of Harleybury on Saturday mornings, instead of applying dutiful noses to the grindstone during private study periods. (All public schools have lessons on Saturday mornings in return for extended holiday periods.) Of course, schoolboys tend to equate free periods with free time: prep could always be done *mañana*.

Two weeks into term, at Saturday morning's Headmaster's assembly, Howson made it quite clear to the school that this practice would cease forthwith, that non-timetabled subject periods were *not* free time and that all sixth form students should either remain in their studies or go to the library during these times: they were certainly forbidden from leaving the campus. Any breach of this latter regulation would lead to automatic rustication. Howson also declared that he would be instituting an extra prep session on a Sunday evening lasting one hour, between 8 and 9pm, during which all pupils would be confined to their work desks, in order to prepare themselves for the ensuing week's lessons.

Enever called an emergency meeting of the college prefects, ten pupils, each Head of his respective boarding house, to discuss the various initiatives.

'It's obviously a bit of a blow, this Saturday morning rule,' began Enever, 'but we've got to respect the Head Man's desire to get us back on track as an academic high-flying establishment. Things have been getting pretty slack.'

'I disagree,' retorted Egerton Masters, Head of Raleigh House, and, more importantly as far as the pupils were concerned, captain of the First XV, 'this sort of petty restriction will do little for school spirit. Saturday morning visits into town settle us prior to the start of the afternoon match; does he honestly expect us to pore over Racine or Baudelaire a few hours before a big game? Besides, we're of adult age. Are we really expected to be cooped up all day, every day in this prison camp? It's an erosion of our privileges and, quite frankly, I think he's been too hasty and draconian. He's only been here five minutes, for Christ's sake; you think he would've waited to see how the land lay before bombarding us with these petty, churlish regulations.'

There was general consensus amongst the 'gods' (a traditional term for the college prefects) that Masters was right and that Enever should see the Head Man as soon as possible to represent their feelings.

The subsequent conversation between the Head Man and the Head Boy was brief and to the point. Dr Howson made it clear to Enever that town visits on a Saturday morning had never been part of the school's curriculum, so he was not so much removing a privilege, as reminding the sixth form as to actually what the timetable stated. If the existing policy was to be changed, then the prefects needed to make their case to him. He would then put it in front of the school's Coordinating Committee (a body comprising the senior masters representing the various sections of school life, which met once a month in the conference room). In the meantime, there would be no town visits on a Saturday morning. (Howson omitted mention of the fact that under his Headship, the Coordinating Committee was little more than a rubber-stamping body, as indeed were all meetings which he chaired).

Enever returned to his prefectorial body to explain that the Headmaster was immoveable on the issue. Some of them were not satisfied and inevitably, led on by the influential Masters, it was decided that a group of five Upper Sixth-formers would sneak off, via the rear drive, past the gardener's lodge, at 10.20 a.m. the following Saturday. If anyone was looking for them, they were told to say they were working in the Upper Library (which, in order to reach, one had to negotiate ninety-two steep steps and, not surprisingly, was rarely visited by the staff). Besides, 10.20 was coffee break and one rarely saw an adult out of the Staff Common Room at this time. Unfortunately, as chance would have it, Benjamin Fine happened to break his routine on that particular morning and had decided to pop into town to buy an assortment of refreshments for a soirée he was putting on that evening for his house prefects. As Masters *et al* were passing the gardener's lodge and bearing right on to the A284, to take the twenty minute walk into Harleybury, along came Fine in his rather battered Saab estate; he looked straight at the group, rolled down his window and announced to all.

'I have seen nothing; be very careful, he's on the warpath.'

Relief pervaded the entire body and it advanced gingerly into town in a high state of both anxiety and excitement. If they could pull this off, reputations would be strengthened. Besides, it was felt that, even if they were caught out, no Head would consider rusticating five members of the First XV.

Inevitably, rumours about the incident of the town visit defiance very quickly circulated around the College community and Benjamin Fine's name was mentioned in an almost heroic context.

At 11 a.m. on Monday morning – break time during weekdays – Fine was telephoned in the Common Room by the Headmaster's secretary, Sarah Cox. Could he come to the Head's study at once? During almost three decades at Cranford, this could be only the third, possibly fourth, occasion when the very experienced housemaster had been summoned – the last occasion, some eight years previous, on a Saturday afternoon, when two of his boys (as members of a house are known) had been caught shoplifting in Harleybury, which they had no right to be visiting in the first place. On that occasion, Fine had been refereeing an inter-school under-fifteen football match – the Head had requested that he drive immediately to the local police station to supervise their release. This, of course, was a particularly serious matter and Fine, although furious at having his Saturday afternoon favourite pastime interrupted, quite understood his bounden duty in *loco parentis*, to attend these rogues' formal police warning.

Why on earth was he being summoned on this occasion? Like all employees when sent for by their boss, Fine spent five anxious minutes, as he traipsed to the Head's study, reflecting on exactly what had been going on in his "house" since the beginning of term: nothing out of the ordinary, he thought; the usual odd incidents of bullying, extortion of tuck, smoking, etc, but nothing particularly serious. The only time Benjamin made this short walk to the Head's offices these days was to see Sarah, his dear friend and weekly bridge partner. This morning she was inscrutable as she led Benjamin into the Head's sumptuously furnished study; Howson himself was sitting at his desk, holding a number of pieces of paper.

After a curt salutation, the Head enquired, 'Did you or did you not come across, at approximately 10.30a.m, on Saturday morning, a group of five sixth-formers, who, in direct contravention of my specific instructions, were taking themselves off into town?'

There was no way out.

'Yes, Headmaster, I did.'

'Did you order the aforementioned to return immediately to their study areas, and did you then inform their housemasters? Indeed, one of the boys is a member of your own house.'

'I did not, Headmaster.'

'Why not?'

'Because if the truth be told, all five chaps have represented this college tirelessly in all sorts of areas; none has asked for much in return and a Saturday morning outing is something of a treat for them. I think we should try to keep these fellows on side; this sort of petty restriction does little to maintain a healthy school spirit.'

'Oh, that's what you think, Mr Fine, is it? So you are of the opinion that it is your duty to make unilateral decisions about whether you think one of my rules should be broken or not, regardless of school policy?'

'That's not quite what I said.'

'I find your attitude irresponsible, arrogant and wholly unprofessional; you have flagrantly disregarded my instructions and, to exacerbate matters, you have deliberately undermined my authority. I am left with no alternative other than to suspend you from your duties as Housemaster of Sternberg, pending further enquiries.'

It took some time for Howson's final statement to permeate. Fine suddenly felt he had temporarily left the land of the living. What did he mean 'suspended'? Pupils are suspended on occasions, but members of staff? Fine could recall no such incident during his faithful nigh on three decades' service at Cranford.

The torture continued.

'For the time being, you may remain in the housemaster's quarters, until I have had the time to speak with the Chairman as how best to proceed. I cannot say when, or indeed if, you will be returned to your duties.'

Fine had been educated at Harrow and Oxford; he had never married, not so much, he asserted, because he would not have enjoyed sharing his life with someone of the contradictory gender, it was just that he had never found his perfect match. He had, accordingly, devoted his life to his beloved profession, subsequent to securing the top First in his year, in Physics, at Balliol. In spite of his academic ability, Fine consciously felt a calling as a schoolmaster and, not surprisingly, had found little trouble in finding a teaching post at his old school. Before long he was promoted to the post of Head of Physics at Cranford, at the young age of twenty-five, some twenty-five years previously. He had a reputation as a fairly humourless workaholic; he was not the most sociable animal but more discerning colleagues respected him for his intellect, dedication, single-mindedness when under pressure and his integrity. Some assumed that Fine was a homosexual, simply because he had never married. What was not generally known was that, as a student, he had fallen in love with a beautiful young Romanian violinist, a sadly unconsummated love, which had not been reciprocated. Benjamin Fine had been very slow and shy in his early, clumsy courtship attempts and, on this occasion, the young lady left to visit Romania, ostensibly for a few weeks, but never returned and he was never able to locate her again. He never really recovered from this and threw himself into a career as a bachelor public schoolmaster.

Fine was not exactly a barrack room martinet but his quiet dignity and superb teaching were sufficient to earn the respect of the boys and he always demonstrated the same high standards of effort and conduct, which he demanded of them. There is perhaps one incident which gives an indication of his commitment to those in his care:

On one occasion, as a young master, it was brought to his attention that three of his tutor group members had been placed into a Saturday detention, which, short of a suspension (sent home), was as serious a punishment as the school could administer. Fine summoned the three boys to his study to ascertain the details as to why all three were to be punished in this way. It was 13 year old James Prior who spoke on behalf of the assembled trio.

'Yesterday morning, Sir, during a History lesson, Mr Horne left our class to pick up a book from the Resources room next door and, as soon as he went out of the room, Andrew Dale farted loudly, Sir. Mr Horne came back in immediately and shouted at the whole class, saying we were in trouble and that he was going to put us all into Saturday DT. At the end of the lesson Smith and I stayed behind to tell Mr Horne who it was who had done it and he told us he couldn't care, we were all going to be punished. He told us to go away unless he would get very angry.'

'Is this exactly what happened? It was definitely Dale?' enquired Fine'

All three boys nodded.

'Prior?'

'Yes, Sir.'

'Mortimer?'

'Yes, Sir.'

Smith?'

'Yes, Sir'

As in all public schools, at Cranford there was an unwritten hierarchical structure: few junior teachers would have the temerity to involve themselves in an issue between a pupil or pupils and a senior member of staff; this was the prerogative of the all-powerful housemasters who could, if they wished, overrule disciplinary actions taken against pupils in their charge, although they would have to answer to the Headmaster if such a decision was questioned. However, it was virtually unheard of for an ordinary, young master even to question such a matter as what came to be known as the 'farting affair'

The following morning, at break time in the Staff Common Room, after securing himself a cup of coffee, Benjamin Fine approached Andrew Horne, who was sitting in the bottom corner of the lounge, in what was referred to by most staff as 'Old Gits' Corner'.

'Mr Horne', (young Fine would not have had the temerity to address his experienced colleague by his first name), 'I'd like to speak to you about 2b's class detention for this coming Saturday evening.'

'What about it?' was the curt rejoinder.

'If you don't mind my saying, I think it's preposterous that you're punishing the whole class, when the culprit has been identified.'

The resultant verbal explosion was enough to silence the entire room.

'As it happens, I DO mind your saying. What the hell's it got to do with you? Who do you think you're questioning? You've only been here five minutes.' Horne's face had turned puce with rage.

Ben remained calm. Horne continued:

'I don't wish to discuss this matter further with a junior member of staff. Now, go away before I say something which I later regret.'

'And there I was thinking that experience brought superior judgement,' was Fine's final contribution and it had the desired effect as, Horne immediately jumped to his feet and stormed out of the room in high dudgeon, much to the shocked amusement of most of their assembled colleagues.

The courage that Benjamin had shown in this matter did not go unnoticed among the staff and this tale, with various embellishments, become part of the folklore or the annals, as some described such unusual events, in the ongoing history of the school.

Fifteen years into his career at the school, Benjamin Fine was rewarded with what he had always wanted – a house; i.e. he was appointed Master of newly-built Sternberg House, at the age of thirty-eight. Since he had taken over, the house had always been considered to be first rate in every way: Fine was a strong disciplinarian, idiosyncratic and immensely popular with both pupils and parents alike. During his tenure as Head of Physics, he had written a ground-breaking textbook on classical mechanics, which was widely respected for the originality and depth of its insights. The physics department under his guidance had the reputation for producing the most outstanding examination results of any department and Fine's own classroom reputation extended well beyond the Cranford community. Furthermore, Fine, who had been Captain of the Oxford University Bridge Squad, had founded the Cranford Bridge Club, subsequently leading the college to many victories in inter-school competitions.

He had endured a *mensis horribilis,* six years into his stint of housemastership, when a recalcitrant fifth-former accused him of assault, claiming Fine, in a temper, had slapped his face: there was an internal inquiry but the matter was quickly dropped, Fine receiving total backing by the school. When the boy's mother subsequently wrote to the school to complain, the then Head wrote back to state that he quite understood the mother's disquiet and that he would allow her to withdraw her offspring forthwith, and would not charge her the statutory term's fee in lieu; she, of course, declined the offer: the boy did not even request a change of house.

Fine's nickname was 'Pecker', which was derived from the adjective impeccable, a word which Fine used regularly. He liked everything to be impeccable in his house: manners, discipline, dress, quality of work, as well as the boys' efforts on the field. Although, for the most part, an avuncular figure among his boys, he could be particularly forceful when needs be and would stand for no nonsense, although he preferred to lead in a quiet, non-confrontational manner. In his way, he had built a reputation for metamorphosing even the most wayward adolescent into a flourishing student.

This proud man, who had striven to set high standards in every area of school life which he touched, left the Head's study and returned home in a state of utter shock. He sat on his Chesterfield and placed his head in his hands. There he remained for what felt like hours. In reality, it was no more than forty-five minutes when he started at the sound of his internal telephone ringing, it seeming so much louder in the quietness which pervaded the room on that Monday morning. It was Howson.

'Benjamin, could you come and see me in the study now, please?'

More torture, no doubt. Fine reluctantly dragged himself into the magisterial presence.

'I have spoken at length both to the Deputy Head and Judge Harris, Chairman of Governors, about the serious matter of Saturday morning. Both agree that your decision flagrantly to undermine my authority is a serious breach of school discipline; Nathan Worsthorne has spoken up for you with respect to your outstanding reputation as a teacher and housemaster. He believes that removing you from this position would be a most unpopular decision and would be ill advised. As you will be aware, I do not worry in the slightest about my popularity ratings. I ought to make an example of you, but fortunately for you, the Chairman, who is prepared to support my decision whatever it is, has permitted me to show clemency on this occasion. You will be issued with a formal written warning, which will make it abundantly clear that any future failure to follow my clear instructions will result in your removal from your post as Housemaster and could, in some circumstances, even lead to your dismissal from Cranford.'

The sense of relief was overwhelming. Fine realised that he had escaped ignominy by the skin of his teeth. On the other hand, he now knew that his card was very definitely marked and that Cranford would be, for him, never again the same.

The miscreant rugby truants did not escape as lightly: they were to be suspended for a fortnight with immediate effect, particularly embarrassing as two of them were college prefects.

As Fine was leaving Howson's study, he met Russell Graham, the Master in charge of Rugby, standing at the door, waiting to see the Head. Graham was concerned about the high probability that he would be without five of his First XV for at least a fortnight, which would affect three matches – the first of which was against arch-rivals Millhall, Cranford's oldest enemy, that very weekend. Both men glanced anxiously at each other.

'Trouble?' whispered Graham.

'You'll know soon enough,' was Fine's curt rejoinder, as he hastily descended the stairs. A perturbed Graham proceeded into the Head's study.

'It's not official yet, Russell,' exclaimed Howson, 'but I'm afraid that you are going to have to make contingency plans for the forthcoming matches and, of course, you will need to appoint an, albeit, temporary captain.' Graham was given a blow-by-blow account of the events of the previous Saturday, the details of which had become distorted as the rumour-mill worked overtime.

'Is there any way that you could make your decision after the weekend, Sir?'

'That's palpably impossible; parents have already been informed. Arrangements for collection of the five are being supervised by Mr Worsthorne,' rejoined Howson curtly.

So it was that at precisely 2.10 the following Saturday afternoon that Cranford's makeshift First XV took to the field in their traditional black and red hooped shirts, to face the might of Millhall, in their gold and white. Howson donned his wellington boots and cap and, with Marie-Christine in hand, made his way across Field Gate, where the colts were playing, down on to the Dell, where the First XV were endeavouring to secure a hat trick of wins, in successive seasons, over their arch rivals (which they had failed to do since the Great War), this season having their strongest team for a decade. The match had been running for nigh on eight minutes when the couple approached. Both touchlines were packed with supporters, almost exclusively shouting for the home side.

'What's the score?' enquired Howson to a couple of pupils making their way back up to watch the colts.

'We're trailing 10-0, Sir,' said one of them disconsolately.

As Dr and Mrs Howson made their way to the halfway line area, suddenly pupils on both sides of them walked further along 'touch', leaving the couple to stand alone, ill at ease, cheering on their depleted First XV. They tried to move along to catch up with the retreating pupils but it was like the parting of the Red Sea. Wherever they moved, a significant space was maintained on either side of them. Like a pair of lepers, Dr Joseph Howson and his wife found themselves in not so splendid isolation.

Chapter Seven
NO SINGING FROM THE HYMN SHEET

'When people are free to do as they please, they usually imitate each other. Originality is deliberate and forced, and partakes of the nature of a protest.'

E. Hoffer

In 1985 Cranford had, for the first time in its history, admitted girls but only into the Sixth Form. Entry was highly competitive and only about one female applicant in eight was admitted. The presence of teenage girls in the school had many side effects. On the positive side, the ranks of the choir and orchestra were strengthened; drama improved, at least insofar as female parts were actually taken by girls, as opposed to boys in drag, and, furthermore, senior boys tended to be a little more cognisant of their dress, manners and language.

However, with the arrival of the girls, it was inevitable that the school had to contend with the problem of the proprieties which the parents and public expected of Cranford. Sexual activity between pupils was absolutely forbidden and any instance which came to light would result in automatic expulsion. Chadwick had been the first Headmaster to set standards of publicly acceptable behaviour. He had on one famous occasion announced to his staff that any conduct between a boy and a girl which could cause any member of staff to feel the need to avert their eyes with embarrassment was deemed unacceptable. To ensure that this was obviated, he introduced 'the six-inch rule', indicating the distance to be kept between the two genders at all times. Chadwick's rule was well understood by staff and pupils and rarely did any Cranfordians dare to overstep the mark in public.

Inevitably, romantic attachments blossomed and the eleventh commandment became paramount, namely 'thou shall not get caught'. Most of the new entrants had come from single-sex girls' schools and, on the odd occasion, a shy, demure, virginesque, ex-convent girl would become flattered and excited by all the attention she received. Some of these girls needed little persuasion to experiment with extra-curricular activities of a type which they had previously avoided under the watchful eyes of the dragons who tend to roam the corridors of the average independent girls' school.

The one girls' boarding house, named Nightingale, had been purpose-built and was surrounded by a garden area with an eight-foot high brick wall. The only unlocked legitimate way into the house after 10p.m was the front entrance, equipped with security code. Late entry triggered off a floodlight for about twenty seconds and the housemaster's quarters were at the front of the house. Thus, Nightingale's presented a fair challenge to any potential unwelcome visitor. Unfortunately, this challenge, combined with the desirability for visitors of many of the occupants, enticed some of the more high-spirited and athletic Cranfordians. The college prided itself on its Combined Cadet Force – it had produced a fair number of military heroes. For a young man heading for a career in the Parachute Regiment or SAS, an assault on Nightingale's was not merely a proverbial walk in the park, it was almost *de rigeur*.

A recently appointed young housemaster, David Prosser, with his own rather attractive Swedish wife, was extremely protective of his charges.

Maybe it was unrealistic of him, and somewhat overzealous, but one Saturday night, about eight weeks into term, while still up at midnight, marking a long backlog of history essays, he was disturbed by noise coming from the garden. He lost no time in donning wellington boots, collecting a powerful torch and investigating. Within a short time, he noticed that part of a flower bed around the side of the house, adjacent to the garden wall, looked somewhat flattened. A careful search unearthed a carrier bag, which contained a rope, a hook and other items which looked like wall-scaling equipment. He returned to the house, exchanged boots for slippers and gingerly made his way around the boarding house, placing his ear against each door in turn. It took him about half an hour before his search yielded a result. There were faint sounds of conversation and heavy breathing coming from a room occupied by Sophie Lyons, an upper sixth-former, who had developed more of a reputation for her social interests than one for delivering her academic essays on time. Prosser knocked on the door. There was no immediate answer. Everything went silent. He knocked again and called Sophie's name, asking her to let him in. After a few moments, Sophie announced that she was 'making herself decent' and would be with him in a few moments. Prosser waited impatiently and eventually Sophie appeared at the door, wearing slacks and a blouse and, putting on a pretence of being somewhat bleary-eyed.

'What's the matter, Sir?' she asked Prosser in innocent tones, 'has there been some bad news from home?'

'Two questions, firstly why is your light still on, well past midnight, and secondly, why can I hear voices emanating from your room?'

'That's impossible, Sir, I'm working.'

'I want to come in to check, if I may.'

Somewhat reluctantly, she moved away from the door and Prosser switched on the light. At first he couldn't see anything suspicious. A more experienced housemaster might have decided that this was the time to let sleeping dogs lie, but Prosser was now determined to unearth the reason for what he had heard.

'Sophie, I have reason to suspect that you have been entertaining someone in your room.'

'Certainly not, Sir!'

'Sophie, I insist on searching your room right now.'

Sophie responded nervously.

'Honestly, Sir, I would never ...'

Prosser ignored her. Within seconds he had opened a built-in wardrobe, where a very uncomfortable and embarrassed young man, naked except for a pair of boxer shorts, was hiding.

We will spare the reader the full details of the ensuing investigation. Suffice to say, Prosser had no trouble in discovering physical evidence of sexual activity and Rory Duncan, a popular young man, with high rank in the CCF and the school's Fives champion, was standing before his Headmaster the following morning.

Howson was quite sympathetic towards the young man.

'I'm really sorry, Rory, but there is no way that Cranford could sustain its reputation if we allowed you and Sophie to get away with this. I will do everything I can to persuade one of my colleagues at another public school to accept you, but you and Sophie will have to leave Cranford immediately.'

Rory had feared this outcome.

'I'm really sorry for the problem I have caused you, Sir. I couldn't resist the chance I was offered. I'm sure you understand, Sir.'

'I do indeed, but, as you know, we have to live by community rules. I'll do everything I can to help. Obviously, I shall have to call your parents without delay.'

From that point, events moved swiftly and Howson was surprised when later that day he received a knock on the door. It was James Enever, the head boy.

'Sir, as you can imagine, the news about Sophie and Rory has spread like wildfire.'

'Yes, James. It is very sad; most unfortunate.'

'Sir, I've been asked by a number of my peers to plead for clemency. Both Rory and Sophie are extremely popular. They are very nice people and Rory has been an absolute stalwart for the school ever since he came.'

'I agree with you, James. Both will be looked after. I have already spoken to the Head of Millhall and he will accept both of them immediately. Apparently their relationship is strong and they have begged to be sent to the same school. Both sets of parents have agreed. They have promised not to misbehave in this fashion again, at least not on school premises. Both sets of parents have taken it well and are supporting them.'

'That's good news, Sir, but their friends don't want them to leave Cranford. Is there any way they could have another chance?'

'I'm sorry, James. I've consulted the Chairman of Governors. He confirmed that I have no choice and I have already issued a press release, which I'm happy to share with you.'

Howson thrust a sheet of A4 paper, printed on College letter-heading, into Enever's hand:

"Following an incident in which two pupils of the contradictory gender were discovered in a private bedroom, in a state of semi-undress, the Headmaster of Cranford College has announced that the two pupils have been required to leave the College."

'I don't think this will go down very well, Sir.'

'I don't suppose it will, James. I have not enjoyed making this decision. It is your job, as my ambassador among the pupils, to explain why this course of action was necessary.'

Howson fixed Enever with a determined glare. Enever knew from past experience that this man was not for turning.

Both miscreants were collected by their parents on the following day.

On Sunday morning, at 11a.m, the entire school assembled in Chapel for the traditional Sunday Communion Service. The Headmaster sat, as usual, on a special high chair, at the front of the Chapel, with his wife on the opposite side, in a similar chair. The Anglican Service was pretty traditional. The processional hymn chosen for the day was "Praise the Lord, the King of Heaven". The normal ritual was for the organist to set the key and the pace by playing the first few bars, whereupon the school and choir would rise and commence singing. On this occasion, everything went to plan until the point at which the entire school rose, but then something very embarrassing took place: as the staff commenced singing, they discovered that there were only a few lone voices joining with them. Virtually the entire pupil-body remained silent, standing at attention but not singing.

The few pupils who had commenced soon stopped. The organist continued until the end of the verse. Howson immediately stood up, waved to Jonathan Caffery, aka Lord Snooty, the organist, to stop playing and, without saying a word, beckoned to his wife. Both commenced the traditional exit from the chapel without musical accompaniment. Howson had not legislated for anything like this. He realised that this was a protest about his decision to expel the two pupils. He realised that there was nothing he could do for the moment. He would, of course, summon Enever in due course.

The confident Joseph Howson did not consider for a second that he may have ill-judged the whole expulsion affair. All that preoccupied his mind was the challenge to his authority, which he would not tolerate under any circumstances.

His response was characteristically robust.

At the next school assembly he berated the school for their infantile behaviour, telling the pupil-body that they had betrayed him and the high standards expected at Cranford and that if anything similar were to occur in the future he would seek out the ringleaders and have them summarily expelled. As a punishment, all exeats were cancelled for the following weekend and instead there would be an extra congregational singing practice (nicknamed Conga Singa Praga) on Saturday evening, between 7.30 and 9p.m, about which the Director of Music, Peter Compton, aka Spider, was as irritated as the pupils.

Chapter Eight
THE SINGING OF PRAISES
'Ones religion is whatever one is most interested in; mine is success.'
J. Barrie

Towards the end of his first year in post, Joseph Howson had already made a considerable impact on the school. The Founders' Day concert, on the eve of Speech Day, attended by most of the Governors and many of the parents, was distinguished by a number of features: firstly, the entire school was in attendance; the choir, which used to number only some forty pupils, enhanced by a few parents and staff, now numbered over one hundred. Howson had invested £3,000 from a separate budget for the weekend, as the music one did not extend to such luxuries as importing four distinguished soloists, (including an Old Cranfordian).

The programme began with a rousing rendition of Haydn's oratorio *The Creation*, followed by Gershwin's *Piano Concerto in F*, brilliantly performed by the Senior Music Scholar, Jonathan Goldberg. The second half of the concert opened with Brahms' *Academic Overture*, which had originally been written for the opening of a new university in Germany. Instead of the usual safe and sedate Mozart symphony, Howson's hand was evident and the atmosphere was more like the last night of the Proms, with works such as Walton's *Crown Imperial* and Arne's *Rule Britannia*. The concert finished with a performance of Elgar's *Land of Hope and Glory*, followed by all standing for the *National Anthem*. The musicians were obviously very well rehearsed and many experienced listeners remarked that they had never before heard a school concert of such rousing quality. The following day, in front of an assembled company of nigh on 2,000 – governors, staff, parents and pupils, Howson excelled himself with a brilliant speech:

'...We have, as a school, enjoyed an excellent year academically: you will all be aware that last year the proportion of those obtaining three or more A grades at A level was a mere 26%. According to the mock A levels, held three months ago, we are expecting this figure to exceed 40% this year. Cranford has won the inter-schools' National Rugby Competition, the *Daily Mail* Schools' Bridge Competition and made the final of the National Chess Competition, sadly losing to Downson's, by just half a point. However, I am even more pleased to report that, during the Lent term, only twenty-two Saturday detentions were given, compared with in excess of a 100 the previous year. This term, there have been fewer than a dozen and there are those colleagues who had been timetabled to supervise these unpopular sessions, who have found themselves with a free Saturday evening: the good behaviour of our pupils is of paramount importance to me in my single-minded quest to establish Cranford as the leading public school in the country.'

There were smiles and appreciative nods from all areas of the hall.

'I have, regrettably, had to expel two pupils and rusticate nine over the course of the year and my hope is that every pupil here realises that no one is exempt from the rules, which have been put in place for the benefit of the whole community: no one.'

Howson then produced valedictories for a number of retiring members of staff, not all of whom were leaving entirely of their own volition. Phrases such as "outstanding dedication to Cranford", "the community will miss their charm and kindness", "thirty-five years of exemplary service to the school", dropped liberally from Howson's silver tongue, regardless of the reasons for that member of staff's departure.

The Head then mentioned that he had secured the appointment of six new members of staff for the forthcoming academic year, all of outstanding calibre, which included a Cambridge-educated chess player for the mathematics department, a distinguished Russian virtuoso violinist for the music department, an award-winning novelist for the English department and a cricket coach, who had just excelled himself by scoring a century in his final county match, joining the already talented PE department. This appointment was met with considerable enthusiasm, as Cranford's cricket had been struggling for a number of years and had been a source of disquiet to sports-keen Howson since his arrival.

During the course of the afternoon, Sir Marcus Silver took Howson aside:

'Well, young man, I must admit that you have made an excellent start. Many have remarked to me about the purposeful academic atmosphere, which you have wasted no time in establishing and how clean looking, well dressed and polite the pupils are. I have not seen a single item of litter in the wrong place. The singing and demeanour of the pupils in chapel this morning were beyond anything I have witnessed in this school. I and the Governors are delighted that you have already eased out some of the "dead wood" of the Common Room, without any comeback on the school, and the Bursar remarked that you have achieved this with minimal cost. Things are as good as we could have hoped for at this early stage of your tenure as our Headmaster. I hope you and Marie-Christine feel able to take a good well-deserved vacation at some point this summer.'

'Well, Marie-Christine is going to spend a month at her parental home in Tours. I hope to get away for a week or so here and there, but there's still much work to do prior to the new school year.'

'What are the numbers looking like for September?'

'All places have been filled; however, the average calibre of the new intake is considerably higher than last year's. According to the Director of Studies, the new year group has the potential, with careful nurturing, to knock our rivals out of their league-table dominance, but, of course, we may have to wait for a few years for that benefit to show. Meanwhile, we're making the best of the material we have, which is not at all bad, but, as I keep telling the staff, they need effective teaching and we'll only be as good as our weakest link in this department.'

'Quite so. How have you managed to dispense with most of the traditional punishments?'

'Very simple, we have created very high expectations. It took me a little while to train the staff to sing from my hymn sheet but we eventually got there, with the odd exception. The pupils have learned to take pride in themselves and in their school. The culture I have encouraged is one whereby even a telling-off has become stigmatic. I've instituted a training scheme for all house prefects, so that the older pupils all feel involved in maintaining high standards. They've learned to enjoy being good. Punishable offences are now so rare that I can afford to involve parents, if necessary. They all seem to be remarkably supportive and fully understand Cranford's philosophy.'

'Fine a problem for you?'

'He doesn't like my direct methods, probably doesn't like me. I may need your continued support in this area.'

'He's basically a very good schoolmaster but, nevertheless, you can count on the Governors' support if there are any on-going problems with him. Let's hope not because he's served the school well. I think we've heard the last of the Cohen problem, thank goodness. It was a good move to award him the Queen Victoria medal. Anyway, once again, very well done, Joe. After first meeting you I had little doubt that you would lead Cranford in this direction. I am, nevertheless, astonished at the speed with which you have raised the standards.'

'If you get the staff to toe the line, although there's still work to be done in this area, and you put the right prefectorial body into place, things change pretty rapidly.'

The friction between Benjamin Fine and Howson had been an on and off issue throughout Howson's first year in post. The latest tension between the two proud, strong men had resulted from the appointment of school prefects for the following year, which the staff came to refer to as the 'Cohen affair'. Traditionally, Cranford's Heads of Houses had been appointed by their respective housemaster. Normally, those heads were then automatically appointed as school prefects as well. Although Howson was generally happy with the choices (which were normally obvious), he was not entirely content for such an important matter to be outside his direct control. In particular, he was aware that Benjamin Fine had been telling various audiences in the Staff Common Room that a boy in his own house's Lower Sixth form group, a certain Simon Cohen, was about to be appointed as Head of Sternberg House and, what's more, it would be a disgrace if he were not chosen to be Head of School for the forthcoming year. Cohen was a quiet, introspective but very self-assured pupil. He was not only academically outstanding, but also the son of Professor Monty Cohen of Trinity College, Cambridge, distinguished world expert on the origin of languages. The young man was also captain of the chess team, which had a near-unbeaten record in the county. This very well spoken individual, with an immaculate record of community service, was an obvious candidate, in spite of his reserved character. Howson was well aware of Benjamin Fine's fierce support for the boy but it was a view not entirely shared by Howson himself and he was particularly irked by Fine's, in his view, rude and presumptuous announcements to colleagues with regard to the whole matter. What's more, Howson found Cohen to be somewhat aloof, almost arrogant and found him to be almost icy in character, the exact antithesis of most of his contemporaries. (It did cross his mind that perhaps Fine had, at some stage, made an indiscreet comment to the boy about his personal view of the Head: such things happened in schools, as unprofessional as they are). Cohen was certainly a fiercely independently minded pupil and, disappointingly in Howson's view, possessed little or no interest in sport. The Head knew he had to make a stand and felt this difference of opinion to be a good opportunity to show Fine, yet again, just who was boss. He decided to do so at the final housemasters' meeting.

'Gentlemen, as you know, I have full confidence in your ability to choose the correct pupil to lead your house prefectorial team. However, as the Headmaster is effectively obliged to appoint your choices as college prefects, it doesn't seem appropriate for that Head Man not to have a say. Therefore, as from now, I will exert the right to veto these appointments. I may not use that power often but I'm sure you will all understand my reasons for making this change.'

The housemasters had all learned to think very carefully before expressing any views, especially if they were likely to appear to be in opposition to those of the Head. However, once again, and now with a professional guillotine hanging over his head, Fine was not to be deterred:

'Headmaster, please forgive me for questioning this decision but, as you are aware, this has been a long-standing tradition at Cranford and has worked very well. We are the men on the spot. We know our own house members better than anyone, even though we're all aware that you have made an exceptional effort to get to know every single pupil. I would respectfully ask you to reconsider this decision because I believe that it could undermine our work in the houses and possibly lead to severe embarrassment, should one of our choices not meet with your approval.'

There was rumour in the rounds that Howson intended to use his veto to prevent the appointment of Cohen.

All awaited the Head's response, amazed that their colleague, Ben Fine, having already received a formal warning from this autocratic boss, had dared to put his head once again above the parapet.

'Benjamin, we know that you are a diligent housemaster and classroom teacher and we value your opinions,' Howson replied, somewhat disingenuously, 'however, I will remind you that before I arrived here Cranford's standards had slipped considerably. I know you may see me as a youthful revolutionary but the question of the choice of college prefects is paramount, if we are to maintain the new level of good order achieved this year.'

Most of the other studiedly sycophantic housemasters showed their approval by nodding. Fine knew he was isolated once again, even though there were others who would be bound to express their dissent discreetly to him after the meeting. He also knew that not many colleagues were likely to stand up and be counted in the event of a suggestion from Fine of suspected anti-Semitic discrimination, which he thought could well be part of Howson's objection. Many of the older housemasters regretted that the proportion of Jews and foreigners at Cranford had increased over recent years and there were those who, over their gin and tonics, referred to Sternberg House as the 'Yid Bin', or 'Little Israel', to name but a few disrespectful epithets, usually accompanied by puerile snorts and sniggers. Fine suspected that Cranford's new Head shared their racist attitude, having heard about remarks he had made, on a supposedly light-hearted level, at various staff drinks' parties.

Indeed, when the time came for Fine's nomination of next year's Head of Sternberg House, he was summoned to Howson's study.

'I'm sorry about this, Ben, but I agree that Cohen is an excellent pupil but I feel he is too much of an academic to make an effective head of house and college prefect.' (This was ironic in view of Howson's own academic standing.) This house needs a rugby fellow at the helm, as this is the sort of chap who the boys automatically respect.'

Fine knew that, in truth, Howson was using his authority to set himself up as *agent provocateur*, not believing the Head could possibly consider Cohen not to be the obvious choice of Head of House.

'But Cohen is undoubtedly one of the most impressive pupils Cranford has had during my time here and I predict he'll achieve distinction in later life that may even exceed that of his brilliant father,' bleated Fine.

'Well, I do respect your views on this matter, Ben, but on this occasion you will have to bow to my judgement. You know that Simon finds difficulty at times connecting with the sporty fellows, not to mention the less-academic boys and I feel he is not the right chap. I'm sorry.'

Fine left the Head's study with a real sense of despair and concern. He had already told Professor Cohen that Simon was his choice for the appointment and he would have to explain now that the Head had vetoed his decision. He had no doubt that the brilliant and sensitive linguist would sense that the decision had been prompted by bias and anti-Semitism. Within a few days, the Head received a fairly scathing email from Professor Cohen. Howson's response was to re-summon Fine.

'I have told you before that it is your job to support my decisions. You will have to re-contact Simon's father and explain that long and careful consideration was given to this matter and a decision was taken by me, only after much deliberation. You can tell him that Simon's achievements will be recognised at next year's Speech Day.'

Fine knew that he was walking a professional tightrope after the incident of the Saturday absconders, and he didn't want to be accused again of any kind of disloyalty. Professor Cohen received a bland reply from Howson, who told him that Fine would be in touch with him in due course. The Professor came immediately to the school to speak to Fine – and did not mince his words.

'You, a man with Jewish parentage, know full well that this is blatant anti-Semitism. You cannot find fault with my son on any front. He doesn't play rugby – so what? I am very disappointed that you are waffling as a paid lackey of Howson.'

'I'm terribly sorry; I *have* spoken up for Simon. I have done everything I can. I can make Simon Deputy Head of House and I will give him the full privileges of a Head. Off the record, I share your concerns but this Head Man is the most determined, single-minded and ruthless I have ever come across and he will brook *no* opposition. He'll certainly not admit to any anti-Semitic tendencies.'

The Professor shook his head sadly.

'Throughout history our people have been wronged simply for being Jewish. I know your heart is in the right place but my son's *Curriculum Vitae* will be blighted by this decision and I do not rule out the taking of legal advice over this matter.'

Fine nodded sympathetically and secretly hoped that Cohen would unleash Rottweiler-like Jewish lawyers on Howson, although he suspected that he would do little while his son was still at Cranford.

'I will tell you, Mr Fine, that, even though everyone seems to be in awe of this man, I consider him to be lacking in integrity, and prone to ruthlessness; not attributes a Head should possess. As sure as eggs are eggs, these shortcomings will destroy him and, worryingly, could harm this magnificent school.'

Fine did not respond but it was these words from Professor Cohen which confirmed Fine's personal viewpoint of this supposed 'golden boy'.

The following correspondence subsequently took place between Professor Cohen and Chairman of Governors, Lord Justice of Appeal Harris.

June 12, 2001:

Dear Lord Harris,

Congratulations on your recent appointment to the Law Lords.

I am sorry I feel the need to complain about the conduct of the Headmaster of Cranford. I am the father of Simon Cohen of Sternberg House, who is about to enter his final year at Cranford. I think you will find that Simon has an excellent behavioural and academic record, having obtained thirteen A stars at GCSE. He is predicted A grades at A2 level in Latin, Greek, Mathematics and Further Mathematics. He is captain of chess and, personally, has not lost a match for the last two years. His housemaster, Mr Fine, told me three weeks ago that I should be very proud of Simon and that he was far and away the most suitable choice of Head of Sternberg House for the next academic year and would make a first rate Head of School.

I now understand that the Headmaster, Dr Howson, has just introduced a power of veto over Housemaster choices and that he has exercised this power in Simon's case, giving the unconvincing reason that "Simon is too academic and lacks the breadth and strength of personality required to be a successful leader", something I wholly repudiate.

It is obvious to me that this is not a principle which is consistently applied at Cranford and that the loss of the opportunity, which Simon has clearly earned, will damage his Curriculum Vitae. I am aware that legally I cannot take action against the school over this matter but I must protest in the strongest possible terms. I know that people of my faith are often accused of being paranoid about anti-Semitism but I cannot help but suspect that the real reason for this decision is that Dr Howson would be obliged to appoint a Jew as a College Prefect.

If my concerns are accurate, then I fear for the future of Cranford College, with a racist in charge.

Yours sincerely,

Professor M. Cohen
Trinity College, Cambridge

The response was as follows:

June 21, 2001

Dear Professor Cohen,

May I congratulate you on the publication of your fascinating book on the Evolution of the English Language.

I am sorry to hear that you feel as you do. You will appreciate that the Governors cannot interfere with the Headmaster's internal decisions. I have nevertheless spoken to Dr Howson, who assures me that his reasons are that he does not consider Simon a sufficiently strong character to wield the level of authority required of a college prefect. This, as you know, is purely a matter of personal judgement but Dr Howson does have the full confidence of the Governors and I must respectfully ask you to accept that this is his genuine opinion, even if you, as a parent, do not agree with it.

Knowing Dr Howson as I do on a personal level, I utterly repudiate any notion of racism on his part.

Cranford has a very clear written policy with respect to any form of racial or religious discrimination and I can find no evidence whatsoever that the policy has been breached in this case. The Board of Governors considers Dr Howson as a man of the utmost integrity.

Yours sincerely,

Lord Harris
Cranford College
Encl. copy of Governors' 'Anti-Discrimination Policy'.
cc. Dr Joseph Howson

This was indeed the end of the matter but the already strained relationship between Howson and Fine had now been done irreparable damage. Howson, for his part, convinced that Fine had added fuel to the fire in Professor Cohen's mind, resolved that his *bête noir*'s days would be numbered. As far as Fine was concerned, any vestige of confidence that he may have had in Howson's good faith had been utterly destroyed. Humiliatingly, he was obliged to appoint a worthy but non-academic sportsman as Head of House.

Howson's sop to the Cohen family was to award the prestigious Queen Victoria Memorial Medal to Cohen for his 'outstanding contribution to the academic and extra-curricular life of Cranford'. This was hardly underserved, as Cohen was not only the outstanding classicist of his year but could demolish a Further Maths practice examination paper with full marks in less than half the allotted time. There were those among both the staff and the pupils who felt young Cohen would have made an excellent Head of School. How the Headmaster could have overlooked him, they innocently pondered, even to be a College Prefect? Benjamin Fine had convinced himself it was the workings of a treacherous mind.

●

Chapter Nine
EXTRA-CURRICULAR ACTIVITIES
'When you don't have money, the problem is food; when you have money, it's sex.'
J. Donleavy

Late in June, Marie-Christine gave birth to Karl, a very proud moment for both parents; their pride increased on this occasion because they had been trying for a child for nigh on eight years. The labour was troublesome and Karl's birth had to be induced. Marie-Christine had long lost the desire to make love and the physical problems suffered on that day meant her desire to resume carnal pleasures with her husband was clearly not to be forthcoming in the foreseeable future. Post-natal depression exacerbated matters and Joseph was denied any physical access to his beloved wife. When he attempted even a cuddle, she apologetically declined. It became clear that she could not bear even to be touched and Joseph, a man of high sex-drive, became increasingly frustrated.

In the final week of term, Joseph Howson stayed at a hotel in central London for a night, as he was attending the biannual financial planning meeting with the school Bursar, James Riley, along with the school auditors. After dinner, Riley and the others joined Howson at the bar before retiring to their individual rooms just after 10p.m.

Earlier, Howson had noticed an elegantly attired young lady sitting at an adjacent table, seemingly unaccompanied. She had been sitting there ever since the financial party had arrived nearly an hour earlier. There was little doubt in Howson's mind that this slim, blonde individual, probably no more than mid-twenties, had spent much of the time focusing on he himself. Intrigued, he wandered over to her.

'Are you waiting for someone?' he asked politely.

'You,' she retorted with a faint smile.

'Now, why would you be waiting for me?'

'Well, what do *you* think? Actually, I was due to meet a client here, but he hasn't shown. I'm beginning to feel glad about the fact.'

As soon as Howson heard the word 'client' he knew exactly what he was dealing with. This woman was a prostitute, by her looks a high-class one at that. He knew he should take his leave there and then but he hesitated.

'Would you like some company?' she enquired.

After hesitation, Howson replied:

'How do I know you're not a journalist?'

'Oh God, no. Every journalist I've met has been dowdily dressed with dull, lank hair. Anyway, why should a journalist be interested in you, are you famous or something?'

'No, but I *am* married.'

'So are ninety percent of my clients, darling. Look, you're... we're not breaking any laws, are we? We're just two responsible adults, enjoying each other's company - at least, you enjoying my body, I enjoying the hundred quid coming my way.' She stared at him, a wicked glint in her eye. 'Look, darling, relax. What's your room number? I'll be up in five.'

As Howson sat on the bed, awaiting a knock on the door, he could feel his heart pounding against his chest. Was he mad? What if this were made public? What if she *were* a reporter? What if one of his colleagues saw her entering his room? All reason told him to stop there and then and to send 'goldilocks' packing.

He heard a quiet tap on the door and his new acquaintance entered, locking the door behind her.

After a few preliminaries, Chantelle, as she had announced herself, started to disrobe her latest client.

Beads of sweat collected on Howson's brow. He had felt tense, nervous when he had arrived at Sir Marcus Silver's residence for that all-important preliminary interview, but the feelings he had now were much more uncomfortable. Of course, he experienced a frisson of excitement – who wouldn't? – being undressed by a beautiful young woman, but Howson knew this *liaison dangereuse* could jeopardise everything he had striven for since an early age.

Off came his shirt, then his immaculately tailored suit trousers, his shoes, his socks. Chantelle began to remove her own clothes. Within moments a naked sex goddess, with the figure of a catwalk model, emerged. Her breasts were medium-sized, firm and perfect. Her legs seemed endless. Howson could no longer control himself as months of pent-up sexual frustration finally got the better of him.

Although he had hitherto been completely faithful to Marie-Christine, he was neither shy nor lacking in experience. He started by lying side to side with Chantelle and, taking her in his arms, he started gently kissing her lips. His tongue searched for hers and within minutes they were both passionately engaged. She then withdrew her tongue and asked him to lie on his back. She proceeded to kiss his neck, followed by his chest, gradually going lower until she positioned her head between his legs and took his penis gently into her mouth. At that point, Joseph had an overwhelming desire to 'taste' Chantelle and within moments, in the customary sixty-nine position, they were engaged in passionate, mutual, oral sex. After ten minutes or so, she asked him if he would like to mount her from behind and the thought of holding that perfect bottom and thrusting his manhood into her filled him with excitement. After Chantelle had handed him a wafer-thin condom, Joseph quickly and deftly slipped it on to his now-erect penis and proceeded to mount her 'doggie-fashion', pushing very slowly at first, gradually quickening, as his partner began to pant with pleasure.

They then reverted to the missionary position and, within minutes, he felt he was close to orgasm. At that point, Chantelle whipped off the condom, took his swollen penis full length into her mouth and it was not long before it was too sensitive to endure any more of, what had become, exquisite torture, Joseph thus relieving himself of many months of frustration with a copious ejaculation.

This entire process had lasted less than half an hour. Chantelle, after running to the bathroom and returning with tissues, lay down beside him and gently cuddled him for a further few minutes. The whole business had been emotionless and Joseph Howson could not prevent immediate strong feelings of guilt overcoming him. He quickly dressed, handed over the cash and accepted the mobile number she handed to him, but doubting he would ever see this woman again. He wasted no time in ushering her to his hotel door.

This experience was something of a watershed in Joseph's life. Within the value system to which he had hitherto adhered, this was arguably the first time he had done something which he considered significantly wrong. He'd always liked having his own way and could be unkind, but, in his mind, only when there was a conflict and he had no other choice. However, in terms of offending against what was written in the 'big book', he had now committed adultery. Furthermore, he had done it with a call girl, a fact which, if it came to light, could destroy his career, as well as his marriage.

When he returned to Cranford, his awareness of the untouchable, attractive females around him sprang to life. Like many men living in a boarding institution, it was inevitable that he would entertain a passing fantasy of dalliance with some of the more winsome female members of that community, but for the first time he began giving the topic more than a cursory thought.

Not all of the Cranford wives were plump and dowdy. Some of them were quite striking and it was widely known that there were a few who were available for intimate attentions from men other than their husbands. Indeed, there had been a recent occasion when a member of the Physics department had caught one of his colleagues *in flagrante* with his own young wife. The scientist had sought an audience with Howson and informed the Head that if he saw that colleague again, he would be taking matters into his own hands, indeed fists. Howson realised that the community sympathies would be with the cuckolded husband and he had to call in the adulterer and gently inform him that he would need to pack his bags and seek pastures new. The young man was an excellent teacher and not easily replaceable. Needless to say, the man left, taking his lover with him and leaving the bereft husband with three young children. Howson gave the errant philanderer a good reference and within a short time a rival public school was very happy to benefit from the services of the excellent young teacher, accompanied by his concubine, who rapidly obtained a divorce and made herself fully socially acceptable within another boarding community. Such staff trafficking between schools was not unusual. Indeed, a few years previously at Cranford, a twenty-five-year-old languages teacher was appointed, who brought his pretty, twenty-year-old wife with him. He had to leave his former school because the wife he had taken happened to be an alumna of the school. Indeed, the romance had arisen when A level French lessons, while she was still a pupil, had, it was rumoured, led to additional tuition in matters arguably related to French culture, but not stated on the syllabus.

Following the hotel room incident, once Howson had managed to overcome his feelings of guilt, he surprised himself by, for the first time, looking at some of his colleagues with a more interested eye.

In particular, hitherto fleeting longings became increasingly focused on his secretary, Sarah. He knew that there was no realistic chance of a physical relationship with her, besides which, the risks were wholly unacceptable. However Sarah, at the age of thirty-seven, was a pretty woman, petite, with perfectly formed curves in the right places and possessed an attractive air of innocent virginity. What changed in Howson's mind was the fact that he, for the first time, was looking at women other than his wife in a longing sort of manner. So it was that the soirée in London was certainly proving to be a watershed in this 'perfect' man's hitherto unblemished life.

Chapter Ten
ON THE SKINNING OF CATS

'Experience shows us that every man invested with power is apt to abuse it, and to carry his authority as far as it will go.'

C. de Secondat

Since the incident of the Head of House appointment dispute, Benjamin Fine had become even more of a thorn in Howson's side. Howson took enormous pleasure – always had done – in portraying himself as a perfect specimen of humanity but Fine considered him to be a control freak and duplicitous and was always ready to voice his opinion over coffee in the staff common room. Word had got back to Howson.

It is not unusual for a Headmaster to seek to ease a housemaster out of his post. On occasions, housemasters can prove mischievous; sometimes upsetting influential parents. If some multi-millionaire is in the process of donating a million pounds to the latest building appeal, but then objects to a housemaster's attempts to discipline an errant son, the Head will usually have a quiet word in the housemaster's ear, in order to ensure all donations continue to arrive.

It was unfortunate for Howson that Fine had an excellent record on all fronts as a housemaster. Sternberg boys were known for their smart appearance, good manners and high achievements. Colleagues rarely experienced difficulties with the boys in that House and, if Fine was called upon for support, it was certain that the pupil concerned would be dealt with thoroughly and professionally, and whatever the problem, it would be put right immediately. Fine was always approachable and courteous with his colleagues. Howson was not going to find a chink easily in Fine's armour. Howson had always believed that there was more than one way to skin a cat; however, this particular feline seemed to have a pretty impregnable hide.

Many headmasters glean a lot of information about their housemasters via college prefect meetings. At the final meeting of the year, Howson decided to engage in a little fishing expedition. He led his senior pupils on to the subject of different methods used by housemasters to deal with internal disciplinary problems. Many useful snippets came to light and Howson made a mental note that he would need to look into some of the more bizarre stories; however, there seemed to be a universal consensus that if you were a member of Sternberg's, you had better watch your step because Benjamin Fine was not a person with whom to mess.

Howson looked for an opportunity to pose an innocent question, primarily directed towards Sternberg's current Head of House, one Malcolm Braithwaite.

'Give us an example of how Mr Fine would deal with a senior boy who had behaved badly,' he enquired.

'No one of any sense would behave badly, or at least they would make sure they weren't caught,' replied the prefect.

'Surely there must be occasions when someone gets things wrong?'

'Oh yes. After last weekend's summer ball, Jeremy Major was ten minutes late for call over. When Mr Fine asked Jeremy why he was late, Jeremy contradicted him claiming that he was wrong about the time.'

'How did Mr Fine react?'

'Oh, he grabbed Jeremy and gave him a severe telling off. People could hear him shouting in a neighbouring boarding house by all accounts.'

'Major is a difficult boy, isn't he?'

'Oh yes. His parents split up a couple of years ago and since then he's been a pain in the neck; always chats back, lazy at work, won't pull his finger out on the games field, argues, complains. Mr Fine does his best with him but he is the most difficult boy in his year group, in fact in the entire house. I can't stand him, neither can the rest of the Upper Sixth.'

Howson made a mental note that he would follow up the information he had gleaned. Later that day he sent for Jeremy Major.

'Jeremy, I hear that things haven't been going that well. I understand that your teachers were less than impressed with your preparation for your GCSE exams. Major hung his head rather shamefully:

'I find it difficult to concentrate on my work, Sir.'

'Also, some teachers have commented negatively on your attitude.'

'I find Cranford too pressurised, Sir.'

'I do agree that we expect a lot. Am I right in believing you had an altercation with your Housemaster last weekend?'

There was a pause.

'Sir?'

'Tell me what happened after the Ball.'

Jeremy hesitated, searching in his mind for what the Headmaster was referring to.

'Come on Jeremy. What happened between you and Mr Fine?'

'Oh, yes. We had to be in by 11p.m. Mr Fine thought I was late.'

'Were you?'

'According to my watch, I was on time.'

'How did Mr Fine respond?'

'He was very annoyed with me, Sir, because I contradicted him about the time. I was rude, I suppose.'

'And what did he do?'

'He grabbed hold of me, Sir, and bellowed in my face.'

'Did he hurt you?'

'Not really, Sir, but it was a bit frightening.'

'Where did he grab you?'

'On my shirt collar, Sir.'

'Had you been drinking, Jeremy?'

'A few of glasses of punch, Sir.'

'Had Mr Fine been at the Ball?'

'Yes, Sir.'

'Did he have anything to drink?'

'Well everybody did, Sir.'

'Did you smell any alcohol on Mr Fine's breath?'

'I can't remember, Sir.'

Suddenly, Howson changed tack:

'Jeremy, would you like to become a House Prefect next year?'

'Of course, Sir, but my record isn't up to much.'

'Well, I would not rule it out as a possibility. With the right people on your side, you just might. Your father would be very pleased, I imagine.'

'Of course, Sir. He's disappointed by my progress here and accuses me of wasting his money.'

'Well, this is an opportunity to show your father that you have turned over a new leaf by being mature. It would help me in my end of year report to your parents if I could write that you were, at last, being helpful. Now listen Jeremy, I am going to ask you one final time, are you sure that Mr Fine hadn't been drinking excessively?'

Jeremy remained silent.

'Did he choke you at all when he grabbed your shirt? Did you become short of breath?'

'I can't really recall, Sir...'

'Come on, Jeremy. If you want to progress in this school, if you want me to say nice things to your father, you'll need to be more precise about your recollection of this sort of incident.'

By this time Jeremy Major, who was not unintelligent, realised that his headmaster wanted to hear things to his housemaster's detriment. Major knew that the opportunity, with his poor behavioural record, of securing a position of house prefect by conventional means was very slim. He would have to give the headmaster exactly what he wanted.

'Well, to be honest, Sir, I think I was a bit shaken. I noticed a red mark around my neck that night and I seem to recall the smell of alcohol on his breath.'

'You mean Mr Fine touched your neck?'

'No, Sir, but when he grabbed hold of my shirt, he twisted it and it pulled my collar tight around my neck. I had trouble breathing.'

'I will ask you this question only once, Jeremy. Do you wish to make a formal statement against Mr Fine?'

Jeremy hesitated.

'Well, yes, Sir, I suppose so.'

'I want a detailed record of what happened, Jeremy; I shall be happy to assist you.'

Howson was all too aware of the modern-day sensitivity about teachers 'assaulting' pupils and he knew it was not going to be difficult to use this incident against Fine. Howson used his own computer to prepare the statement. After obtaining Major's signature, he was dismissed with the clear warning that details of their discussion were to be kept entirely confidential and that if he breathed a word, either to a fellow pupil or to a member of staff, he would find himself in serious trouble.

After Major's exit, Howson scanned the signed statement back into the computer and then added the heading:-

"FORMAL COMPLAINT AGAINST BENJAMIN FINE"

He was then able to reprint the document, so it looked more serious. The boy had naturally exaggerated the incident, which was all that Howson needed: physical contact under the influence of alcohol is a damning cocktail for any teacher.

Howson lost no time in sending for Fine. He immediately thrust the document in front of the bewildered housemaster and gave him a few moments to read it.

After a pause, Benjamin Fine spoke:

'Headmaster, this is a gross exaggeration.'

'Did you manhandle this boy? Had you been drinking alcohol?'

'I did grab hold of his shirt but I did *not* touch any part of his body; nor do I accept that I caused *any* tightening of his collar. I'd had a drink, I admit, but the implication that I may have been drunk is preposterous. Why has it taken so long for the boy to complain? This incident happened last weekend. Jeremy Major may be a difficult boy but he and I have a very good relationship. He would never've complained about me.'

'Well, there you have it – he has. It's in black and white. What did you drink at the Ball?'

'I may've enjoyed one or two plastic beakers of punch, but that was about it.'

'The punch contained alcohol?'

'Well, yes, but an insignificant amount.'

'Well, I'm sorry, but, as you know, we have a strict policy at Cranford concerning any form of manhandling pupils and you have breached that policy. Furthermore, even a hint that you may have been under the influence of alcohol and it could be very damaging to the school. Allied to all this, you have already received a formal warning from me for a previous disciplinary incident.'

'I can only reiterate that there was no violence. It was little more than placing my hand on the boy's collar.'

'Which is forbidden in this country, particularly when that teacher has consumed an alcoholic drink. I'm very sorry, I cannot tolerate this sort of conduct. I regret that I must require your immediate resignation as Housemaster of Sternberg. There will be no reduction in salary and you will be given excellent alternative accommodation. I will do my best to find you some other position of responsibility.'

'This is unjust, Headmaster. I cannot accept your decision.'

'If you do not offer me your resignation as Housemaster, then you will be accordingly dismissed from the position and, in this case, I might not be quite as generous over the matter of your special allowance, or indeed your new accommodation. Under the circumstances, considering this is the second occasion you have come in front of me on a disciplinary issue, I feel my offer is more than generous.'

Fine knew that he had no redress against Howson. The latter had him on a technicality and any appeal to the Governors would be pointless. They were bound to support their very successful Head.

The truth of the matter is that Heads of independent schools wield enormous personal power, comparable to those of a medieval monarch. They can move their staff around like pawns. They are subject to the judgement of employment tribunals only in the case of dismissals or salary reductions. Howson knew that, so long as he maintained Fine's financial package, he could make his life very uncomfortable. Furthermore, without their Head's goodwill, schoolteachers are unemployable, since any independent school would be loath to engage them without a good confidential reference from the existing Head.

School masters are not primarily motivated by money: power and influence are often the primary driving forces. Being a housemaster in a public school is a much sought-after position and losing that status involuntarily is a massive blow to a professional's self-esteem. To Fine, his position meant everything and to lose it on a trumped-up charge, issued by someone for whom he had a deep mistrust, was simply intolerable. He was not prepared to accept the ignominy which the manipulative Howson had in store for him. 'Headmaster, once I have consulted my professional representative body, I shall come back to you with their recommendations. However, I make it plain now that I am not happy to remain in your employ. You are a thoroughly manipulative and unscrupulous man.'

'That is your choice and your opinion. I am sorry you feel this way. You must do as you see fit. One other thing – I forbid you from talking to Jeremy Major about this incident or to discuss this with any other member of the community. If you do, it will make your situation untenable.'

Fine could not resist a parting shot.

'Dr Howson, you are having your day now, but, believe me, I shall have mine, and I shall not rest until I have exposed you for what you are.'

'Unprofessional threats do nothing for your professional integrity but cast you in an even worse light, Mr Fine.'

The now ex-housemaster turned on his heels and swiftly exited. Howson knew that Fine's days at Cranford were now at an end.

As did the beleaguered, resentful Fine himself.

Chapter Eleven
THE TURNING OF STONES
'Detection is an exact science, to be pursued in a cold,
unemotional manner.'
A. Conan Doyle

Advice from the *AMMA (Assistant Masters and Mistresses Association)* was partially helpful: Fine was allocated an experienced negotiator, who was extremely sympathetic. However, he warned Fine that his organisation was constantly dealing with such cases and that there was little chance of him securing reinstatement as Housemaster without a retraction from the pupil. (Fine had been immediately suspended from his position at Sternberg, although he was allowed to remain in his accommodation while negotiations took place). Howson appointed Sternberg's senior under-tutor (Cranford's term for a house assistant) as Fine's temporary replacement, until the end of term. Fine found himself unable to face his teaching duties and obtained a medical certificate stating high stress levels and he set off for Cornwall, where he owned a holiday cottage. The best the AMMA was able to achieve was a generous ex-gratia payment and, within a matter of weeks, Fine and Cranford formally parted company, just as Howson had wanted and anticipated.

After a brief period of reflection, Fine put up his Cornish cottage for sale and arranged to purchase a small terraced house in Cranford village. His plan was to maintain close observation of Cranford College, simultaneously to dig up what he could on Howson himself. Fine was convinced that, at some point, this ruthless egotist would have overstepped the accepted line and he was determined that no stone would be left unturned until he exposed his true nature. Ironically, Fine shared certain characteristic traits with Howson in that they both possessed a single-minded fanaticism in pursuit of a particular goal, coupled with a ferociously powerful intellect.

As a practising Christian, Fine lost no time in joining the local Anglican congregation; in fact, he volunteered himself immediately for the church choir. The Rector of Cranford, Reverend Stuart Sanderson, was of an evangelical persuasion and welcomed Fine's services as a tenor. Men who could read music and sing within the higher range are like gold dust and there were occasions in which the Church of St Mary's, Cranford, had had to make do without a single tenor voice. Before very long, Benjamin Fine had cultivated a friendship with Stuart and his wife, Eileen, which proved to be a comfort and source of strength during his lonely sojourn in the village. Although he had many friends and supporters within the College community, Fine felt it prudent, for the time being, to keep his distance.

Although unsure how to begin, Fine was determined to dig into Howson's background. His first point of reference was *Who's Who*, for, as Headmaster of Cranford, Howson had managed to make it into these hallowed pages. The entry there was unremarkable. It described Howson as born in 1960; parents Michael and Margaret Howson in Maidstone. It named the schools he had been educated at and detailed his degree; all his posts and his publication were mentioned, along with details of his wife. There seemed nothing of assistance.

Fine was aware that Howson's parents were, or had been, respectable publicans: this was generally known information. Accordingly, he started by tracking down a telephone directory for the Maidstone area. Howson is not a terribly common name but he failed to unearth anyone of that name in the town itself. He managed by internet search to obtain a list of all the public houses in the area and decided to make an early trip to Maidstone, to embark upon a systematic 'pub crawl'. Moving on from pub to pub, purchasing a large number of still mineral waters, his attempts to find anyone who had heard of the name 'Howson' proved to be futile and, after five hours, he decided to return home. Two days later, he made a second trip. After locating a further six public houses, he ended up in 'The Mitre', which was a large Tudor-style building, with its own car park and beer garden, on the town's outskirts. It was advertised as a **FREE HOUSE** and included a restaurant and accommodation. He entered the bar area, ordered his customary bottle of water and asked if the landlord was present. Within a short time, a stout, red-faced man of about mid-fifties appeared. He realised immediately that this publican was far too young to be Howson's father. Nevertheless he asked if the name Howson meant anything to him. The beer-bellied publican immediately responded:

'Well of course – Michael Howson was the previous owner. I purchased this establishment from him and his wife over ten years ago. The Howsons must be in their eighties by now. They're very well respected. In fact, their only son is Headmaster of a famous public school. I forget the name but it's one of the great ones.'

'Do they live locally?'

'I used to have their address, but I doubt whether I could find it after all this time, but I do know that, when they retired, they went back to live at their cottage in Wilton-cum-Studely and they may well still be there. They used to pop in during the early years after their retirement to keep us updated about their son Joe's progress. We haven't seen them for probably seven or so years.'

'Where is that village?'

'It's about six miles out of town, off the A2, going towards London.'

'Thanks for your trouble. I'm most grateful.'

With a sense of some excited anticipation, Benjamin immediately set off to find Wilton-cum-Studely. He had taken a map with him and it was not long before he had turned off the main road onto a small track, signposted to two or three villages, which included the village in question. He was in the heart of the rolling, flat Kent countryside and before long he saw a left turning, signposted:

Wilton-cum-Studely ½ mile.

When he eventually reached the village, he was pleased to discover that it was very small. It boasted a church, a post office, a pub, a general store and the mandatory fish and chip shop. He decided to try the pub first. He ordered yet another bottle of water before asking the young barmaid:

'Do you know Mr and Mrs Howson?'

'I'm new to the village, I've never heard the name. George, you ever heard of the name Howson?'

A pensioner sitting at an adjacent table, playing cards in hand, immediately replied:

'I know the Howsons – they don't come out very often these days. They're very old, you see, very old. Mr Howson suffers from something – could be Parkinson's. Mrs Howson, she's very frail too. They live only a few minutes from here. Go out of the pub, turn first left and you'll see a row of three cottages. Theirs is the end one.'

His entire explanation was delivered without his eyes leaving the cribbage game in progress.

Benjamin made his 'thank yous' and, after his fourth visit that day to the gents, he made his way to the Howsons' home. He was not sure how to present himself but, as uncomfortable as it was, he knew that he'd have to engage in a little deception, if he was to gain the confidence of the old couple. Fine was also unsure what good visiting two very senior citizens would do: even if there were skeletons in their son's cupboard, they were hardly likely to share them with a complete stranger. Nevertheless, he had to start somewhere, and meeting members of Howson's family was as good as any starting point.

He opened the small wooden gate and made his way through the front garden to the cottage door and rang the bell. After about a minute a reasonably well-spoken, elderly female voice from behind the door asked:

'Who is it?'

He decided to give a false name, stating that he was a former colleague of Joseph, who happened to be in the area and wanted to meet his parents.

The door was opened and a short, slightly stout, elderly lady greeted him:

'Oh you are one of Joseph's friends. Very nice to meet you – please come in.'

His first reaction on meeting Margaret Howson was her total lack of resemblance to her son. However, at her age, obviously over eighty, this was not that unusual. He couldn't tell whether she had ever been beautiful but certainly there were no signs of the striking features and bearing of the tall, aristocratic-looking Joseph.

Before ushering Fine into the living room, Margaret came up close to him and said:

'My husband Michael is not terribly well. He has difficulty remembering things, but don't be put off by him.'

Seated in an armchair, Michael Howson, slightly unshaven and looking very pale and gaunt, was awake, although he showed no expression.

'Michael, this is Marcus Stuart. He is an old friend of Joseph.'

Michael Howson didn't look like he had been tall in his younger days and certainly there was nothing about *his* features, either, which suggested a resemblance to his son. He managed a faint smile.

'Very pleased to meet you, please sit down,' the old man stuttered.

As Benjamin took a seat, he immediately noticed a family photo standing on the mantelpiece. It showed an ordinary-looking couple in their early fifties and a smiling, tall, gangly, fair-haired boy, which was obviously the young Joseph. There was no resemblance whatsoever between the beautiful vibrant-looking young boy and the very plain middle-aged couple. There were further framed photos dotted about the room, including a smiling picture of the young Howson in academic garb, and a wedding photo of Howson and his stunning French bride. On the wall was a print of a drawing of a school main building, which Fine didn't recognise. There was also a school photo of Highdown, with the young Howson sitting centrally next to the Abbot, which must have been taken in his final year at school. All in all, the room was a shrine to Joseph.

At this point the full English tea ritual took place: a teapot encased in a tea cosy was produced, china cups with saucers appeared and Benjamin was actually quite happy to partake of a hot drink, having been awash with endless bottles of water in various local hostelries.

'How is Joe? We see so little of him nowadays, he has been so busy running schools. When did you last see him?'

Benjamin proceeded to fabricate a story about his own background and association with Joseph. Artifice did not come naturally to Ben and he felt distinctly ill at ease purporting to be one of Joseph's university friends. With nearly ten years' difference in age between them, Fine could hardly have claimed to be a close friend.

Eager to leave the topic of his own background, Fine then said:

'Forgive me for asking, but you know your son has an enormous reputation for his academic achievements – you must have given him a fantastic upbringing and education.'

Margaret responded very modestly.

'Oh, Joseph was a very gifted child. He was reading at the age of three. He asked incessant questions but neither my husband nor I had had a great education. Michael left school at fifteen and went into the family business. In my day, girls were not treated very seriously as far as education was concerned. I was very good at English at school but I never developed. I worked in a shop and then met Michael when I was only eighteen. We were married shortly afterwards.'

'Does Joseph have any brothers or sisters?'

'Oh, no – Joseph's our only child.'

'And he wasn't born until many years after your marriage?'

At this point Margaret grimaced.

'Not many know this, but we adopted Joseph. Michael and I desperately wanted a child. However hard we tried, there was no success. We spent hundreds on medics, I mean a lot of money in those days, but it was never established why I couldn't conceive.'

'You were very lucky to adopt such a beautiful and gifted child.'

'Yes, we were indeed fortunate. It was a private arrangement. I can't really speak about it, but the circumstances were very unusual. Joseph was far too gifted for us to feel that we could do an adequate job as his parents. Fortunately, we were in a position to ensure that he obtained the best possible private education and I'm sure you know the rest.'

The adoption information aroused Benjamin's curiosity and he politely asked if he could use the lavatory. Margaret directed him upstairs. As soon as he reached the landing, he took the opportunity for a quick snoop. He peered into what seemed to be the master bedroom. The only thing he noticed above the bedpost was a photo portrait of a very young man with a moustache, wearing grey trousers, held up by a prominent black belt, and what appeared to be a dark shirt. His bearing was military and it was clearly a picture of Michael Howson as a young man. Fine felt a sudden shiver, as if he had seen a ghost. In a flash, he remembered seeing a similar photograph in a book of the young Sir Oswald Mosley. Could Michael Howson have been one of Mosley's Blackshirts in his youth? He was the right sort of age: if he was now in his mid-eighties, it would correspond precisely. He lingered, staring at the picture for a while. His mind was filled with a mixture of surprise and fascination. In any case, he thought he had better pull the lavatory chain quickly and reappear downstairs.

'Well, I cannot tell you what a pleasure it is to meet you and how grateful I am for your hospitality. You are rightly proud of Joseph and so are we all and I hope you continue to enjoy many years of retirement. Don't mention to Joseph I popped in because I have every intention of surprising him up at Cranford.'

'We're hardly likely to do that, as you'll be seeing him before we do. He hardly ever phones us these days.'

As he left, he felt that he had perhaps been unfair on the old couple, but he was certainly excited with the information he had acquired and was already racking his brain as to how he could find out more about Howson's genetic circumstances. He thought about what Margaret had said concerning the adoption and wondered why she was prepared to admit to the basic facts but was reluctant to talk further about it. He pondered whether it was likely that a former fascist would be permitted to adopt a child. However, he also wondered whether, in reality, the fascist connection might have been central to the adoption. So, with his head full of thoughts of further lines of enquiry, he drove home.

Chapter Twelve
THE GARDENER PLANTS A SEED
'Somebody needs to yield to temptation, otherwise it becomes absurd.'
A. Hope

Mary Anne Marshall was born on June 17, 1982. Her father, Monty, was a minor rock star and very much a child of the sixties and, although not an actual hippy, he was very much into the cannabis and drug culture of the era. He had not made a lot of money from music but had developed a lucrative sideline in selling marijuana, or 'grass', as it was popularly known. Mary's mother had been a very young groupie, who had hardly stayed around long enough even to bond with her child, who had been born by accident, after being conceived in an atmosphere of free love and random sexual activity at a music festival, where guitarist, Monty, and his group of hirsute musicians, had been one of the less prominent acts. Mary was brought up by Monty and a stepmother, who went on to produce several siblings for her.

When Mary was about ten, Monty was arrested over a drugs deal and was fortunate to be sentenced to only eight years in prison. He had already laundered sufficient money to purchase a villa in Spain and accumulate several hundred thousand pounds' worth of investments in various offshore accounts. Mary remained with her stepmother, who acquired a new partner and new home during Monty's detention at Her Majesty's Pleasure.

Mary developed into a somewhat rebellious teenager, who did not get on with the acquired stepfather and, although she had been a very bright child, by the time she was fifteen she had got into a fair amount of trouble at the private girls' school she attended on the back of her father's ill-gotten gains; it was mostly for rude and uncooperative behaviour. She was also a very pretty girl and when Monty was paroled after five years, Mary, to the relief of her stepmother and partner, opted to join her father at the villa in Spain. Monty found a sixth form boarding school in the Devon countryside, which had a reputation for looking after the offspring of those in the entertainment industry, as well as those parents who had a generally more relaxed approach to the rearing of teenagers. She was not the only child from a rock music background at St Michael's, a non-denominational foundation, with a loosely Quaker tradition, (although the serving Headmaster was an avowed atheist). The school had always been strictly vegetarian, discipline was lax, there was no school uniform and members of staff were generally addressed by Christian names. The school had a reputation for drama and, while music was a major preoccupation at the school, the corridors were dominated by ghetto-blasters, rather than by the sounds produced by dead German composers, usually associated with fee-paying schools. Although St Michael's did not figure highly in the academic league tables, it did have considerable success in propelling its pupils into higher education, although an Arts course at a minor university was a more common result for departing pupils than studying Classics at Durham. St Michael's was widely believed to have a major drugs' problem, especially with regard to the use of the soft variety. The school had a somewhat *laissez faire* policy towards the use of soft drugs, although any hint of hard drugs or dealing or supplying illegal substances to other pupils, even on a non-profit making basis, were dealt with by using the school's ultimate sanction.

Another offence deemed serious at St Michael's was bringing meat or meat products onto the premises. However, it was generally believed that the local hamburger joint did extremely good business with the pupils, many of whom being seemingly unable to get by on a diet of rennet-free cheese, nut roasts, ratatouille and vegeburgers. Nevertheless, the Headmaster's wife pursued vegetarianism with an almost missionary zeal which was, in many respects, stronger than the religious fanaticism often pursued in some of the more conventional Christian foundation schools. The atheistic head was a closet meat eater who, it was rumoured, indulged in carnivorous orgies at various local restaurants whenever he could manufacture an excuse to get away from the school, or, more particularly, his wife! Indeed, on one occasion he was unable to take disciplinary action against a group of pupils, who were simultaneously engaged in meat eating at a popular local hotel, which provided an eat as much as you like carvery, for a very modest price.

In this co-educational hothouse of teenage sexuality, smoking, drinking, joint rolling and illicit burgers, Mary Anne was a popular student; she studied A levels in Art, History of Art and Theatre Studies. She was developing into a slim brunette of remarkable beauty, with an air of sweet innocence and an infectious charm. Her sylphlike figure led to copious offers of dating and indeed it was not unknown for her to attract the attention of some of the younger male members of staff. By the time she reached the upper sixth, she had developed sufficient social skills to steer clear of confrontations with the extremely tolerant and rather 'arty' teachers, but she showed less skill in producing coursework essays on time. Although she showed only a modicum of interest in her studies, on a social level her friends considered her to be caring and generous and there were many others from sad backgrounds whom Mary Anne would counsel patiently. If anything, she had quite an ability to empathise and, like many children who had come from an unstable and somewhat unloving home background, she was certainly compassionate and understanding about the plight of others.

Meanwhile, things were becoming increasingly unhappy during the holidays in Spain. Although she loved her father, in spite of his frequent absenteeism, Monty had acquired a new partner who found the somewhat temperamental teenager too difficult to handle and, accordingly, Mary-Anne was spending less and less holiday time at their Spanish villa, instead preferring to stay at a friend's house in South London drinking, smoking spliffs and snorting cocaine.

At Easter in her final year, Mary Anne left St Michael's without even sitting her A level examinations and, following another major argument with her dad's partner, she simply walked out, boarded a 'plane and joined her friends in London. It was not long before she found a lucrative job as a stripper in a nightclub and gradually increased her recreational use of various drugs. The point at which a recreational habit develops into an addiction can be hard to define, however Mary Anne's descent was accentuated when she met one Kenny Churchill, a drug addict of Caribbean origins, who would regularly visit the capital 'on business' from his squalid home in a rundown area of a town in Surrey. He had no inclination towards work or gainful employment, but nevertheless afforded Mary Anne such undivided attention, so lacking in her life to that point, that the two were soon inseparable. It was Kenny who introduced Mary Anne to two substances, which were to prove to be her ultimate downfall. One was heroin and the other was crack cocaine, known on the street as 'brown' and 'white' respectively. The brown was physically addictive and, initially, Mary Anne found that it was very effective at numbing her sense of mental pain, which her dysfunctional family background had engendered. The white produced an instant high, which contrasted with the effect of the heroin. She found the psychological addiction brought about by the crack was, in many senses, more powerful than the physical craving for heroin. She also found, as have many others, that crack is not really a suitable drug for recreational use. At least with heroin she was satisfied with a modest smoke about three times a day, but she found that the craving for crack was continuous and any money she acquired would be rapidly converted into little stones of the irresistible white substance. It was not long before her timekeeping and reliability became so bad that she was sacked from her job as a stripper and, at this point, she began the descent into a hell of prostitution and drug addiction. The hit from smoking heroin ceased to be sufficiently strong to bring her down from the highs produced by the crack and she started injecting. Initially she serviced clients produced by Kenny, the latter buying drugs for the both of them with the proceeds. As client after client told her how beautiful she was and how well she spoke, Mary Anne, prompted by Kenny, decided to offer her services at an upmarket escort agency, *Paradise Babes*, which was located on the outskirts of Harleybury, not far from Kenny's flat. Although such agencies took a larger cut than ordinary massage parlours, the well-to-do clientele were prepared to pay much larger fees for professional services than could be obtained via the usual outlets. High-class agency clients, or 'punters' as they are known, are more demanding and expect more time and a higher quality service, but the rewards for the so-called professional are correspondingly greater. Furthermore, the interaction was safer and clients were often sophisticated, attractive and well to do. Meetings often involved dinners at fine restaurants and rides in luxurious cars, and even the odd visit to the theatre.

Mary Anne, young, pretty and seemingly undamaged by drug abuse, was just the sort of girl that *Paradise* sought to employ and she was immediately hired. She rapidly learned to provide the kind of service sought out by the affluent clients. They were demanding in their sexual requirements but Mary Anne had developed a proverbial buffalo hide and simply closed her eyes and focused on the wad of money coming her way. With tuition from Kenny, she had even learned techniques that produced many very satisfied customers, a good few of whom became regulars. A particular speciality was a tantalisingly slow act of fellatio in which she would pause and look up towards the face of her client with a combination of sweet innocence but wicked sexuality, which had them begging for more.

She often received tips as large as fifty pounds, to add to the agreed personal financial arrangement between her and the client, all of which would go towards an orgy of 'scoring' with Kenny. One might presume that Mary Anne's boyfriend would be jealous of the intimacies which his girlfriend had to endure with other men but, like many of his type, Kenny saw Mary Anne as a meal ticket and his personal interest in either her as a human being or as his sexual partner were subsidiary to the satiation of his massive drugs habit. Of course, Mary Anne told Kenny that she never tongue-kissed a client or allowed cunnilingus, but she learned rapidly from experience that she could increase her earnings substantially, if she was prepared to provide more of a love fantasy than cold and sanitised sex acts.

Kenny was, in fact, almost twice Mary Anne's age, a selfish lover, who would often treat her with contempt, bordering on violence. Certainly, he was a well-built, tall man, who could be quite frightening and, although Mary Anne soon realised that she had made a bad choice of partner, she also realised that she was locked into this relationship. Kenny had her manacled to him and there was no conceivable safe way out for her.

Buying the drugs was risky and stressful and involved meeting shady characters in dark places. There were risks of robbery, scams and violence, which many street prostitutes live with on a daily basis. Mary Anne, who did not come from this sort of background, found that she depended on Kenny, who at least produced the drugs without her having to become involved in the sordid and dangerous transactions.

When Mary Anne first enrolled as an escort for 'Paradise Babes' she was a mere nineteen years of age and was listed as:-

"a beautifully-spoken, angel-faced, nineteen-year-old, long-haired brunette, with small breasts and a pert backside".

In fact, Mary Anne had already lost a fair amount of weight and, although not emaciated, her stomach was concave, with not an ounce of spare fat. She was viewed by many as a sylphlike goddess. As her addiction had not been hitherto long lasting, there was negligible visible damage and, with a healthy all-over suntan, acquired largely from her time in Spain, she presented a beautiful, sweet appearance of young womanhood in early bloom, which many of her clients found irresistible.

Joseph Howson's encounter with Chantelle in the London hotel in late June had had a profound effect on him. Initially he had been engulfed in feelings of guilt-ridden betrayal and was quick to dispose of the piece of paper on which Chantelle had written her mobile number. At first he even found it difficult looking straight into his wife's eyes. As the days went by, however, he became more and more comfortable about the whole matter and Joseph began to look forward to concluding matters each evening at school, to make his way home in order both to cuddle his newborn before his bedtime and to spend as much time as possible relaxing with his wife, even though he knew that marital sex would not be on the evening's routine. His feelings of guilt now gone, Joseph had decided that, if his wife felt unable to provide him with regular sex, then he was going to have to once again look elsewhere. The problem was there were no more school meetings in London until late September.

On a professional level, Benjamin Fine's departure late in the summer term had certainly unsettled the whole school community; matters exacerbated by a major incident, which unfortunately reached the national tabloids, involving a fourteen-year-old boy who had managed to acquire a full-sized sex doll, which he had been renting out to other pupils. When a housemaster caught one of his boys *in flagrante delicto*, the resultant fallout was particularly embarrassing for Joseph Howson and his governing body, albeit commensurately amusing for the pupils and the newspaper readers. Although there was no doubting the academic revival of Cranford, and its overall much-improved disciplinary record, Joseph Howson felt under constant professional pressure and Marie Christine was an enormous support and strength to him at this time.

It so happened that Jasper Wilson, Cranford's head grounds-man and gardener since 1983, had decided to retire as he approached his 65th birthday, at Easter of Howson's first year in office. Although Jasper had earned considerably less than any member of the teaching staff, he had enjoyed free accommodation in the school lodge, a three-bedroom bungalow adjacent to the rear school gates. The Bursar had difficulties finding a suitable replacement and finally decided to appoint Stephen Wicks, already on the ground staff and who lived in nearby Cranford village. As he would not be using the lodge in which to live, Wicks was offered a commensurate top-up of his modest salary.

Accordingly, the lodge was now empty. The Bursar mentioned to the Head that he may like to offer it to one of the teaching staff, but Howson stated that he would like to use it himself in the short-term as he needed a bolthole in which to write his on-going diary; he needed somewhere quiet, away from both the school and from his noisy child. It had certainly occurred to Howson that the lodge would be a convenient, quiet, out-of-the-way bolthole for him, but it had nothing to do with writing memoirs. He had a plan.

As the school year came to an end and Marie-Christine and their son departed for Tours, Howson remained in situ, dealing with writing reports for every child in the school and having endless meetings with the Bursar and the Head of Property Services about the various building projects which were to be undertaken during the nine-week break. One of these was the start of the construction of an Arts Centre, housing both a theatre and concert hall.

After another long day, some eight or nine days into the holiday, for the first time, Howson felt lonely. Although in some ways relishing some time on his own, it was this very solitude which brought to the fore Howson's vulnerability. Indeed that evening he felt mildly depressed.

After Mrs Minns, the cook, who attended at Cranford House whenever Marie-Christine was ill or away, had left, Howson took himself upstairs to his computer. He had done some tinkering around on the internet, exploring escort agencies of various kinds but had not had the opportunity to pick up the phone: now he had that opportunity. One title had often caught his eye, 'Paradise Babes', which advertised beautiful and sophisticated lady escorts for the professional man, for all occasions. It was reasonably local. The advert was illustrated with a female silhouette, a bottle of champagne and various coloured hearts and he was sure that this was the sort of agency for which Chantelle, his company in London, had worked.

Joseph plucked up the courage and, with a sense of nervous excitement, tapped the advertised number into his mobile phone. The call was answered by a well-spoken, female voice, who first asked for Joseph's name and number. He gave his name as Maxim Horton.

'What exactly are you looking for, Sir?'

'A girl.'

'Yes, Sir, I'm aware of that, but is there a type of girl you'd prefer?'

'Young, slim, if possible.' Joseph did his best to play down his naturally cultivated accent. 'And how long do you want, Sir?'

'An hour or two, if possible.'

'We merely supply the company, Sir, at a charge of £50 an hour, a minimum charge of seventy-five. You will have to either supply a credit or debit card number to pay for this and, on top, pay for transportation. Alternatively, you can pay cash directly to the escort and driver. It's up to you to negotiate with the escort for any additional services you may require.'

'We do have a website, Sir, which has photos of all the young ladies who work for the agency. Do you have a computer?'

'Of course,' replied Howson.

'Do you have a pen handy?'

'Sure,' responded Howson.

'It's www.paradisegirls.com'.

'OK, I'll have a look and call you back.'

It didn't take Howson long before he was scrolling through a number of scantily-clad images of young women. Most of them didn't appeal to him: many of the faces looked a little hard, others looked rather too fleshy, while many of the poses were rather lacking in good taste. However, one image did catch his eye: it was that of a slender brunette, obviously very young , with long dark hair and the face of an angel. She was smiling sweetly and adopted a tasteful, reclining pose. Nor was there a total exposure of her assets, as it were. He was intrigued by this image of a stunning looking 'girl next door' type, who looked far too sweet and innocent to be portrayed on what was, after all, a hooker website. The name given was Mary Anne.

Howson lost no time in calling back 'Paradise Babes' and he indicated that he would very much like a two hour visit from Mary Anne. He gave the address of the lodge, along with explicit directions, offering its number on the Cranford Road, thereby not mentioning the school. The arrangement was for the following day.

So it was at 2.30p.m on a hot July afternoon, when Mary Anne Marshall turned up. Joseph met her at the door and introduced himself as Maxim, Max for short, a gardener and caretaker. His naturally rugged appearance and carefully chosen garb lent themselves well to the deception. There was no doubt about Joseph's increased confidence and reduced anxiety following his London hotel rendezvous. He certainly felt considerably less guilty.

It occurred to Mary Anne that his vocabulary and speaking voice were somewhat above the level she would have expected of a man in such a role but when he offered her £250 in cash for two hours of passion, she did not look the gift horse in the mouth too closely, and so proceeded with him to a master bedroom, where he already had the foresight to produce a bottle of champagne waiting in an ice bucket. Within a short time, the two were sipping champagne.

Mary Anne began slowly to remove her clothes.

'Please don't rush. I want to help you undress, if I may. Please, sit down on the bed.'

He took her in his arms.

'You are so beautiful.'

She smiled demurely and he kissed her on the lips. He searched for her tongue and she responded quite sweetly.

After ten minutes or so of kissing, he started slowly to remove her clothes, followed by his own. Within a short time she was lying back naked on the bed and he began kissing her all over. She gently felt for his manhood, which by now was quite robust. She then repositioned herself and began to perform on him orally, very slowly. Within five minutes or so, he gently pushed her away and told her to lie back and relax. He lowered his head between her legs. She had a small, neat triangle of dark pubic hair but he had no difficulty in locating her tiny clitoris and began to use his tongue very gently and slowly. She actually found his ministrations quite pleasant and when he supplemented his oral efforts with the insertion of a finger of his right hand inside her now wet vagina, she realised that this was going to be one of her more pleasurable sexual encounters. Joseph then started using his left hand to stimulate the entrance to her anus. This three-pronged attack proved quite effective and, within a short time, Mary Anne was holding Joseph's head and making various noises to indicate that this was more than simply business. In fact, much to her own surprise, she felt an orgasm coming on and when she announced that she was going to cum, he became very excited and increased the speed and strength of his activities. Finally, she had a shuddering orgasm and he could feel the contractions of her vagina.

Joseph indicated that he would like to penetrate her, so she produced a condom and deftly worked it on to him, using her tongue and lips. He then mounted her in the missionary position and, before very long, he exploded, while tongue-kissing her throughout.

Exhausted, he lay back on the bed as Mary Anne wasted little time in taking a mobile telephone from her handbag to call the driver.

'That was very, very good. You have a great body and are a great performer. It'd be nice to see you again, if you'd be willing,' said 'Max'.

'You've been very nice, thanks, I'd love to see you again, just give a ring.'

Joseph handed her the required sum, including the driver's fee.

As she made her way to the door, she checked and kissed him once again on the lips, saying, 'Thanks, babe, hope to see you again *very* soon.'

Turning on her heels, she made her way out to the waiting car, Howson swiftly shutting the door behind her.

He immediately showered, put on his suit and made his way back up to the main school building, passing the various offices, which were full of secretaries, working away on their computers. If only they knew, thought Howson, as he climbed the stairs to his study.

Chapter Thirteen
REPEAT FIXTURES
'Sex is the most enjoyable thing I do without laughing.'
Woody Allen

Dr Joseph Howson's annual salary ran to six figures and, indeed, nearly all of the hefty sum was disposable income inasmuch that he did not have to pay rent nor household bills, and even had meals provided in the school dining hall whenever he or his family wanted; as well as this, he and his family could avail themselves of a 'gratis' housekeeper-cum-cook, although Marie-Christine preferred to produce the family's evening meals herself, very much *à la française*: Mrs Minns took care of the laundry and cleaning side of things.

In such a comfortable financial situation a £250 lay-out to Mary Anne was obviously not going to break the Howsons' budget. Nevertheless, Joseph was mindful that any sudden change of spending could arouse the suspicions of his wife, even though she rarely afforded more than a cursory glance at their joint account, if she glanced at all. Anyway, he pondered, this was purely a temporary fling, until his wife rediscovered her sexual appetite.

A week later, Howson arranged another rendezvous. The routine followed was similar to the first, apart from the fact that this time he felt a very faint stirring of emotion, which had certainly not been part of the plan. Mary Anne had a sweet, girlish way of talking and a very attractive throaty, almost dirty, laugh. On this occasion there was a little more conversation and the overall experience was even more enjoyable than the first. After orgasm, Howson managed more readily to come to terms with the inevitable feeling of post-coital guilt.

Realising that such periods of living alone were going to be rare, Howson was back on the telephone to the agency within forty-eight hours and this time he requested three hours. He had only a couple of weeks' opportunity, so he was determined that Mary Anne's visits should become regular and more and more intense.

This is exactly what came to pass. On one occasion when Mary Anne arrived, he greeted her like a long-lost girlfriend, telling her how much he'd missed her and how he'd been looking forward to this latest assignation. He had bought her a large bottle of expensive perfume, a grand box of high-quality liqueurs and a single red rose, tastefully gift-wrapped. After two hours of lovemaking, both lay on the bed, physically exhausted. Mary Anne, too, was starting to enjoy this particular gig, which was most unusual for her, as she hated having to make love with people she certainly did not love and most of whom were the last people on God's planet she would offer even a second glance, all things being equal. Tall, slim, well sculpted, Joseph Howson was a world away from the fat, balding, unprepossessing oddballs she normally had to share a bed with. It was not unknown for her, while taking a post-coital shower, to be physically sick.

Mary Anne interrupted the silence:

'How the hell do you afford to pay for me?'

'Oh, I've put a bit away over the years. I'm single (Howson always removed his wedding ring prior to her arrival) and I ain't got no sprogs, at least I don't think so. No harm in treating myself now and again.'

'Now and again? We've been at it like rabbits.'

Even though Howson laughed off the comment, it did make him think of Marie-Christine and baby many miles away. Momentarily he considered asking Mary Anne to leave, but was all too aware that he had entered a liaison from which he would not find it so easy to extricate himself. The whole 'affair' was beginning to grip him like a drug... purporting to be someone else, the intrigue, the deception and, last but not least, the lovemaking.

'Look, what would you say if I asked you to stay the night next time?'

'I'd say five hundred smackers, but the agency needn't know,' retorted Mary Anne.

There was a silence.

Joseph Howson began wondering whether he was losing his mind... this whole business couldn't last, it would all end in tears... he, the Headmaster of one of Britain's most prestigious public schools, she a call girl. Everything told him he had to stop it all, *now*. He owed it to his family, he owed it to his school. Howson convinced himself that he could afford, both financially and emotionally, one very last tryst, and it would be an all-nighter.

'OK, five hundred it is.'

Mary Anne could not believe that her gardener friend would possibly agree to half a grand for one night's fun. His response caught her off-guard. If this was to be the case, she knew she would be unable to spend an entire night deprived of her usual 'medicine'. She had to explain.

'There's something I need to tell you,' she started.

Howson turned his head towards her. Gazing into her pale blue eyes, he suspected what was coming next.

'I use drugs pretty regularly – no needles, just smoke stuff,' she said untruthfully, 'I'll need £250 in advance, so I can buy sufficient for that length of time.'

What she failed to admit was, a) she did inject regularly and, b) most of the £250 would have to be given to Kenny, as he charged her a hefty handling charge when supplying her with the shopping list.

So the arrangements were finalised. Mary Anne would return the following evening, without informing *Paradise Babes*, and she would bring with her an array of illegal substances, to help her get through the night.

She was looking forward to a night away from the somewhat dirty two-room slum accommodation that she shared with Kenny. Furthermore, she enjoyed the company of the handsome and unusually intelligent gardener, whose conversation was more sophisticated and interesting than might be expected for a man of his social class. (Occasionally, Howson forgot himself and she once remarked with irony that he sounded more like a headmaster than a gardener. Little did she know at that time how perceptive her off-the-cuff remark had been).

A further little matter that became a subject of negotiation was the question of the performance of intercourse. He explained how frustrating it was for him to use a condom. He assured her, and she believed him, that he did not see any other working girls. On her part, she did not apprise him of the fact that she had a boyfriend who did not use a condom and that she had every reason to suspect he did not confine his sexual activities exclusively to her.

Howson eagerly anticipated the final night of full, unfettered love-making with Mary Anne. He now had the opportunity to get to know her a little better. She told him her life story and he started calling her 'hippy girl', which she quite liked. Of course, she omitted that part of her life story which involved Kenny and was generally very discreet about her sexual history. Joseph was not so naïve that he failed to realise that, in spite of Mary Anne's air of sweet innocence, she must have learned a thing or two from other men, as his recollection of sexual encounters at Oxford with girls of her age were of somewhat inept fumbling in comparison. He also began to realise that Mary Anne was far more intelligent than he had realised hitherto and that her chaotic background had probably led to considerable under-achievement. He was amazed at her vocabulary and general knowledge. She seemed to love talking about literature, which she did with insight and imagination. He imagined that she could have been a writer or at least a literary critic, if familial circumstances had been kinder.

After a session of drinking champagne, as Joseph was entertained by Mary Anne's life story, both eventually sat down to a feast of seafood to start, steak as the main course, *bombe maison* to finish. After a couple more hours of relaxed chat and laughter,

Mary Anne having complimented Max on his outstanding culinary expertise, it was early to bed but not early to sleep. Mary Anne was wearing a very short denim skirt and a purple blouse, but not for long. After several minutes of passionate tongue kissing, Joseph slowly removed her blouse, followed by her bra and, still standing, started to kiss her sweet, firm, perfect, but tiny, breasts. He then gently led her onto the large double bed and laid her down. He removed her panties and started to tease her clitoris with the tip of his tongue. He was very excited by her faint feminine odours and he used her mouth to lubricate the index finger of his right hand. He then started stroking the entrance of her anus very gently, while continuing the tongue action. Within a short time Mary Anne began to moan quietly, muttering, 'that's beautiful, you really do know how to suck pussy,' and such-like encouragements. He then inserted a finger inside her vagina and his tongue action became stronger. Mary Anne started rotating her pelvis in small circular movements. Her breathing became heavier and he would alternately lick and then suck her clitoris, while using his index finger to simulate intercourse. He found it very exciting when Mary Anne gasped things like 'please don't stop', 'that's great', 'oh, suck my pussy', in the conventional, unrestrained manner of these things. After several minutes, Mary Anne quietly announced that she was going to cum, saying it with the girlish excitement of a child who was about to tuck into a large ice cream. Joseph felt quite overwhelmed by the femininity and sweetness of this child-woman.

This time, when she reached orgasm, he could not only feel the powerful contractions of her vagina but the vibrations of her whole body. After the motion subsided, Joseph continued to minister to her and, to his pleasant surprise, she did not push him away but started to build up to another orgasm. The second one was just as powerful and, when she recovered her breath, she told him that 'no one had ever made her cum like that'.

'It's your turn,' she added.

Joseph lay down on the bed and she started to kiss him, first on his chest and then lower and lower, till she slowly, without using her hands, took his penis inside her mouth. She kept looking up at him wickedly and, while holding his organ in her mouth, she gently used her tongue to stimulate the underside. She seemed to keep hitting his g-spot with just the right amount of pressure and Joseph felt as if he was proverbially being taken to heaven and back.

Within a short time he was straining hard to avoid a premature explosion and, just before he reached the brink, he gently pushed Mary Anne's head away and told her to turn over. She rolled onto her stomach and then raised herself up onto her knees. The sight of her sweet little bottom raised in the air was almost too much for Joseph. He managed to contain himself and proceeded to mount her from behind, thrusting in and out very slowly, savouring each insertion for as long as possible. Before very long, he had pumped a copious quantity of semen into her vagina. He then withdrew and lay down exhausted.

With Marie-Christine all this would have been sufficient for the week; with Mary Anne it was to be repeated at almost hourly intervals throughout most of the night.

The next morning, Mary Anne complained of feeling unwell. The truth of the matter was that she had already used up all her heroin and was starting to go 'cold turkey'. The symptoms were somewhat flu-like and she certainly was in no condition to be touched. Somewhat disappointed, Joseph decided that he would have to make do with a cup of coffee and forgo the breakfast he had planned for them both. Mary Anne needed to be returned to an environment where she could obtain some heroin as quickly as possible. Joseph drove her back for the very first time.

As the two travelled along in silence, his mind was awash with many thoughts and emotions. He realised that he had gone too far in this relationship and that he was a fool to have become so involved with a junkie. For her part, Mary Anne was irritable and impatient and whenever the traffic became heavy, she kept urging him to try and go faster. In spite of the annoyance and stress caused by the situation, Howson remained calm. He could not prevent his thoughts turning to Marie-Christine and his child. He did feel guilty but he knew that his lovemaking with Mary Anne did not detract from the love of his wife. It was in Howson's mind, as he dropped off Mary Anne, that he must call a halt to their meetings – this had to be the end.

Mary Anne was so desperate for a fix, that she decided to take the risk of buying her own drugs and went directly to a nearby dealer to purchase £40 worth of heroin and £80 worth of crack. She returned to her flat, at Manchester Street, one of the back streets off the Cambridge Road, and found Kenny still asleep. She woke him up and immediately waved the stash in front of him. He was up very quickly and wasted no time in producing his pipe and other kit for dealing with the two substances. Within a short time both of them had dealt with their urgent needs for heroin and began to enjoy a session of 'batting', a popular street term for smoking crack.

'How much cash you got?' asked Kenny.

Mary Anne dutifully produced the remaining £130.

'You must've been a right dirty little tart to get so much dough out of one punter.'

'Fuck off, you cunt, I hardly did anything at all. He happened to be very generous, just a poor lonely sod.'

Mary Anne made another mental note of how ungrateful Kenny was and toyed with the idea that next time she might keep some of the money back. The trouble was she was frightened of him: he was capable of forcibly searching her and beating her, if he suspected her of holding back her earnings.

When Kenny had satiated himself with drugs, he always felt the need to assert his rights, as he deemed them.

'Get undressed,' he ordered.

'I'm tired; I want to get some sleep.'

'You fucking filthy bitch, you've been shagging some bloke's arse off all night but I don't get any, eh?'

As usual, Mary Anne had no choice but to relent and she immediately stripped off her clothes without even bothering to wash. Kenny removed his and, without preliminaries, rapidly mounted his girl, pulled her legs up over his shoulders, penetrated her fully and began to thrust in and out, hard and fast, within a few minutes, ejaculating into her while saying:

'Take that you fucking whore. I'll show you how a real man can fuck your brains out.'

The truth was that Mary Anne was tired and sore and that, for her, this experience was no better than being raped. She desisted from remarking that she had just made wonderful love to her idea of a 'real man', and that to describe Kenny as an animal would have been complimentary to the thug on top of her. Like so many battered women, for this was Mary Anne's lot, she complied with her partner's orders for fear of yet another beating.

Orgasm complete, Kenny announced that he was hungry and he left her alone while he went in search of some food. Mary Anne cried herself to sleep, fantasising how much she would like to get away from this brute and spend more time with Max. She was falling in love with her gardener friend, of this she was sure.

Chapter Fourteen
SCHOOL ON A HIGH
'There are times when everything goes well; don't be frightened, it won't last.'
J. Renard

It was the last time that Joseph Howson saw Mary Anne that summer. Within days he had left damp Britain for the sunnier climes of the *Val de la Loire*. He had taken care to ensure that his mobile number remained secret and, even though he was aware he was going to miss continued relations with Mary Anne, he also felt a sense of relief, of freedom. When Marie-Christine and his son met him at the arrivals lounge of Tours airport, he could hardly hold back his tears.

Se absente, Mary Anne spent each day swallowing, sniffing, smoking, injecting and waiting for the ring on her mobile from Max which never came. As her distress heightened, her dependence on her brutish partner and squalid habit intensified. She could not understand why her new lover made no contact.

The Howson family flew back to Heathrow in mid-August, where they were met by the school driver, Clive State. He handed Joseph a letter. From the envelope the Head recognised the handwriting of Sir Marcus Silver. What could this be about? Had Mary Anne discovered who he really was? Had she contacted the school authorities? Or worse, gone to the papers?

Under the pretext of going to the lavatory, Joseph separated from the party, so they couldn't witness the reaction on his face as he read the letter's contents. He found a spare seat (unusual at Heathrow) and slowly opened the envelope. With his heart racing, Joseph looked down at the enclosed single sheet of paper.

Joseph – well done! 4th in the National League Tables! What a transformation from last year's 37th! Governors ecstatic!
Marcus

Joseph looked upwards and silently praised the heavens. The A level results weren't due to be published until the following day, but in his capacity as Chair of the Educational Advisory Committee, Sir Marcus had already been made aware of them.

It was a very happy and bronzed Howson family which arrived back at Cranford on that hot August afternoon.

As Marie-Christine supervised the unpacking, Joseph made his way over to his study to look through the post which had arrived in his three-week absence. His secretary, the immaculate Sarah, had started her summer holiday, although she would be in the following day to coincide with the arrival of the results. He had hardly closed his study door when the telephone rang.

'Yes?' said Howson curtly. He hated answering phones without knowing who was at the other end.

'Joseph – it's Anthony Harris. How was France?'

Joseph relaxed.

'It was as beautiful as ever.'

'Well done on these results, old boy. Marcus rang me last evening. I think you're going to be ecstatic when you see them. I knew we had a winner in you. Now, when are we dining?'

'What about tomorrow evening? It'll take me a little time to get a babysitter, as we've left Marie's parents in Tours.'

'Tomorrow it is. Speak later re arrangements.'

After speaking to Lord Harris, Joseph decided to walk down to the lodge to pick up some clothes he had left in the wardrobe of the main bedroom. As he put his key into the lock, thoughts of the trysts he had enjoyed with Mary Anne came flooding into his mind. It made him uncomfortable. His discomfort was about to be increased. Behind the door, lying on the mat, he saw a scruffy envelope on which was written:

The Gardner [sic]
Cranford School
Surrey

He opened the envelope and read the contents:

Max – where are you? Phone me immediatly [sic]
M-A
x

There was no stamp, so presumably Mary Anne had delivered this letter herself. Once again, Joseph Howson was besieged by a multitude of possible scenarios and his hands began to shake so speedily that he dropped the letter and envelope back onto the mat. As much as he had enjoyed her body and her company, the recurring anxiety about the whole affair had brought Joseph Howson to the conclusion that he had been playing Russian roulette by engaging in a sexual relationship – or any sort of relationship – with a woman practically young enough to be his daughter; her being a call girl exacerbated things tenfold – something, Howson imagined, one of his yearling pupils could have told him. He had given her a plethora of compliments, even courted her; did he honestly think that she would simply disappear out of his life now that he had decided to wave his farewell wand? He had read once that a man's decision-making is governed principally by his sexual drive: so it had proven to be in this case.

The Cranford College A, AS and GCSE results, which arrived over the ensuing eight days, were outstanding. Indeed, they were the best at the college since the inception of GCSEs in 1988. News travels fast and, before term started, Howson had to do a myriad interviews for the local media. While enjoying both his personal exposure and the publicity for his school, at the back of his mind was always the thought that, however unlikely, Mary Anne could be watching or listening to the news.

The atmosphere at Cranford, as Joseph began his second year in situ, was better than it had ever been for a generation. Buoyed by the academic success, both staff and pupils carried out their daily lives with gusto: work in the classrooms was purposeful, all thirteen rugby teams set the pace in the region and few disciplinary problems reached Howson's study – the latter always a positive sign of a well-run, successful school.

As September came and went and, with no further contact from Mary Anne, Joseph Howson was just about managing to work her out of his system. It had been difficult, but the fact that both his professional and familial life were settled helped him to put full focus on these areas. In fact, Howson was feeling, as he watched the First XV secure their fifth win in succession, that life couldn't get much better. However, as so often happens at these times, there was an assortment of problems waiting around the corner.

Chapter Fifteen
HEY, BIG SPENDER!
'Man's best friend is a sympathetic wife.'
Euripides

Marie-Christine's morning routine came to a sudden halt as she glanced through the bank statement of the account that she and her husband had shared for the past seven years. It had been Joseph's idea to share a private account, at the time against *her* better judgement. As things had turned out, it had proven to be practicable, as her husband's career had become ever more time-consuming, with fewer and fewer opportunities for him to dally over any personal balance of payments. Marie-Christine had not found it an onerous task to oversee the account, mainly due to the fact that her husband's six figure salary, plus courtesy car, plus six bedroom full grace and favour mansion, plus generous entertainment allowance and all household bills paid, meant that their monthly expenditure during term-time was negligible. Marie-Christine routinely transferred about £5,000 to a high rate deposit account, without looking closely at individual withdrawals. When the funds deposited exceeded £20K, they were accordingly invested into some other form of savings.

On this particular morning, what caught Marie-Christine's attention was that the money available for transfer had been reduced for the second consecutive month. She noticed two withdrawals on the account, both in the sum of £450, and she also noticed that the aforementioned withdrawals were from a branch in Oxley, a small town about twenty minutes' drive from the school. What was her husband doing there? For the very first time since the day she met Joseph, Marie-Christine was perplexed by something he had done.

For Marie-Christine, life seemed to be going from strength to strength. She had borne a beautiful child as the wife of someone rapidly becoming one of the country's most successful headmasters; dinner invitations to the homes of some of the most eminent celebrities in London regularly dropped onto their doormat – politicians, entertainers, sports personalities (many of whom desired their son or sons to be educated at Cranford). All were keen to spend time with Joseph and his beautiful, intelligent wife.

Although Marie-Christine spent many hours deprived of the company of her beloved husband, she appreciated that this is what came with the territory; she endeavoured to enjoy, accordingly, all the more the time that they did have together, usually late at night chatting about the day's events, a glass of claret in hand.

Marie-Christine said nothing to her husband about the withdrawals but decided to look carefully at the following week's statement. Sitting at the kitchen table, perusing the morning mail, she sliced open the envelope marked *Lloyds Bank*. Her eyes skimmed the deposits and withdrawals and, as she was just about to place this latest statement onto the pile of assorted, already-read circulars, she noticed a withdrawal of £600. Once again the money had been issued at a bank across the county boundary, in a town she had never heard her husband mention: strange. Marie-Christine sat in the quiet of their spacious kitchen, contemplating the figure on the statement and wondering why her husband had withdrawn such a large amount of money without telling her, and from a cash point in a town they had never visited together or even mentioned in conversation. Surely he wasn't going to surprise her with an expensive gift? This would be very much out of character. Although he could be very expressive of his love for her when both were together under the duvet, Joseph had never been someone to show his feelings openly by way of presents, surprise or otherwise – not even a bunch of roses, a brooch or a simple card (even on her birthday his message bordered on the perfunctory). Although he possessed a high sex-drive, Joseph had never been a husband to touch her tenderly, to smooth her brow and express his feelings of undying love. She had put this down to his having been brought up in a boys' boarding school, where one learns from an early age that it is unseemly, somewhat effeminate, to express openly one's feelings. All that was expected was that you manifested your loyalty to your friends by making a covering tackle on the rugby field or making every effort to stop that cricket ball reaching the boundary. Expressions of love – be they *agape* or *eros* - were certainly taboo at an all boys' school. No, Marie-Christine was certainly not expecting the £600 to have been spent on a lavish gift for her from her husband.

So why would Joseph remove such a sum of money and not mention the fact to her? And it wasn't the first strange withdrawal. Marie-Christine decided to scrutinise the pile of previous statements, which she had placed, almost mechanically, into the top drawer of his study bureau. Her hands were inexplicably shaking as she delved into the drawer. Throughout her relationship with Joseph she had never acted surreptitiously or clandestinely. Now she felt as though she were being dishonest. How could she have any doubts about the man whom she loved more than life itself? She was numb and, as she sifted through the plethora of statements of account, she could barely focus on the figures in front of her. Would he forgive her? Would she ever be able to forgive herself? Initially, there appeared no previous unexplained, sizeable withdrawals... had she imagined seeing them? Somewhat confused, she looked more closely: all she saw was the usual assortment of standing order charges and regular withdrawals, the vast majority of which she herself had undertaken. Nevertheless, she decided she would have to challenge Joseph. She certainly didn't wish to irritate or embarrass her husband – she was very much aware that he worked under relentless pressure over at school and that it was incumbent on her to make his life as stress-free as possible once he had crossed the quad and negotiated the leafy footpath, which meandered up to the main door of Cranford House.

On that particular evening, Joseph was tardy in his return home – a regular occurrence – but, when he eventually arrived, on this occasion he wore the air of a troubled man.

'I've had to expel Ben Mason,' he complained, 'I had no other option. He's been selling weed to some juniors. The parents are in tears, he's in tears. Bloody hell, I feel like crying myself. The fellow's one of the brightest boys in the school. Pity he didn't use his intelligence outside the classroom. I've recommended him to Sandford School, near Brighton. Their gain is our loss. How could he have been so utterly stupid?'

'Ne t'inquiète pas, chéri, ces choses se passent de temps en temps: c'est une partie inévitable de la vie d'un Directeur.'

Marie-Christine put her arms around her beloved husband and kissed him tenderly on his left cheek. She made her way over to the drinks cabinet and poured him his favourite pre-prandial, a schooner of dry sherry.

'Il y a un message sur le répondeur, de la part de Marcus. Il veut que nous dinions chez lui samedi soir, si nous serons libres.'

'Oui, d'accord.'

Marie-Christine disappeared into their spacious kitchen to serve up her husband's evening repast. She insisted on doing all the evening cooking at Cranford House. Mrs Minns, the housekeeper, would stay late only when there was an official dinner party. For special occasions, when Marie-Christine was expected to adopt the role of host, alongside her husband, a chef was hired, with Mrs Minns in attendance. As well as preparing her husband's meal, Marie-Christine would always dutifully wait until Joseph returned home to have her own, no matter how late this may be.

Joseph was still evidently tense.

'Whenever I lose a pupil in this way, I feel as though I've failed in my responsibilities. I realise it's irrational, but I just can't help myself.'

'I know, Joe, it's that perfectionist approach to life which has made you the golden boy of your generation,' purred Marie-Christine, as she placed a copious plate of beef wellington in front of him. She watched him devour his food as if there were no tomorrow. She had it in her mind that she wanted to bring up the issue of the withdrawals, but felt it prudent to wait for him to finish eating.

'Joe, I was looking at the bank account today; we seem to be spending pretty freely lately – there's under £2,000 in the current account for the first time since I can remember.'

There was no response from the other end of the table.

'I bought a number of outfits of late, but we seem to be thousands down.'

Try as she may, her husband refused to be drawn. After Joseph finished his *crème brûlée*, he repaired to the spacious lounge. It was usually the province of total relaxation, of laughter and of winding down. On this particular evening, Marie-Christine had to eradicate the nagging disquiet which was occupying her mind.

'Joe, those withdrawals from our account; I noticed a couple of sums for an odd few hundred, which you cashed in Oxley. What were you doing there and what was the money for?'

Her husband looked at her straight in the eye but said nothing.

'It's just that these withdrawals have become pretty regular and you've never mentioned anything to me.'

'And your point?' he asked with obvious irritation.

'The fact that you've been spending hundreds and hundreds of pounds from *our* account and you didn't deem it worthy to let me know.'

'May I make it perfectly clear,' retorted Howson, 'that the vast majority of the money being paid into *our* account emanates from my own salary. You know I was afforded a hefty pay rise last September, as pupil numbers topped 1,000. I felt it in order to treat myself to a few extra personal luxuries; it did not occur to me that my wife would have any objections. I was obviously wrong.'

'I didn't say that I had any objections,' faltered Marie-Christine, 'I was simply pointing out that it's so unlike you not to have mentioned anything.'

'Well, now I know; I do apologise if it's caused you any concern. I shan't make the mistake again.' Joseph's tone reeked of sarcasm.

With this final rejoinder, he stood up, turned on his heels and with a cursory, 'I'm awfully tired, I need to go up,' he ascended the grandiose, winding staircase, leaving a suitably admonished, upset and somewhat perplexed Marie-Christine alone to finish her freshly-made coffee.

Chapter Sixteen
A FINE MISSION

'Beware the man who does not immediately return your blow – he is likely to be set on revenge.'

G. B. Shaw

After his investigative day in Kent, Benjamin Fine was completely exhausted. He was certainly pleased with the relative success of his day's efforts. After all, he could not have expected to achieve more than he had done so. Equally, he was aware that he had a long hard road ahead and there was no guarantee that his enquiries would ultimately lead to anything of value. The adoption issue would really be a real tough one to crack; it had been a private matter, so the usual public records might not be terribly helpful. If only he could obtain Joseph's birth certificate. The trouble was he didn't have a real name. He decided that the only way forward was with the help of a detective agency. He had plenty of personal financial backing, which had been supplemented by the generous severance award from Cranford.

The next day, after a fairly lengthy trawl of the internet using various search engines, he obtained a list of agency numbers. There was the usual series of unobtainable numbers and answer phones but, after the fourth attempt, he finally received a response from a real live person! Benjamin gave his name and briefly explained the nature of his enquiry. The telephone receptionist said that she would transfer him to one of the company's operatives. He found himself repeating the nature of his request to a man named John Snuggs. The latter's immediate response was that his firm specialised in surveillance, obtaining photographic evidence and asset discovery. He felt that this particular request was an unusual one and that he wasn't confident that the matter was within the scope of his agency's capabilities. However, Snuggs, who described himself as a retired Police Detective Sergeant, suggested an agency named *Frosts*, which he said had an excellent reputation for conducting far-reaching and international enquiries. He said that it was run by two partners, one of whom had been a senior detective with Special Branch, named Karl Frost. The other partner, he said, was known to be a brilliant retired Customs Officer, named Martin Trench, who had made his name as the mastermind behind a major drugs' money-laundering prosecution some years previously. Snuggs warned him that *Frosts* was a specialist firm and was often used by Government agencies, especially when they needed information which needed unorthodox, possibly illicit, methods to be used. They were likely to be expensive, he warned. Snuggs helpfully provided a telephone number.

Within a short time, Benjamin was speaking to another telephone receptionist. He explained a brief outline of his problem. She asked him to wait and then, after about five minutes, she returned and said that a Mr Trench would be prepared to see him, offering him an appointment for the very next day at 9a.m. So it was that Fine undertook a fairly lengthy car journey to Streatham, South London, on the following morning.

At 8.50a.m, he found himself outside a tall, narrow, modern building with a heavily secured entrance. On the wall, adjacent to the front door, there was a list of organisations, with floor numbers and a button to press for each. He pressed accordingly and a voice asked him for his name and whom he had come to see. He gave the details and was invited to push the front door as soon as he heard the buzzer.

When inside, he was confronted by a uniformed security guard who informed him he would need to undergo a body-search. This he duly complied with and was then led to an elevator and was instructed to alight at the third floor, where Mr Trench would be waiting for him.

The latter was a surprisingly small man, in his fifties, with grey hair. He looked wiry and fit. Benjamin was led into an inner sanctum and invited to sit down.

'What can I do for you, Mr Fine?'

'I am trying to trace the true parentage of an adopted acquaintance.'

'What reason do you have for this?'

'The man is well known in public life. I believe him to be corrupt and it's my intention to expose him for what he is; this is my first line of enquiry in that process. Are you willing and able to help me with this?'

'Give me some more detailed information,' said Trench, pouring himself a cup of iced water and offering one to Fine.

'OK, the man is Dr Joseph Howson. He has the top First of his year in History from Oxford, a D.Phil. and is currently the Headmaster of Cranford College.'

Fine gulped a mouthful of the refreshing water.

'Of course, I've heard of Cranford. Actually, one of my best investigative officers, back in my Customs days, had been a pupil there.'

'Small world, isn't it? Howson was adopted at a young age and brought up by a couple, Michael and Margaret Howson, who used to own the Mitre Public House in Maidstone, and are now elderly and retired, living in a nearby village.'

'How do you know that Howson was adopted?'

'Margaret Howson told me! The only other information I have is that I believe that Michael might have been one of Mosley's Blackshirts, in the 1930s.'

'And how did you come by this information?'

'Oh, I went to the toilet at their home but *accidentally* popped into the Howson bedroom on the way. There was a large photo on the wall, which seemed to indicate that this is the case.'

'Well, I am impressed. Pity I haven't got any vacancies here for budding detectives. Mind you, at your age, I could hardly consider you as a possible apprentice!'

'Can you do anything with this, then?'

Trench leaned back in his chair and stroked his chin, before saying:

'I'll be frank. This is an unusual and difficult assignment and I can't guarantee any success. It's hard to put a price on the job. I charge government agencies about £100 per hour, plus expenses. As regards private clients, it depends on the nature of the work and their financial means. I can't work for less than £40 per hour, plus my expenses. I'll also need to charge £20 an hour for secretarial-type work. Of course, we operate economically here and I do my best to keep costs down but I'll have to ask you for an initial deposit of £2,000. Further to this, there's a minimum charge of £500 and I retain the right to abort the job at an early stage, in which case I'll return the deposit, less the 500. Is it really worth it to you? Are you that keen to, um, expose this man?'

'He's ended my career; more importantly he's called my integrity into question and I believe him to be a duplicitous, scheming racist and a bully.'

'Well, that sounds pretty strong stuff. My job is to detect for you. What use you put the information to is your own business. Do you want me to proceed?'

'Your terms are acceptable to me. Yes, I would like you to work on this matter and start as soon as possible.'

Trench handed him a blank sheet of A4.

'To start, could you please write down all the details you have about this Mr Howson: approximate date of birth, education, etc, the address of the parental pub and their retirement home and all your own contact details'.

Benjamin Fine made his journey home in a more positive frame of mind than he had been able to enjoy since his showdown with

Howson. He surprised himself that he had become so single-minded in his pursuit of the man. Throughout his career he had always been at pains to ensure fair play and justice between pupils. Now it involved himself; he wouldn't rest until this wrong had been righted. If it meant damaging the reputation of the school he loved, or had loved, then so be it. Fine was on a mission.

Chapter Seventeen
A RAPID RESULT
'If you open Pandora's Box, you'll never know what Trojan horse will jump out.'
E. Bevin

It was 10a.m the next morning, a very hot August day, when Fine answered the telephone and was greeted by the dry, deadpan tones of his detective. Trench was not a man given to undue verbosity and simply said:

'Good morning. You'll be interested to know that I have unearthed a little matter of significance. Your target Michael Howson was a member of a rather nasty little Blackshirt cell, known as C2. It was believed that they planned and executed nice little stunts, like the murders of prominent Jewish East End community figures. In particular, Howson was suspected as one of those responsible for the assassination of a Jewish shopkeeper in 1936. Hymie Lazarus ran a bagel shop in Whitechapel and was a popular figure in the local community. He and his wife were known to be determined anti-fascists and probably involved themselves in counter-Blackshirt activities. One day two masked men entered his bagel shop in broad daylight, jumped over the counter, summarily slitting the poor bloke's throat – in the struggle, a colleague of Lazarus managed to pull the mask off one of the assailants and initially Howson was identified by name, not merely by description. However, by the time the case reached court, the colleague was mysteriously suffering from doubts and memory confusion and the trial was aborted at the eleventh hour.'

'My God! You aren't joking, are you? That's amazing. Would it be impertinent of me to ask how you unearthed such an amazing series of facts so quickly?'

'Not at all. It was comparatively easy! I made a routine computer search of newspaper reports between 1934 and 1938.

Two short reports mentioned Howson by name – I just punched his name into the computer and told it to search through all the London rags of the time - hasn't even seriously dented your deposit!'

'I knew it. There had to be something, but I'd never have imagined there was anything as extreme as that.'

'By the way, that isn't all. C2 was believed to have direct connections with Hitler's mob – links with the Nazis.'

Benjamin remained silent for a few seconds. His mind was racing.

'Do you think that any of this could have anything to do with Howson's adoption in the early 1960s?'

'I don't speculate. I deal only in facts. I presume you want me to pursue further enquiries into the adoptive father's connections. I'm not going to charge you my full rates for this. Your Dr Howson obviously comes from a pretty dodgy background and I'm not that partial to fascists, anti-Semites or murderers, or their offspring. Most of our jobs here are fairly big but we also have quiet periods. I've got a fair bit of time on my hands at the moment and I'm happy to work partly for the good of the cause and partly for the publicity-benefit to the agency. My next set of enquiries will take a little longer. I'll send you a copy of the facts so far established and call as soon as I've got something new.'

'Talk about Pandora's Box; I thought it was likely that something untoward would be discovered, but nothing as significant as this and so quickly. Thanks again for your hard work. Speak soon.'

Within a week, Benjamin received another one of the characteristic deadpan calls from Trench.

'I've been looking into the Howson finances. There's no way that Michael and Margaret Howson could've afforded Joseph's school fees.'

'How could you know that?'

'I did some routine searches, as well as some enquiries with local estate agents. I also had a chat with the Mitre's current landlord: managed to dig up old records from Company's House. Basically, the Mitre Pub was owned by a company called Mitre Holdings Ltd. In 1988, the company sold its major asset, namely the freehold of the Mitre Pub, for the sum of £450,000. In addition, a sum of £50,000 was paid for goodwill, fixtures and fittings. However, there was a mortgage of £250,000 on the freehold, a bank loan of £60,000 and a bank overdraft of approximately £20,000. When the company was wound up, it had sundry further debts of some £60,000. This left the sum of only £60,000 in the kitty. There was capital gains tax of about £15,000 to pay, so the Howsons only realised £45,000 on their retirement. However, more interestingly, the company had shown virtually no profit since its inception in about 1970. The Howsons only drew nominal salaries each year. The family cottage was only a small, two bedroom affair, which they'd purchased on mortgage in about 1955. Michael had worked in his father's small hardware store until the latter's death in 1970. With their modest inheritance, they were able to borrow sufficient to buy the Mitre Pub, which at the time was apparently extremely run down. There was no way their financial structure could've supported boarding school fees. You either need access to a very large source of capital or a very high after-tax-income to pay those kinds of fees. The Howsons were not in that league. DVLA records, which I know how to access, show that they owned a succession of modest second-hand vehicles, of average value, no more than a few thousand at most. Their whole financial profile is not consistent with fee-paying parents at an independent boarding school. In fact, their combined salaries from the Mitre Pub would've been insufficient in themselves to meet such fees.'

'So where do you think the money came from for Joseph's fees?'

'I don't have a clue as yet, but I do know they must have come from elsewhere. I am going to try to access old bank records, but that will be difficult, although probably possible. As you can imagine, after years in this business, I have a lot of contacts in financial institutions.'

Another week passed before Trench called again.

'I have more news. From 1962 until 1978, Michael Howson received regular international transfers from a coded account. From the codes I was able to trace the source to a small bank, which incidentally no longer exists, called JNK Friedberg, headquarters in Basle, Switzerland. As it happens, some years ago I was involved in a major money-laundering case, in which Friedberg was one of the conduits for drugs money which'd been circulating from Columbia, to Lichtenstein, then to the Cayman Islands and finally disappearing down a black hole at Friedberg. The evidence we unearthed resulted in the arrest of the bank's principals and the Swiss Government closed the bank down. That was in 1988. It appeared that there'd been a lot of movements between Friedberg and Argentina, which appeared to have no connection with drug trafficking but we suspected at the time that Friedberg held a number of closely guarded accounts connected with former Nazis, who were resident in Argentina. Certainly, one of the directors, one Herr Erwin Steinmann, was an Austrian suspected of having questionable origins and connections. The directors were ultimately released without charge, due to the complexity of proving complicity in anything illegal, but there was sufficient irregularity for the authorities to close the bank down, although a number of apparently innocent accounts were transferred to other more respectable institutions.'

'So it seems possible that someone connected with Nazism was acting as Joseph's fairy godmother?'

'In a nutshell, that seems to be a reasonable hypothesis. I'd certainly think it justifies further investigation.'

'Absolutely.'

'Look, I must tell you that on our original charging basis, you've already lost your deposit and owe us another £2 to 3,000. However, I've discussed the case with my partner, Karl, and we're prepared to continue investigating at a 50% discount. It must be in the public interest to uncover the truth here and we don't trust 'plod' to deal with it – in any case they wouldn't be interested because no one has reported a crime, although I suspect that there were probably some illegalities associated with the adoption and the likely forging of citizenship papers, etc, but minor crimes... much too old.'

Fine was temporarily lost for words. After a small pause he spoke:

'This is exciting news. I can't find a way of expressing my gratitude. I suspected something, but this beggars belief. Invoice me what I owe you and thank you once again for your work, interest and support.'

Benjamin Fine slumped into his armchair in a state of combined shock and elation. He had always been convinced that Joseph Howson had more about him than his perfect exterior. However, never in his wildest dreams did he imagine he was connected, however indirectly, with one of the most heinous and ruthless criminal organisations of recent world history.

Chapter Eighteen
REVELATIONS AND REVENGE
'To be betrayed, you must first belong.'
K. Philby

Mary Anne Marshall, now aged twenty, had lost contact with most of her school contemporaries. As one of the girls said soon after they had all left, the only companion Mary Anne would go out of her way to stay in contact with was her drug dealer. She was almost right. In fact, the only pupil she even bothered with was a girl called Caroline who, on leaving school, had shared a flat in Balham with Mary Anne for a few months until the latter disappeared one weekend with Caroline's shopping money. There was some reconciliation and the money was eventually returned but the damage had been done and both parties agreed it would be prudent to go their separate ways. They still contacted each other by mobile from time to time, although more often than not it was Caroline who took the initiative: for some reason – schoolgirl loyalty perhaps – she felt it was incumbent on her to check from time to time upon the academically bright, but emotionally vulnerable, Mary Anne.

Two years had passed since they had left school. It was late August 2001, and Caroline had not heard from Mary Anne for a number of months; she was simply not answering her mobile. After contacting Mary Anne's father, Caroline ascertained that her contemporary had moved in with a man called Kenny and both were living in a run-down flat in Harleybury, a small town in Surrey. She decided that she would have to make the short trip south, down the A3.

'Run down' seemed something of an understatement as Mary Anne answered the front door. What Caroline found inside was unadulterated squalor. Private schoolgirl Mary Anne had moved from the immaculate, spacious Spanish villa of her youth to a tiny, dark, suffocating flat in a run-down backstreet.

'Look, come and stay with me for a couple of weeks. We can go out, buy a few nice clothes, have a laugh. It'll be like old times.'

'I can't, he won't let me.'

'Who won't let you?'

'Kenny, my boyfriend. He only lets me go out to earn money. If I was away for a couple of weeks, he'd expect me to return with thousands.'

'That's crap. How can you call him your boyfriend? Jailer more like!'

Mary Anne looked pathetic as she sat on the moth-eaten, ash-strewn carpet of the dimly-lit lounge. She drew on the joint, which hung loosely from the corner of her mouth. Since the contact with "Max" had ceased, she had felt more wretched than ever.

'Listen, keep that phone on – you've got my number. If you need a bolthole, I can come and pick you up. You're no one's slave,' said Caroline, as the two girls embraced.

The latter departed, reluctantly leaving her friend at the mercy of this so-called boyfriend. If he'd been there, she might well have given him a piece of her mind, as the saying goes. He sounded little more than a drugged-up control freak.

It was two months to the day that Caroline received a text from Mary Anne:

'Come quick! Fuckin Kennys gone beserk recked the flat and beaten me to a pulp. Please come. MA x'

Mary Anne spent two days in a south London hospital, having her wounds treated – broken nose, three broken fingers, a patchwork of heavy bruises, including two black eyes and, most seriously, heavy concussion – Caroline was finally allowed to drive her back to her own flat in nearby Stanton.

She soon ascertained the reason for Kenny's anger, as Mary Anne produced a supply of heroin, which she had been systematically hiding from Kenny over a period of weeks. It was her intention that, once she had stored up enough to see her through a month or so, she would leave Kenny for good and settle down with gardener Max. When, on a particular occasion, he realised his girlfriend was being less than honest about drug distribution, he gave her the pummelling of her life.

Even though Caroline was uncomfortable about having a plentiful supply of a hard drug in her own home, she realised that Mary Anne could not function without it. She felt she had little choice in the matter and busied herself tending to Mary Anne's recuperative needs; she had never seen such a flagrant example of bodily harm in her career as a paramedic but understood Mary Anne's reluctance to press charges, given the reason for the assault. Mary Anne was resolute – not only was she not prepared to entertain any notion of police involvement, she was even in a state of anxiety about how Kenny would react to her leaving the flat and not telling him where she was going – such was her desperate mindset.

The swelling eventually subsided, her nose had been re-set and within a couple of weeks Mary Anne was back on her feet – she still suffered from intermittent headaches but most of her concern came from her need for a fix.

One October morning, Caroline, concerned that Mary Anne had not left the house for nearly a week, made a proposal:

'Mary Anne, why don't you come with me back to St Michael's next Friday? The school is having its annual Autumn Awards Day and I've got a couple of tickets. It'll be a chance to catch up with some of the old teachers, and some of the girls from our year.'

'I've not got much to say. We didn't have much in common at school, even less now.'

'Will you do it for me? I don't want to go on my own, just in case there's no one there I was friends with. We could pop in for an hour or so. We could even visit our favourite café at Budleigh. Please?'

Mary Anne reluctantly agreed, on the condition Caroline allowed her to ring a number each morning, to arrange for a daily fix to be delivered. Caroline once again agreed, realising that if Mary Anne was to get better, it would have to be a gradual process, emanating from a change of lifestyle – and that principally meant keeping her away from Kenny. She reckoned if she could supervise Mary Anne's drug taking, she hoped, gradually, she'd be able to wean her off. Just as importantly, she would endeavour to get Mary Anne back into a life routine, so often missing among drug-users. She was also fully aware that her effort could well backfire; still fresh in her mind was the incident of theft when they last shared accommodation. Caroline resolved that, once Mary Anne was over the current shock, she would find for her a flat nearby, some distance from Harleybury.

The sun was shining on a cold October day, as the two friends drove down the A303, out of London, on their way to Devon. On arrival at St Mike's, as it was commonly called, some three hours later, they parked the car and made their way along the main drive, observing the VIPs on the lawn to the left, who had spilled out of the enormous marquee. They proceeded up to the main hall. Ascending the steps, leading to the front doors, they were greeted by Deputy Head, Mrs Wellbeck, who extended a welcoming hand, smiled warmly and engaged Caroline in a brief conversation as to how she was doing – she didn't seem to recognise Mary Anne. Caroline assured her how well things were, told her about her new life as a recently qualified medic and accepted a programme from the pile Mrs Wellbeck was holding. Both alumnae then proceeded into the hall. Already virtually every one of the thousand seats was taken, Mary Anne and Caroline settling for a couple which were spare, right at the back, in the corner. Caroline surveyed the plethora of backs of heads, hoping to recognise someone of their

146

year group. The hall was a hubbub of conversation and within minutes those who had been enjoying lunch in the hospitality marquee began filing in from the rear, to take up their reserved seats at the front of the hall. Caroline started to read the day's programme, wondering if there were any recognisable names. Caroline herself had been back on a couple of occasions, but for Mary Anne it was her very first visit. After a while the audience went very quiet as the Principal Guest and the Headmaster made their way in through the rear doors. Mary Anne was finding it hard to concentrate by this point and had closed her eyes, wondering what Kenny was doing, how mad he would be and how he would react when he eventually found her. The Headmaster started to address the assembled company and this seemed to push Mary Anne into deeper contemplation: she could feel her fingers and toes tingling, sensations which she had become accustomed to when she felt in need of another

fix. As the Headmaster concluded his opening address, Mary Anne briefly opened her eyes, asked Caroline where the nearest lavatory was and quietly slipped out. She was gone for a good ten minutes. As she regained her seat, Caroline could smell cannabis emanating from her friend's newly purchased jacket. The presentation of the various awards seemed to go on forever (St Mike's was run along such egalitarian lines that it was usual for nearly half the number of pupils to receive at least one award). Mary Anne showed little interest in the proceedings, barely glancing at the stage as the fellow in the gown and mortarboard handed out the final assortment of books, plates and shields. As the applause petered away, the academically bedecked Principal Guest took his place at the centre of the stage, his six-foot frame towering over the modest-sized lectern.

'Ladies, Gentlemen, pupils of St Michael's...'

Mary Anne sat bolt upright and focused directly on the speaker. Her blood seemed to have drained from her head, and momentarily she lost track of where she was. Caroline glanced at her, wondering what had excited her sudden, undivided attention.

'It's him,' she said aloud, causing a number of audience members in the immediate rows in front to turn their heads. 'It's Max...it's Maxim.'

Perplexed as to what Mary Anne was talking about, only very much aware that she was drawing attention to herself, Caroline ushered what had become a somewhat excited and shocked Mary Anne out into the fresh air.

'What *is* the matter? You look like you've seen an extra-terrestrial.'

Mary Anne sat on the grass, trying to put some understanding into what she had just witnessed.

'Can I see your programme for a moment?'

Caroline duly handed it over. Mary Anne read:

Awards presented by – **Dr Joseph Howson, Ph.D., Headmaster, Cranford College, Surrey.**

Mary Anne wanted so much to tell her faithful friend the whole story, but something urged her to hold her counsel for the moment. She had to come to terms with the fact that it wasn't a gardener with whom she had been making love, but a Headmaster, and a very important one at that. Although she did understand why someone in his position should not want to divulge too much about themselves, at that moment she felt very much deceived by so-called Max the Gardener. After all, he had not contented himself with straightforward sex. In a bid to elicit more and more passion from Mary Anne, he had led her to believe that she meant more to him than a routine call girl. As a result, Mary Anne had found herself becoming more and more emotionally entangled with him. Was he pretending all along? Perhaps he was married and had children. If Mary Anne had known that, she certainly wouldn't have allowed herself to put anything more into their meetings than the usual routine sex. When their rendezvous had ceased, she'd been very upset, something she had never been when any other client had moved on.

'I saw someone in there who I thought I knew. I think I made a mistake.

'Who did you think you saw?'

'I thought the Guest of Honour was one of my clients from the escort agency, but he's simply a look-alike. I don't want to go back in there, it's hot, stuffy and it's difficult to see much from the very back.'

Caroline burst out laughing, entwined her arm with Mary Anne's and both decided that, after a visit to their old boarding house, they would drive the short distance to their favourite café in Budleigh Salterton, where they'd often been during their school days. No mention was made of the client look-alike during the long journey back to London, but Mary Anne could think of little else.

Ensconced back at Caroline's flat, Mary Anne waited until her host had left for work on the Monday morning before ringing *Directory Enquiries* to ascertain the Cranford College main number. They put her through to the main switchboard and Mary Anne asked for the Headmaster's office.

'Could I speak to the Headmaster, please?' she asked Howson's secretary.

'May I ask who's calling, please?'

'Could you tell him it's Mary, a family friend?'

'Just one moment, caller.' There was a pause. 'I'm afraid the Headmaster is not picking up his phone at present. Could you ring back later, please?'

'Yes.'

She replaced the receiver of Caroline's phone.

As the days passed, Mary Anne made a series of unsuccessful attempts to contact Max, as she knew him, but each time she managed to reach only his secretary. She was told that he was in a meeting, away from his desk, teaching, etc. She left her number time and again (each time leaving the name of Mary) but, unsurprisingly, he did not call back. Mary Anne, at this point, felt genuine empathy for Max's predicament – she understood why he had purported to be the school gardener. Indeed, she felt a certain admiration for his thespian talents. However, she'd immediately recognised the unmistakable timbre of his voice at the Awards' Ceremony. He had taken on a definite rustic tinge during their sessions, which he had maintained throughout and which had convinced her utterly that this man sharing her body and his bed, was a full-time tender of gardens. He had delivered an acting *tour de force*. Even though she felt he had taken advantage of her, she nevertheless understood why he was nervous about now even talking to her. He felt embarrassed – ashamed – that he had summarily brought a halt to their trysts. If only she could allay any such concerns, Mary Anne felt they could once again enjoy each other's company; she might even be able to do it without Kenny ever knowing.

At last, on the umpteenth occasion of trying, she was put through to his study, only to be greeted by the words:

'I don't know why you keep calling or what you want, but I do not wish you to call me ever again – ever.'

He hung up.

It was not quite what Mary Anne had been expecting. She realised immediately that Maxim knew exactly what he was saying. She sat on the edge of Caroline's sofa, staring out of the window, wondering how she should react – walk away and treat the whole affair for what it obviously was – a client paying money for professional services – or should she make a stand and make this arrogant man realise that telling people you love them over and over again is wholly unfair if you're simply interested in unalloyed sexual gratification.

The more she turned over in her mind his perfunctory rejection of her, the more slighted and angry she felt. Mary Anne decided that if Max wanted to play dirty, she could too. It was at this point that the image of Kenny appeared in her mind – he'll know what to do: indeed, if Maxim refused to allow her back into his life, she had ways of insisting that he did so. He had always teased more and more adventurous sex out of her on the grounds of his emotional attachment – he'd been lying. He'd been happy to accept a first-class service but had always paid only second-class sums of money. The number of times he'd told her that times were difficult financially and all along he had been earning probably a six-figure sum.

The more she contemplated the whole affair, the angrier she became. She'd been well and truly duped – he didn't love her at all – he desired her on one level only: she'd been lied to, totally used and abused.

'Well, Mr Headmaster, you had better get your chequebook ready because now it is *your* turn to be taken advantage of,' she said to herself.

Within minutes she had collected her minimal belongings, shoved them into her rucksack, written a quick note to Caroline thanking her for the three weeks' rehabilitation and sauntered off down the road towards Streatham station, to pick up the train back to Harleybury.

Kenny was asleep when she got back – stoned. She thought it best to leave him until he naturally stirred: depending on what he had injected, swallowed or drunk, that could be a couple of days. Waking Kenny was equivalent to stirring a sleeping bull terrier. When he at last did come to, even this heartless crook was unable to disguise his pleasure at seeing her.

'Sorry, babes, I lost my temper and all that, 'cos I thought you was rippin' me off,' Kenny said.

'Kenny, I'm telling you straight, man, if you lay a finger on me again, you can just fuck off, man, because I'll fuck off for good!'

'I won't. I promise.'

'You said that last time and I believed you. You won't get another chance. I've had enough of your beatings.'

Whenever the two had heated discussions it was always the uneducated, slow Kenny who had to concede. He had only one area of superiority over Mary Anne – physical strength. This, coupled with an uncontrollable temper, which was Kenny's means of survival on the streets was, on occasions, his response to Mary Anne's much quicker tongue. When his mind was free of drugs, Kenny was like a puppy in her arms but, with a mind unbalanced by smoking his favourite marijuana and simultaneously riled, he could be brutal.

'Kenny, I mean it – this is the *last* time. You touch me again and you'll never see me again. You're lucky I've come back this time.'

She proceeded to fill in Kenny on all that had happened during the previous three weeks. As her tale unfolded, Kenny's jaw dropped lower and lower.

'Babes, this could be an on-going Christmas for us,' he said, 'we'll bleed that fucker for every last penny he possesses – he's screwed you, now we're gonna screw him, the fuckin' bastard.'

'We need to be careful. He's a clever bloke, in a powerful position. He'll not take too kindly about being screwed by the likes of you and me.' As usual, it was Mary Anne who spoke sense.

The two sat together for hours, mulling over the possible courses of action best suited to extracting some golden eggs from their, as yet unaware, soon-to-be benefactor.

Chapter Nineteen
HOWSON'S CHOICE
'Most of the time we have to choose between the unpalatable and the disastrous.'
J. K. Galbraith

It was the day after the Carol Service, the final week of the Michaelmas term. Joseph Howson sat alone in his study. The words uttered to him as he progressed from the chapel were few, but crushing: *"**We know who you are, Mary Anne fucker... be in touch**."* The instant the Rastafarian came into his sight, Howson knew instantly that this individual was in consort with Mary Anne. It was the moment he had been dreading since she had gone out of his life nearly five months previous.

"Be in touch".

Three short words but they were torturing his mind, as he played them over and over again. It wasn't just the words which were a source of disquiet, it was that glance – those dark, threatening eyes. How long would he have to wait for him to 'be in touch'?

He sat at his study desk in a state of anxious contemplation. He had a choice: either he was to go along with the blackmailer (because there was little doubt in Howson's mind what the Rastafarian and Mary Anne were planning), or he was to reveal all immediately to Marie-Christine and to Sir Anthony, then hope his wife would stay with him (at least for the sake of their son), resign from his position and retire to France with the family. The latter course was dismissed in an instant – Joseph Howson was a proud man and he had striven successfully to become one of the most respected Headmasters in the land; he was not going to humiliate himself, or his family, by putting his indiscretions into the public forum. He would rather die than be exposed by a couple of desperate, grasping drugged up ne'er-do-wells. No, he was going to fight as he had done throughout his life whenever faced by a difficult challenge. Nothing or no one had managed to get the better of Dr Joseph Howson and neither would these two. He would have to go along with their demands initially, while considering and then implementing some sort of plan. In the cold light of day, Howson realised that he would have to destroy them before they destroyed him. He didn't want to hurt Mary Anne particularly, as she was a desperately sad individual, but he had little choice... what must be done, must be done. The Rastafarian may be ruthless and be used to getting his way; unfortunately for him, Howson pondered, on this occasion he had met his match. With this, he got to his feet and made his way back to the Common Room, to carry out the term's final tasks.

Throughout the rest of the afternoon, Joseph made every effort to carry on as normal. He managed, temporarily, to expunge some of the worrying thoughts which lay just below the surface of his mind. When he was finally able to extricate himself from his last commitment of the day, he returned to the Headmaster's grand residence, picked at the *poulet rôti* his wife had prepared for him, poured himself a very stiff whisky and retired to his bedroom, physically and emotionally exhausted. Marie-Christine knew when her husband needed some proverbial space.

As he tried to sleep, his mind was dominated by two major thoughts: the first was his feeling of shame that he had used Mary Anne for his own sexual gratification and the second emotion was the fear of her and the Rastafarian's response. The cat was out of the bag, as it were, and he had laid himself open to blackmail, exacerbated by the fact that one of the potential blackmailers was an obviously very dangerous and unscrupulous character. How could he have been so naïve? Of course, this had been, from the start, a *liaison dangereuse*. His sexual drive had blinded him to prudence and he had ridden roughshod over his usual impeccable carefulness.

Eventually, Marie-Christine came and lay down beside him. She whispered pleasantries to him about how brilliant the Service had been and how a Governor had remarked that Cranford was enjoying one of the most glorious periods in its already distinguished history. She was sufficiently perceptive to realise that the weekend's pressures had taken a heavy toll on her magnificent husband.

Eventually, Joseph managed to drift off to sleep. In the early hours of the morning, he awoke and, unable to get back to sleep, he got up, donned his dressing gown and went for a walk around the school grounds, trying to martial his thoughts.

He was sufficiently worldly-wise to know that it is generally foolish to succumb to blackmail. However, he also knew that he could not ignore the threat. He considered whether there was any point in seeking professional or legal advice; however, he couldn't face the risk or embarrassment of confiding this situation to anyone, including to his beloved wife.

He contemplated how convenient it would be if Mary Anne and the Rastafarian were simply to disappear, but he knew that they were not going away, at least voluntarily. As he wandered around the 1st XV rugby pitch, he contemplated the privileged nature of his own life: leader of this beautiful, renowned, historic educational establishment; he thought about Marie-Christine and his beloved son. Was he prepared to lose everything over his involvement with a junkie and a criminal associate? Why had this potential outcome not been paramount in his mind when he had begun the whole tawdry affair?

Joseph's interests were very broad and he had always enjoyed reading about true crimes, as well as the occasional detective story. He didn't find accounts of the exploits of serial killers generally very interesting. The crimes which had caught his imagination were murders carried out by apparently ordinary people, who had no obvious history of criminality and violence. He had often asked himself what it took to kill in cold blood, to plan murder and execute it. He could never imagine being capable of murdering for financial gain. Nevertheless, he had often asked himself whether there were circumstances in which he would contemplate the most heinous of all crimes. It was inevitable that the dark thoughts which were beginning to engulf his mind included this as a possibility.

Joseph had never held any genuine religious beliefs. He was an unashamed opportunist, who had always been determined to rise to the top. He didn't like playing second fiddle to anyone. He was not generally a moraliser and he'd never spent a lot of mental energy agonising over moral principles. In some of his darker moments, he wondered whether he really did care about anyone other than himself. Of course, he loved his son and cared about his welfare. Indeed, he was as ambitious for him as he had been for himself. He also genuinely cared for and, in his own way, loved Marie-Christine. However, he often asked himself whether his love was selfish. Certainly, he knew that his primary driving force in life was his own ego and not any great sense of public service or genuine care for others. Getting married and having a child was expected of anyone with ambition to rise to the top. His own childhood had been stable but not particularly affectionate. His adoptive parents were somewhat older than average and, although he could never find fault with either parent, he was aware that they had not been demonstrative of their love for him. Added to this, he had known from an early age that they were not his biological parents. The truth of the matter was that Joseph was fundamentally cold, although he could act out great charm and warmth, whenever he wanted to, that is, whenever it suited his purpose.

The thought of perpetrating violence on anyone was essentially alien to Joseph. This was not primarily through a strong moral sense but was simply that he had never had any sort of taste for violence and had always avoided it. He saw violence as something that lower specimens of humanity resorted to, for whatever reasons. Nevertheless, Joseph was in an extraordinary situation. Two people who, in his view, led essentially parasitic and worthless lives were threatening his whole productive, successful world. Would it really be that evil, that wrong, for him to arrange their removal? After all, his professional demise would be to the detriment of so many others in this wonderful community, pupils, parents and staff, who relied on his strong leadership. On the other hand, who, apart from their dreary, tawdry selves, would suffer if the blackguard Rastafarian and Mary-Anne disappeared? **No-one**, reasoned Howson. It was all about natural selection, pragmatism.

Deep in his consciousness, he knew that it was wrong but he had visions of being forced to resign in disgrace, visions of Marie-Christine leaving with Karl for France. He could not contemplate turning up to explain to his adoptive parents that their golden boy had messed up and lost everything. In fact, the thought that he'd never be able to show his face in the circles in which he had always been accustomed filled him with a sense of unbearable despair. What's more, due to his public persona, the press would have a field day.

Of course, it occurred to him that, even if he did bring himself to organise the premature deaths of the pair, he might not escape detection and then he would have added life imprisonment as a cold-blooded murderer to the ignominy. But, if he were left with no alternative, then so be it, this was a risk he would have to take: 'in for a penny, in for a pound', as they say.

Joseph had often been faced with the need to make bold decisions, some risky, but he had realised that making weak or cowardly decisions was also risky. In fact, it was not possible to achieve and sustain important office without taking calculated gambles. He was now contemplating what many would consider the unthinkable.

When faced with a difficult choice, Joseph had always tried to give himself as much space and time as possible. He realised that there was no immediate need to decide what to do for the best. Having given his anguished thoughts some airing, he felt a little better and decided that it was best to return home and attempt to get some sleep. In fact, he had no essential commitments on the following day and he resolved that in the morning he would contact his deputy, Worsthorne, and ask him to 'look after the shop' for the day. He could then take himself for a drive somewhere and engage in further contemplation, without distraction, something he had done in the past when a major decision had to be made.

Worsthorne received a call at 7.45a.m to inform him that the Head would be away for the day, and could he arrange cover for his late morning double period of politics with the Upper Sixth top set. Worsthorne, a perspicacious man, was used to receiving early morning calls from his lord and master, but this one was unusual. Howson usually operated by careful advance planning and rarely skipped a teaching or school commitment at short notice. If he did, he would normally have a very good reason. On this occasion, he didn't even bother to invent an excuse. After all, he didn't have to bare his soul to his deputy. The relationship between the two was not particularly close. Worsthorne was generally available for sound advice and he was certainly an excellent hatchet man, who would efficiently carry out such dirty work as Howson would delegate, whenever possible. However, Howson did not use his Deputy as a close confidant. The latter was an acerbic character who, in his own way, was as intellectually able as Howson, although he had never obtained a D.Phil. He certainly had a First Class degree and contributed to learned journals from time to time. Worsthorne did not particularly like Howson. Although the Deputy was capable of ruthlessness, there was a considerable difference between the two. Worsthorne would reserve his cutting edge for those who, he believed, fell considerably short of his own high standards of professionalism and teaching capability. He didn't generally use his authority for personal advantage, to keep adversaries in their place. He had obtained his position on the basis of obvious merit and had been given administrative responsibilities from quite a young age. He was responsible for producing the school timetable, which is one of the most demanding of tasks in a school, one having to juggle a large number of constraints of staff member availabilities, many of which are quite idiosyncratic. The Worst, indeed, was capable of simultaneously retaining forty or fifty relevant constraining facts in his head and satisfying all of them. There was one occasion when he'd had to apologise to the Head of Mathematics over timetabling a double period for a late afternoon, explaining that, try as he did, he was unable to improve the timetable any further without affecting the A level choices for an outstandingly bright pupil, who had insisted on tackling an unusual A level combination, which had included History and Mathematics.

However, The Worst, who tended to keep his own counsel, had always had serious doubts about Howson's way of thinking and certainly he had been unhappy with the Head's obsessions, particularly his almost fanatical pursuit of Fine. The latter was of a similar age to Worsthorne and was one of the colleagues whom he very much approved of and respected. Indeed, he had serious doubts about the reliability of the complaint made by the pupil Major, but had not been permitted to get involved in the investigation. He couldn't help suspecting that Howson had unduly influenced the boy. He knew full well that his boss was a calculating man and possessed a sinister side. Thus, when early this morning he was asked to arrange short notice cover, it did occur to him briefly that Howson's absence may be connected with the Carol Service incident in some way. In true Worst form, he didn't allow this fleeting thought to develop, but simply shrugged his shoulders and decided how he was going to attend to the day's problems. In some respects, the Deputy quite enjoyed taking charge. He knew that he was good at dispensing authority, although he was aware that he didn't have quite the tact and outward charm of his superior.

For his part, Howson had asked Marie-Christine to provide him with a small continental-style breakfast and, at 8a.m, he left the school premises and drove off to one of his favourite beauty spots, where he parked his car, in order to contemplate his position in peace and solitude.

Joseph realised that he had reached a major crisis point in his life. He considered how he would cope with exposure. Although he had hitherto never entertained suicidal thoughts, he realised that it would be difficult for him to live the consequences of public humiliation. How might he end it all? Fleeting thoughts of drink and drugs combinations, even hanging himself, all briefly crossed his mind. He had never felt as low. Images of his lovemaking with Mary Anne flashed in front of him; only now he saw her face as that of the devil. She had been nothing but a fantasy. In reality, she was the cause of his possible professional destruction. He even felt sick at the thought of what he had done with her. He thought of the wholesome sweetness of Marie-Christine and how much he enjoyed their spasmodic lovemaking. Although his wife did not have the techniques of a great courtesan, he realised that she genuinely loved him and he loved her. How could he have placed himself in such a position with this call girl, simply to satisfy mere lust? Why had he been so foolish? Why could he not have been patient while Marie-Christine had been suffering from post-natal depression? Thousands of other husbands have to cope in such a situation. Why had he not put some effort into helping his beloved wife at that time of need? He should have sought out the best professional help instead of wasting his money on a sordid whore. As many men and women who have sat and contemplated the consequences of their folly, he had the dreadful sense of the irreversibility of time, the onward march of events, the clear recognition that one can never turn back the clock.

Joseph Howson was fundamentally a man of action. He wasn't going to permit events to control him. He still had some hope. He hadn't yet been exposed. As time went on, his realisation was that there was only one certain resolution to his predicament: Mary Anne and her associate would have to 'disappear'. He needed to turn his attention to means and methods and timescale.

In the first instance, he was slightly handicapped. He had no idea how he was going to resurrect his relationship with Mary Anne, in order to put himself into a position in which he could carry out the deed. He knew that the longer he left matters, the riskier it would become. These two reprobates would think nothing of exposing *"the story of the Head Gardener"*, if there were a substantial cheque dangled in front of them.

As the minutes turned into hours, Joseph was able gradually to reconcile himself to the idea of a violent solution. It was never going to be palatable. Was there any point in testing the water of a non-violent outcome with Mary Anne first? Was there a faint possibility that he could buy them off? Surely, if he tried this course, there was never going to be a reason for the demands to end. So long as he was vulnerable, the daily needs of Mary Anne and associate would be paramount. However, things were going to pan out, one thing was for sure – time was of the essence. He could not avoid making contact with Mary Anne and he decided to pluck up the courage to call her as soon as practicable. Joseph Howson got to his feet, jumped into his Mercedes Sports and made the return journey to Cranford College, *his* college – how long for depended upon his courage to do that which was necessary.

Chapter Twenty
THE GOOSE CONTINUES TO LAY
'Most of our relationships begin and continue as forms of mutual exploitation, to be terminated when one or both parties run out of goods.'
W. H. Auden

The Michaelmas term had reached its conclusion, the vast majority of pupils had bidden farewell and the only ones remaining were those about to depart for CCF camp and the small contingent who lived in the Far East, whose flight did not leave, from Heathrow, until the following morning. Most of the staff had completed their term's duties and could now look forward to a month of Christmas relaxation with their family. For his part, Joseph had a full week's work ahead of him, completing school reports, answering emails, correspondence, seeing various parents about disciplinary issues and suchlike. From past experience, Marie-Christine was well aware that their family holiday together in France would not start for well over a week.

Joseph closed the front door of Cranford House and made his way across to his study, to read his morning mail. After an hour or so of letter dictation, he wondered if he should ring Mary Anne. He glanced at his watch – 10am. There was no point in ringing until at least midday as 'street people' rarely arise *ante meridiam*. He tuned into Classic FM on the radio that he kept in his study, while writing a number of reports. That morning some light-hearted Mozart was featured, followed by a full rendition of Brahms's second symphony. Perhaps this was slightly unfortunate – the second symphony is excruciatingly emotional. In many respects its romantic, but powerfully tragic, undertones seemed to underline his own life situation and made it difficult for him to concentrate on the task at hand.

As midday approached, Joseph turned away from his computer screen and decided that he would have to make the dreaded call. He dialled Mary Anne's mobile number. There was no answer. He waited a few moments and dialled again. This time a very sleepy voice answered.

'Yeah?'

'Mary Anne?'

'Max?'

After a few moments she continued:

'I thought you were dead. Why haven't you been in touch? Can't speak now. I'll call you later,' and the phone went dead.

Joseph managed to complete a whole boarding house's set of reports before Mary Anne returned his call. She sounded excited.

'Look, I'm really sorry about what's happened. When can I see you? Have to be quick because he's in the loo at the moment.'

Howson knew immediately that 'he' referred to her Rastafarian accomplice.

'Any time this afternoon.'

They arranged to meet outside a Cambridge Road landmark, the snooker hall, at 2p.m and, with a sense of nervous anticipation, Joseph turned up at 1.45p.m, parking his car in a lay-by opposite. Mary Anne appeared promptly, made her way over to his parked car, opened the passenger door and got inside.

'Let's get the hell out of here,' said Joseph and he drove her as quickly as possible out of town to the same beauty spot where had spent the morning of contemplation. Joseph kissed her insincerely.

Mary Anne lost no time in telling Joseph that, although she had become aware of whom he was, *she* didn't want to cause him any problems but just to continue their relationship together.

'It's my boyfriend, Kenny, who's been a fucking arse about things. It was him who went up to the school. I asked him not to. I swear to God it wasn't my idea for him to go last week. He takes no fucking notice of me. He's a complete bastard at times. Look, Max, I mean Joe, I've really missed you and not just the business.'

'How did you find out who I really was?'

As Mary Anne told him the story of the Awards Ceremony recognition, Howson went cold. He had attended only as a last-minute replacement for a dignitary who had called off. Joseph asked her what she expected him to do now that he was in the firing line.

Mary Anne went quiet for a few minutes and then said:

'Look, Kenny's very dangerous. He's really determined. Any money you give me goes straight to him. I really don't want to use you for your money. I've got a big drug habit and, since we split up, I've not had the stomach to see other clients, so the money's run out and we're in a shit situation. I've clipped a few punters – that's taking money in advance and then pissing off. The agency's dropped me since they suspected I was doing private work without telling them. That was you!'

Joseph felt cool and cynical and was convinced, rather than it being all down to this Kenny person, that Mary Anne was fully up to her neck in any potential blackmail.

'Okay, Mary Anne, what do you want me to do?'

'I reckon £500 per week'll keep Kenny quiet. He wants to bleed you dry but you must believe me when I say I'll do all in my power to keep him at bay. He's as thick as shit and can usually be swayed by the right incentive.'

'That's over £2,000 per month, £24,000 per annum – how can you expect me to find that kind of money without my wife knowing?'

It was the first time he had mentioned his wife in front of Mary Anne.

'Maybe I can persuade him to lay off for 400 quid a week. Look, I'll give you as much sex as you want. You can have me on demand – every day if you want; twice a day even. Whatever you like! You mean more to me than you realise.'

Joseph was silent for a few moments. Unfortunately, he had no interest in receiving services from a woman he no longer believed nor trusted. He didn't have the time or the inclination.

'Can I think about it all?'

'Of course, but he knows it was you who rang me this morning and said that I'd better come back with some dosh or he'd be making another visit to the school.'

Joseph opened his wallet and produced £200 in crisp twenty pound notes.

'Well, this'll keep him quiet for a while.'

'I'm sure it'll help for the present. Do you fancy sex now?'

'I'm really busy at the moment and bloody tired. I'm up to my eyes in school reports, but I promise I'll call you on Thursday.'

He realised that he had to play for time and, although all his instincts were not to give in to blackmail, he decided that he could probably buy a week or two for an affordable couple of thousand, before deciding on the most pragmatic way forward.

As he drove Mary Anne back to the Cambridge Road, he barely listened to her excited chattering. Joseph realised that seeing her in the flesh again had reinforced his growing hatred of her and her boyfriend. After he had dropped her back outside the snooker hall, he drove off, trying to assess the truth about her attitude. For a fleeting moment, he contemplated the idea of having Kenny professionally dispatched, while sparing Mary Anne. Then his thoughts turned to the fact that it was she, after all, who must have given him all the information. She had told him about how to get to the school. She was the one who was following the blackmail through and extracting his money, despite her disingenuous protestations. He resolved that he had to be strong and accept that she was in it as deeply as her boyfriend. It was she who had identified him and was now a party to the blackmail. How naïve he had been. Despite the morsel of affection he still had for her, his overwhelming feelings were anger and resentment. Her attempt to mitigate the blackmail by offering him sex in return for the money did little to help. He certainly had no intention of touching her intimately ever again.

Joseph returned to his duties and spent the following few days trying to concentrate on the hundreds of reports, which appeared, seemingly endlessly, on his computer screen. He was aware that he had lost his customary energy. Certainly, he gave the impression to his office staff of being somewhat lacklustre, a word that he and other schoolmasters were quite fond of using when describing a dilatory pupil effort!

It was Wednesday afternoon when he received a call from Mary Anne. She hurriedly explained that she needed to see him urgently.

'What's the problem?' asked Joseph, being pretty sure exactly what was behind her request.

'Look,' she said, 'I'm sorry, but I need a oner.'

Joseph tried to explain that he couldn't get away, having reports to finish, but Mary Anne was insistent.

'He's going mad – he's not eaten for two days – he's had no drugs for twenty-four hours, apart from a ten pound bag of brown, which I shared with him last night.'

'You mean you've already spent the £200?' Joseph's voice faltered.

Mary Anne explained that her boyfriend had immediately spent the whole sum on drugs and that he had already used most of them.

'He says that he's coming straight down to the school, unless you give me some money.'

Joseph realised that he had little choice, so he made an assignation at the same venue and delivered the requested amount of cash. This incident erased any lasting doubt in Joseph's mind that there was going to be a limit to the demands and confirmed once and for all that he was going to be used as nothing other than a bottomless cash point. Joseph Howson was no longer in control: a position alien to him. To say he did not like the predicament would be a serious understatement; it was this phone call which, in Howson's mind, signed two death warrants. He was now totally resolved that he would devote himself to ending the nightmare in the only possible way; he had no other choice. With a sense of grim determination, his mind was now engulfed in deadly thoughts.

On Mary Anne's return home from their rendezvous, Kenny met her at the door,

'Have you got the bread?'

She nodded limply.

'Then give it here.'

She listlessly handed the full amount over to him. He quickly disappeared, returning twenty minutes later with £30 worth of heroin and £60 worth of crack. He boasted how he had kept a tenner, so that they could get some KFC after they'd scored.

After they had satisfied their most urgent need, they began to prepare and smoke some crack. After a while, Mary Anne spoke:

'Look, I'm worried about what we're doing... shit'll come out of all this. He's too clever to be pissed all over.'

'The bastard's got no choice – he ain't going to want his perversions blurted out, so he'll keep paying – he can spare plenty.'

'He's an intelligent and strong-minded bloke. He's no easy pushover.'

'Well, he gave you enough dosh when he was screwing you. He's not short of the readies when he wants something. Don't start believing any crap he's now telling you about being hard-up, cos he fuckin' ain't. In any case, what the fuck's he gonna do about it?'

'Look, I don't know, but I wouldn't underestimate him – he didn't get to his position being weak and stupid.'

'The guy's a fuckin' perv and there's fuck-all he can do – he shouldn't have shagged you so much. Now he can pay the price. I want him to learn a lesson for shagging *my* pretty little chick's arse off so much.'

168

Kenny grabbed Mary Anne's backside, simultaneously planting a wet kiss on her left cheek.

She had always hated being referred to as Kenny's property. She resented his sense of 'ownership'.

'You know what we're doing is wicked and somehow it'll end badly for us.'

'Look, shut the fuck up, you stupid woman. Let us blokes look after these matters. In any case, I'm fed up with you touting your pretty little butt all over town. We've now got a way of keeping going without all those filthy perverts sticking their cocks in your gob.'

Mary Anne refrained from expressing her feeling that it was he, Kenny, who was the pervert-in-chief and that none of her clients had ever inflicted pain on her like he did or ever shown his level of disrespect towards her. She realised that she wasn't going to get any further with this bully and that she had no other choice but to go along with whatever he said. She cursed the day that she had become involved with him and with the drug scene to which he was inextricably attached, but, unfortunately, she was now firmly manacled to the whole tawdry world as well, whether she liked it or not, and she could see no way out. Although she realised that one day she was going to have to break her habit, she was certainly not ready for rehabilitation. The stress of her life-situation created a kind of vicious circle. The major cause of her stress, the need for the drugs, was also the only immediate solution to it. Like many before her, she knew that the only way out would be in the context of a really supportive relationship, with a decent, solvent man. Joseph would be ideal, were he available, but she knew well that she was only a diversion for him, his plaything, there to suit his needs and availability, and not hers. Mary Anne realised that she had no choice but to do as she was told by mad-dog Kenny and to continue to extract further money from someone for whom, deep-down, she had feelings of love.

Chapter Twenty One
DRESSED TO KILL
'All dressed up and somewhere to go'
G. Whiting

Joseph Howson did his best to limit the financial damage caused by Mary Anne's demands. He soon realised that he could get away with about £100 per day. As long as he kept the two supplied with a reasonable quantity of drugs, it would not be in their interests to carry out any of their threats. On one occasion, he tried to fob off Mary Anne with forty pounds. She said that she'd call him back. When she did, she told him of Kenny's reaction:

'He said you're taking the piss and says he's a good mind to demand £125. According to him, you're a mean bastard and that anything less than a oner and he'll do something you won't like.'

It may, of course, have been a bluff, but Howson felt that he was on the vulnerable end of this particular game of cat and mouse. His grim resolve to change the rules of the game in his favour was now hard and fast. In Howson's mind, it was the lowlife Kenny who was taking the piss, as the latter would phrase it.

As the Christmas holiday reached its second week, Howson was hatching his deadly plan. He first called Mary Anne and explained to her that he was going to France with his family for Christmas, managing to negotiate with her that he would give her £600 in cash and that she and her boyfriend would have to make it last until the New Year. Howson explained that he would not be contactable.

The second step in Howson's plan was to find someone who would be prepared to act on his behalf in eliminating the two blackmailers. He needed also to ascertain where they both lived. Accordingly, he took a suitcase with him and ventured into the school costume department. He rummaged through various items and selected a random outfit of fairly workaday clothes. He was more interested in the various beards. He'd decided on the ubiquitous baseball cap to hide his luxuriant blond hair. He wasn't an expert make-up artist, but he felt confident that he could do a pretty thorough job of altering his appearance beyond recognition. He used his mobile to book himself into a random hotel in the Cambridge Road, Harleybury, in the name of Douglas Smith. It was one of those places with about two hundred rooms, with people coming and going at all hours.

Telling Marie-Christine he was taking the train up to London to meet an old school friend for the evening, he made his way over to the lodge, in order to change clothes and apply a modest amount of face paint to alter his complexion and to muddy the appearance of his features. He then surreptitiously exited the campus, via the rear gate, and walked the two hundred or so yards to the nearest public phone box, to ring for a taxi. He had thought it prudent not to use his own car for his 'work' in Harleybury and was reluctant to walk for fear that a member of the school community might drive past him en route and stop to offer the 'poor old bloke' a lift! He left his mobile phone in the lodge, as he intended to buy another one, so that there'd be no risk of anything about his person which could reveal his true identity.

Once in the local town, his first step was to find a phone shop, where he purchased a pay as u go mobile, plus about £20 worth of credit phone cards. He then checked into the large motel in the heart of the Cambridge Road's notorious red light district.

It was now late in the afternoon. Conscious of being in disguise and uncertain whether or not, in the event of meeting someone, that they would recognise him, Howson decided it prudent not to venture out until after dark.

He purchased a newspaper, went to his room and did his best to while away a few hours with a combination of television, reading and doing the crossword puzzle. By about 9p.m, darkness now having descended, Howson left the hotel to find a fast food kebab house, where he ordered a large doner kebab and a soft drink. There was the odd metallic bench for public use along the Cambridge Road and he sat down, proceeded to eat his supper and observe the developing nightlife: nothing terribly exciting. He noticed that small groups of young men were tending to congregate at various street corners and then disperse. He decided to take a walk up the Cambridge Road, away from the town centre. He passed a 'drive-thru' burger outlet with a car park and continued. He soon noticed a girl, standing at the next street corner, dressed in jeans and sweater. She was on her own and appeared to be glancing at passing cars. He felt his heartbeat quicken and realised that she was almost certainly a 'working' girl. She was white, fairly slender, not remarkably pretty and certainly not dressed to kill. He nonchalantly walked towards her and, as he approached, she made fleeting eye contact. He returned the look with a faint smile. As he got closer, she smiled at him and asked,

'Do you want business?'

He stopped.

'I might.'

'Look, honey, it's not safe to talk here, I'll walk in that direction,' she said, pointing up a side street, 'wait a few moments and then follow me.'

He did as instructed. He couldn't see her at first – she'd apparently disappeared, but then her head suddenly emerged from an adjacent alleyway and she beckoned him towards her.

'Well, honey, what are you after exactly?'

'To tell you the truth, I'm not sure, but have you got time to talk?'

'You got a cigarette?'

Howson didn't smoke but he'd learned to carry cigarettes from Mary Anne, who'd told him how helpful it was to the punters who cruised the streets for a working girl.

'Look,' she said, 'I can't stand around for long just chatting. I need to earn some money. I could do you a good job. It's only £20. By the way, my name's Kelly.'

Howson did not speculate what this somewhat down-at-heel-looking junkie was capable of doing for £20; he certainly had no interest in accepting any offers of casual sex. However, it gave him some indication that he could buy some of her time for very little.

'Look, Kelly, do you know a girl called Mary Anne?'

'Yeah,' she said, 'I do know a girl called Mary Anne. Not well, but she's on the scene. Do you know her? She's very pretty – got a big habit – knocks around with a black guy called Kenny. Don't know how they get their money, but I think they're a couple of con merchants. I'd be very careful if I were you. Kenny's a nasty bit of work. Once beat me up and robbed me of my mobile phone and spare cash – I had a few quid on me at the time.'

Howson was quite surprised that he'd found out so much so quickly. As he would soon learn, almost everyone involved in the street scene knew everyone else.

'Do you know where they hang out?'

'Don't see them often – don't particularly want to see them. Mary Anne isn't really like the rest of us. She's a bit posh actually. Can be quite nice, but no one likes Kenny. I just keep myself to myself. Look, would you be a real sweetie and give us another fiver? I desperately need some 'brown'. Business is lousy and I'm really sick.'

Howson obliged, as Kelly continued:

'Look, if you keep your eyes open around the petrol station, up there on the left, you'll see a tall black girl. Her name's Sophie. She knows everyone much better than me. I'm sure she'll help you, especially if you're as nice to her as you've been to me. Look, if you decide you want business, I'll do a real cheapie for you.'

'Thanks for the offer, Kelly. Maybe some other time but I'm not really in the mood right now.'

With that, the two parted company. Howson wondered whether Kelly was the girl's real name: probably not. He decided to walk up and down the road in the vicinity of the petrol station, keeping his eyes peeled. Before long he was approached by a very tall and surprisingly attractive blonde, who accosted him with the standard, 'Are you looking for business?' She was wearing tightly fitting jeans and a white blouse.

'I'm actually looking for a girl called Sophie.'

'You prefer that thing to me?' she said with open-mouthed incredulity.

'No, I didn't mean that. I'm not looking for business right now, I just want to speak to her.'

'Well, she was here a minute ago, but I saw her walking off that way, with some bloke, a punter.' She was pointing down the road away from the town centre.

'I don't think she'll be long. She usually just goes down an alleyway, gives them a quick hand or blow job. It's all done in ten minutes. Have you got some spare change?'

Howson pulled out a fiver and handed it to the blonde. She smiled, 'That's very generous. I hope I see you again. I'll give you a really nice time.'

As Howson drifted up and down the Cambridge Road, attempting to be as discreet as possible, dreading meeting someone he knew, he mused that he could use this recurring theme of deep dislike of Kenny as a way of finding a hit-man. Surely there must be somebody with sufficient loathing of, what was generally agreed, this nasty bit of work, to be prepared to accept a generous financial reward to pay him his fatal dues.

Eventually, as predicted, a very tall black girl appeared. She could not be described as pretty but certainly she had an attractive figure and a seemingly endless pair of legs, which were well displayed beneath her very short skirt. She was heavily made up and didn't look like she had just emerged from a sordid encounter down a back alley, which was likely to be the case.

He made eye contact. It seemed that the number of variations of the standard direct marketing approach were extremely limited. The girl looked quite hard-faced and had a slightly intimidating air.

'You looking for business, bro?'

'Are you Sophie?'

She responded slightly aggressively:

'Who wants to know?'

'A girl called Kelly told me about you.'

'Well, I suck good cock for twenty and do most other things, but I don't fuck in the arse.'

Howson was a little taken aback by Sophie's immediate frankness and direct language. He began to suspect that there was a rich tapestry of characters to be found on the streets and that this Sophie was clearly a bold and extroverted personality, likely to be well known around town.

'Can we go somewhere quiet and talk?' he asked.

'Time is money – I do hand jobs, blow jobs, shag jobs, and even chat jobs, but they all cost.'

'Look, I'll pay you well for your time but can we get the hell out of here?'

'Okay, but you better not be bullshitting because I need to earn another sixty tonight.'

Howson handed her a fiver. 'That's to show good faith – there'll be more. Can we go somewhere quiet?'

'There's a kebab house up the road, run by Indians – we can sit down there.'

'I need somewhere more private,' explained Howson.

'You're not going to be a timewaster, are you?'

'No, I'll pay you for your time. How about twenty pounds for half an hour?'

'I get that for a blow job. Normally one of mine only takes five minutes; on the other hand, if I've only got to talk, I can be cheaper, but I can't do half an hour for less than thirty.'

'How about twenty, plus a kebab, and you can smoke my fags?'

Sophie looked at him for a moment, wondering what was so important for this punter to want to pay her so much for a mere chat.

'Okay, that sounds fair; you seem like an OK guy to talk to, in any case – I'm fed up with sucking dick.'

She led him further away from the town centre to a small café/takeaway. The décor was very sparse. They stood at the counter and Sophie asked if she could have a large doner kebab, the ubiquitous minced lamb mixture, rotated in a large column in front of a vertical flame grill, which seemed to be on offer everywhere in modern-day Britain, imported from Turkey or somewhere in that Middle Eastern region. It was served with hot pitta bread, salad, chilli sauce, mayonnaise and pickled green chillies.

'Can I have a coke as well?'

The entire meal came to only £3.50.

Having already eaten, Howson contented himself with a diet cola, Sophie leading him to a table in the far back corner, which gave them a modest degree of privacy. She came straight to the point.

'Now, what do you want to talk about?'

'Sophie, do you know Mary Anne and Kenny?'

'Everyone knows them. Kenny's a black bastard.'

This surprised him, given Sophie's own skin colour.

'But you're black yourself. Why do you say that?'

'Oh, I fucking hate black men, I never go with them. My father used to beat up my mother and often sexually abused me.'

Howson couldn't help visibly gulping.

'Is that why you're on drugs?'

'Basically, yes. I was really clever at school but by the time I was fourteen I was on the fucking streets.'

'I suppose there are quite a few black guys like Kenny hanging around the Cambridge Road.'

He had already noticed quite a number.

'Yes, most of them are crack-heads, they'll do anything for money.'

'Like what?'

'Oh, shoplifting, burglaries. They fucking rob the girls, the drug dealers, anyone; some of them live off the weaker girls. Kenny mainly lives off Mary Anne but when they're short, he'll usually beat up or rob one of the other girls. He's a fucking coward, doesn't tend to start with other blokes, but many of the girls are easy prey to him; he's a bleeding coward.'

'Why don't they complain to the police?'

'You're fucking joking, aren't you? Everyone tries to avoid Old Bill. Most of them have got warrants out – *ASBO*s, etc. In any case, they don't want to be asked questions about where they got their cash. And they certainly don't fucking well want to be searched. They all carry stuff like crack pipes, you know, shit like that. Old Bill never does anything in any case. All they fucking do is hassle the girls for soliciting, etc.'

'Do you know any other nasty black guys?'

'Well, there's a big bastard, called Kevin. He's just another fucking version of Kenny but, as he doesn't have a girlfriend, he causes more trouble. The maddest is Murko.'

'Murko? That's an unusual name.'

'It's not his real name, just his nickname. His real name's Dave.'

'What's he like? How come he got that nickname?'

'Oh, he's actually quite small, but very wiry and tough. He uses fucking guns. That's where he got his nickname. He's known to have killed people. Done time for armed robbery – he's much cleverer than the likes of your Kennys and Kevins.'

Howson was becoming interested.

'What about the nickname? What's that got to do with guns?'

'Oh, it's a street term: murk means guns.'

'So where does he hang out?'

'He knocks around with a white guy called Jason.'

'Is Jason dangerous?'

'Nah, he's a complete wimp, but he drives Murko around and helps him with jobs.'

'What kind of jobs?'

'Oh, burglaries, robbing dealers, usual crap.'

'I assume they're both crack-heads?'

'Yeah, they all are.'

'Are you friendly with Murko?'

'There are no real friends around here. Every fucker is out for themselves but I get on with Murko. He don't do shit with me. No one fucking messes with me. I sometimes smoke with him and Jason. They're all right – quite good company and they'll share a smoke, if they've got some, and Murko never beats up girls. In fact, he can't stand Kenny, who has a reputation for hitting any girl who comes his way.'

Howson wondered how an armed robber, who doubled up as a burgling drug addict, could be considered as socially desirable, but he was rapidly realising that, in the dark underclass of the Cambridge Road, values were different. Anyone with a bit of spare crack will always attract a friend.

Howson felt the evening had become extremely productive. He desperately wanted to meet this Murko but didn't want to appear too eager. He decided to change the subject.

'What do you make of Mary Anne?'

'Oh, she's a sweet girl. I like her, she's a class above the rest though she'd never survive on the fucking street on her own; that's why she hangs out with that scumbag Kenny. He protects her, while she's his meal ticket.'

'Why? Does she work?'

'She used to. I think she worked for an escort agency. She doesn't often work the streets. I don't think she generally goes with punters but they say she sometimes does a bit of 'clipping'.'

'Clipping?'

'Yeah, making promises to punters who give her money up front and then fucking off. She's quite convincing – very attractive. Some of the other girls don't like her because she's a big threat to their business. She'd make a fortune if she worked the streets. Why you so interested in her?'

Howson decided he'd better end their meeting. The last thing he wanted was her passing word around the Cambridge Road that some bearded bloke was asking intense questions about Kenny and Mary Anne. He had to play it as coolly as possible, as difficult as that was.

'Do you have a mobile?' asked Howson.

'Yeah, do you want my number?'

'Please.'

'Give me your phone then.'

He passed his newly purchased mobile over to her and she rapidly entered her name and number and returned it to him.

'Sophie, if you can put me in contact with Murko, phone me. I'll certainly make it worth your while.'

'Sure,' she replied.

He handed her the promised £20 and they parted company. Sophie walked away and began calling someone on her mobile, presumably a drug dealer; Howson was convinced that she was already arranging a new 'score'.

Checking out of the hotel that evening, he returned by taxi to the lodge, changed back into his usual apparel and quickly made his way, via his study, back home. The school bell was striking midnight.

For the first time he had a definite plan in his mind that he was about to become instrumental in a double murder. It seemed, paradoxically, to lift his spirits, as he made his way up to bed, his mind more at ease as he looked forward to the following day, when he'd be setting off with his wife and son for a few weeks' relaxation in *La Belle France.*

Chapter Twenty Two
FLUSHING OUT THE TRUTH
'A trick that everyone abhors is strangers opening our private doors.'
H. Belloc

Early in the New Year Benjamin Fine received a call from Martin Trench.

'Hi, Ben, it's Martin, are you able to come up to the office?'

'Is this afternoon okay?' asked Benjamin.

'Make it about four; I have to go out after lunch.'

It was with a certain excitement and anticipation that Benjamin jumped into his Saab that January afternoon and made his way north, up the A3. Although he had to drive a matter of some twenty miles, Benjamin allowed himself a couple of hours to negotiate the ever-increasing number of traffic hold-ups in South London. He arrived at Trench's offices just after 4p.m.

'Come in, Ben, sit ye down. I've got some more news for you. Would you like a tea or coffee?'

'Tea'd be great, thanks; always ready for some refreshment after that ridiculous A3.'

Trench telephoned his receptionist, ordered two teas and proceeded to address Benjamin:

'Sorry I haven't been in touch for a while, like good old London buses, last summer I was waiting for any case to come my way, then three appear, one after the other! Anyway, progress, my friend. When you undertook your little trip to the old Howsons, it was a pity that you only had time to snoop in the master bedroom. Had you chosen to enter the smaller bedroom, you would've been even more gobsmacked.'

Fine's travel fatigue immediately gave way to excited curiosity.

'What did I miss?'

A short, plump woman appeared at the door, bearing a small tray. She seemed to Fine to take an age to place the refreshments on Trench's oak desk. As she closed the door behind her, Trench opened a drawer in the desk, produced a large photograph and thrust it towards him.

'My goodness, I know who that is... I mean, not his name; that, surely, must be Howson's real father,' Fine almost shouted.

Trench smiled. Well if it isn't, one would wonder why a large photograph of a Joseph Howson lookalike, in high-ranking SS uniform, would hang on the wall above Howson's childhood bed.'

'How on earth did you get it?'

'Well, as I once said, some of our techniques are less orthodox than official plod methods. On this occasion, I sent along a young operative who claimed to be collecting money for a church outing for handicapped children. Of course, while he was standing at the door talking to Mrs Howson, he sort of...' Trench cleared his throat, '...sort of got caught short and we took a leaf out of your book, or perhaps I should say a leak! Mrs Howson kindly let him use the lavatory.'

Trench produced a minute object, held it up, saying:

'Smaller than a mobile phone, isn't it? Takes very good pictures, very quickly. Of course, my boy was so excited that he forgot to pull the loo chain, but Margaret Howson is almost deaf and, in any case, I don't think she would've registered the absence of flushing!'

Trench gave another one of his wry smiles, which tended to accompany his occasional dry wit.

Martin Trench was unusually loquacious. Even this dyed-in-the-wool investigator, an obvious expert in covert operations, seemed to derive an almost juvenile glee at his discovery, using the 'need the loo' procedure.

'So, now all we need is a name to the face!' exclaimed Ben with excitement, which seemed to match Trench's.

'Have a look at the small swastika on the breast pocket' said Trench.

'Why, is that of any special significance?' asked Fine curiously.

'Indeed it is ,' said Trench, 'it is undoubtedly the Gold Party badge, which was only awarded to a very small number of Party supporters. It suggests that this officer was held in considerable esteem by the Nazi Party'.

'With this photo,' continued Trench, 'I'm pretty confident I can find his identity, but it's going to cost us a few bob. We'll have to take a trip to the Wiesenthal Institute for starters. Well, as it happens, I'm due to go in that direction to see a client next week, so I can kill two birds, if you can bear to wait a few days.'

'My dear chap, I can't express how grateful I am for what you have done – with the time I've already spent on this matter, a week or so is nothing – I'll have to wait patiently,' retorted Fine, in truth proverbially champing at the bit.

As Benjamin negotiated the revolving door in the foyer, for the first time since his resignation he was starting to feel positive; some spring had returned to his step. Indeed, he felt almost elated. He realised that he already possessed practically enough information to ruin Howson's career. Revenge was on the way; 'a dish', they say, 'that is best served cold'. Moments later, as he walked to his car, Ben reproached himself: he was, after all, supposed to be a Christian, supposed to turn the other cheek, love thy enemy, and all that.

As he negotiated the busy South London streets, his feelings of self-reproach gradually turned once more to satisfaction. Virtuousness was all very well in theory but Howson had taken away his employment, had attacked his integrity, besmirched his name, as he had doubtless done to countless others in his unfettered zeal to reach the top. He wondered whether there was a way in which a Headmaster of one of the great English public schools could possibly sustain his position if it became known that his real father had been an SS Officer, as well as having a

Blackshirt adoptive father to boot. Maybe there would be those who would argue that Howson himself was an innocent – the evil doings had taken place long before he was born. Perhaps much would depend on just what position his father had held – he might just about get away with it if he had been a very young and minor figure in the regime. No, but surely – Cranford had great military connections; many of its sons had given their lives in two world wars; young men with promise swept out of aircrafts into body bags; old Cranfordians drowned and lost at sea due to the action of German battleships; Heads of Cranford Houses gunned down in trenches; the emotions were still high over such matters – Remembrance Sunday was a major event in the school's calendar. How could a Headmaster, a descendant of an active participant in the hostile activities of the Third Reich, the greatest enemy in the history of the land, continue to preside over such solemn ceremonies? To exacerbate matters in Fine's mind was the fact that Howson had kept his father's picture in a place of honour – surely that had some significance – even if, perhaps, he had never known who his father was. The justification for Benjamin's long-standing suspicion that Howson was an anti-Semite was now falling into place. How else could he account for the Simon Cohen incident and indeed Howson's abiding hatred of Fine himself? Howson was certainly very right wing and elitist. There was not a single Jewish, Chinese, Asian or black college prefect in the school, in spite of the fact that there'd been several obvious candidates for such office, including the vetoed Simon Cohen.

Was Howson himself a fascist? After all, he'd been brought up by one. He found it hard to think of the now frail Margaret Howson in that way but, then again, people do mellow with age. Who knows what she was like in her prime? The photograph confirmed that she had been ostensibly happily married to a Blackshirt. Was it so hard to imagine that Howson himself was, at least, a closet fascist? He thought how ironic it was that Worsthorne, his deputy, was not only well known for his left wing views but was also believed to be a card-carrying member of the communist party. Howson had, of course, inherited Worsthorne, but had nevertheless found him very useful. The second-in-command certainly didn't bring his politics into his job. Worsthorne was respected for his sense of justice and fair play. Benjamin suspected that there was little love lost between the two. Worsthorne would have had an abiding hatred of the values for which Howson stood. Ben had to concede that the fact that the two diametrically opposed schoolmasters worked ostensibly so cohesively together was a tribute to them both.

He speculated over various scenarios – he imagined Howson before the Chair of Governors – would the latter ask him to stand down in the school's interests? Would the Lord Justice appeal to his better nature? What if Howson stood his ground? What would an Industrial Tribunal make of it? What would a court of law adjudicate? After all, none of it amounted to misconduct. He could hardly be sacked for, as a child, revering his biological father. Maybe Cranford would simply pay him off; they were wealthy enough. He then reminded himself that, not only did the college boast a Jewish House, there were a significant number of pupils of Jewish origin and they had, in recent years, made a disproportionate contribution to Cranford's academic reputation. What Jewish family would send their son or daughter to be educated, and cared for, in a school run by the son of a former SS Officer? He could foresee the editorials in the Jewish Chronicle. However, as much as he thought about it, he knew that it was going to be a long, hard road – the media were not going to be quick to publish anything without firm evidence that would withstand any onslaught of a libel action, and Benjamin realised that the nature of much of the evidence, and the way in which it had been obtained, would not stand up to much scrutiny. He decided that it was not yet time to open the vintage champagne; there was a long way to go but he still felt that he had Howson in his sights and he knew that he was not going to allow him to disappear from view.

All these jumbled thoughts had flashed before him in only a few moments. He needed to get home, put his feet up and allow things to settle a little in his mind. Although he had expressed patience to Trench, he knew that waiting for the next morsel was going to be excruciatingly slow for him. He had to know more about the handsome, uniformed Aryan, with the chiselled features and the strong jaw. What rank was he? What did he do? What had become of him? He must've been important. He must've had money, connections, influence or Joseph would never have received such a privileged education in England. He must surely have been evil – why was a former Blackshirt, suspected of the brutal murder of a Jewish shopkeeper, chosen to bring up his son? Every fibre of his being told him that the real father had to have been a young man of significance within the *SS* ranks. There was even a possibility of him wielding great power and committing dreadful deeds. Fine's curiosity juices were in overflow.

***

It had been nine whole days since Benjamin had last heard from Trench. Every time his mobile started ringing he would glance down, praying for Trench's number to appear on the lit-up screen. The awaited call came in the evening.

'I've got some very interesting news,' said Trench, obvious excitement in his voice, 'The Weisenthal Institute has put a name to the face. They do have a photo gallery of some of the more prominent figures of the Third Reich. The name is Maxim Englemann. They have also suggested that I get in touch with Mossad, the Israeli Intelligence agency because apparently Englemann had been on their most wanted list! However, they explained that if I required further information about Englemann's past, I would have to write to the records office in Maryland, near Washington, which had microfiche copies of all the records which had not been destroyed. The relevant document was called the

Dienstalterliste . The institute also put me in touch with an old fellow called Solomon Lazarus, a retired caterer, and I've just had a long telephone conversation with him. The old boy is the son of the Jewish fellow who was murdered in East London, I told you about. He was only three years of age when his dad was murdered. He couldn't remember him but he said that it had destroyed his childhood. His mother apparently died of depression and a broken heart when he was about ten and he was brought up by an uncle and aunt. He said that his family had been distraught for years about his father's murder. Their belief was that the police weren't interested in a Jewish bagel shop owner and that after the witnesses, who had obviously been intimidated or bribed, pulled out, the case against Michael Howson fell apart and the police said that they had no further leads and no more evidence and could therefore take the investigation no further.'

'Well, there's no statute of limitation on murder. Is there any possibility of reopening the case?' enquired Fine.

'The trouble is that this murder took place about sixty-seven years ago. Virtually everyone associated with the case will be dead by now.'

'Michael Howson is still alive.'

'Barely. He's unlikely to be fit to stand trial.'

'How does Mr Lazarus feel about it?'

'Oh, he's still very bitter but has long since given up any hope of achieving justice.'

'So, what do you think's the way forward?'

'I don't think that we can do anything at present but I am trying to find out if there are any surviving members of C2. The Institute couldn't help. However, they did help in another way because they've put me in touch with a couple of fairly old men who you might wish to meet. Unfortunately it involves a trip to Tel Aviv!'

'How much suspense are you going to keep me in?'

'Let's say that you might like to hear some information about the identity of someone and the circumstances surrounding his death.'

'OK, I'll say no more. When can we go?'

***

It was a sunny winter morning when Trench and Fine landed at Lod Airport. There was a taxi waiting to take them to the Tel Aviv Hilton. That evening they enjoyed a meal of falafel, pitta bread and salad and retired for the night. The next morning the two taxied to the outskirts of town and Trench led the way to an unimposing little bungalow, typical of the austere and unpretentious architecture which seems to dominate the Tel Aviv suburbs. It was 10a.m. The door was opened by an extremely obese and bearded man of about sixty. He was expecting the arrival of this PI from England and greeted him accordingly:

'Shalom, you must be Martin'.

'Very good to meet you, Yossi,' responded Trench, as he was invited into the old fellow's home. Trench turned to Fine and said:

'Benjamin, this is Yossi Greenberg, retired from Mossad. Yossi, may I introduce you to Benjamin Fine.'

Both men shook hands warmly before Yossi led them both into a small, sparsely furnished living room, where an even older man was seated.

'Can I please introduce you both to Chaim Levi,' said Yossi.

The bronzed and fit-looking seventy-something occupant of the armchair stood and shook hands with Trench and Fine in turn.

'Shalom,' he said to both visitors. Fine was offered the other armchair and the other two sat down on two rather worn-looking, straight-backed, wooden chairs. Yossi produced a sheet of A4 and handed it to Fine.

'Zis is a translation/summary from ze original, vich I obtained from the Maryland archives' he announced.

1912 Maximillian Engelmann, born Cologne only child of Fritz and Helga Engelmann
1930–1933. University of Cologne First Class Degree in English and French
1930 joined Nazi Party
1933 Awarded Gold Party Badge
1935–1938 Military Training
1936 married Magda Wittner
1938 joined Sicherheitdienst Rank: Rottenführer
1939 promoted to Hauptstürmführer
1940 Awarded the Totenkopfring
1941 promoted to Grüppenführer
1942 believed to be responsible for assassination of Jewish financier, Monsieur Nathaniel Dreyfus of Lyon, suspected supporter of French Resistance – wife and three children also eliminated
Awarded Himmler's personal dagger
1943 sent undercover to UK, believed purpose to gather intelligence on prominent intellectuals and leading members of Jewish community
1946 escaped Germany
1961 deceased Argentina (at the hands of Mossad)

'I see that this Englemann appears to have received a number of Nazi honours,' remarked Fine.

'Indeed,' said Yossi. 'Himmler's personal dagger vas awarded directly by ze man himself and vould be a very much valued honour. Zat means that he vould have had to have done some very bad zings!' said Yossi. 'Vell of course, it isn't only ze information vich ve provide. Chaim vas on ze spot.'

Chaim spoke with authority:

'In zose days, I vas a Mossad agent and part of a small team zent undercover to Argentina, in order to locate and arrest a few former Nazis. Engelmann vas one of zem. Acting on a tip-off, ve traced him to an address in ze suburbs of Buenos Aires. We placed ze address under surveillance. After some time ze target emerged and two of us attempted, at gunpoint, to arrest him. However, he drew a pistol and managed to shoot my colleague in ze stomach. He zen put in a shot in my direction, vich just grazed my left ear. He vas clearly very dangerous and I aimed at his head and vun shot hit him between ze eyes. It vas immediately fatal, of course. I managed to get my colleague away and his life vas saved by our medical team, but ve had to get out of Argentina as quickly as possible. Engelmann had shown lightning reactions. I ave never known anyone to respond as quvickly. The gun appeared as if from novere. He had drawn and fired in such a flash – it vas like John Vayne in a cowboy movie.'

'Did you uncover any other details about him?'

'Yes. He had a mistress, who vas a young local lady of dubious professional credentials – apparently a great beauty. He had fathered a child, who vould 'ave been a baby at ze time of his death. He vas, of course, still living viz his German vife at ze time of our visit.'

'What happened to the child?'

'I don't know, but arrangements vould have been made. Engelmann had access to a great deal of money. He vas vell-connected. Zere vas quvite a netvork of former Nazis in zat area.'

'Do you know anything about the mistress?' enquired Fine.

Yossi answered:

'I've checked all ze files. All ve know is zat her name vas Bianca, believed to have been about twenty-eight at ze time. Zat vould make her early seventies now, that is, if she is still alive.'

'What about Engelmann's widow?'

'Not much chance zer. Magda vas born in 1914. Zat vould make her almost ninety, if alive. Probably didn't even know about Bianca.'

Trench interrupted:

'Presumably you have the original address, Yossi?'

'Vell yes, I vould have to look it up.'

It seemed that they had exhausted the information to be gleaned from the meeting and, after thanking both gentlemen profusely, Fine and Trench made their way back to the hotel.

'Do you think we can investigate further?' asked Benjamin, as both men tucked into a welcome dinner.

'Difficult and expensive,' Trench responded wearily, 'we'd have to go to Buenos Aires and ask around, with little guarantee of a result. I'm not sure that Karl would feel that it was justified. We now have a very good picture of what took place. We'll probably never fit all of the jigsaw pieces together. We can infer that the toddler was Joseph and that he was dispatched to England and adopted somehow by the Howsons, funding most likely provided by the Nazi network. Only Margaret Howson would be able to tell us more but it's unlikely she's going to talk.'

Fine was a little disappointed.

'I understand, but do you feel we've got enough to prove the basic facts?'

'I think a good investigative journalist could probably 'firm up sufficient' to get the facts past the libel lawyers,' said Trench. 'The advantage we have is that the press will be gagging to publish this stuff. It'll sell a few rags! In any case, Howson is never going to sue. He'll be too exposed; the more the publicity, the more others are likely to come forward with information. And, of course, *any* connection with the Nazis will be sufficient to damage irreparably both Howson and his school.'

Fine was encouraged. He certainly didn't want to compromise the name and reputation of Cranford College but Howson remaining in post could do even more damage to the school's standing in the long run and, anyway, if Cranford were to suffer as collateral damage in all of this, then, unfortunately and regrettably, so be it. Great schools, like Cranford, nearly always manage to get themselves back to 'winning ways', after a few years, following even the worst of public scandals.

So, in the biting cold of Tel Aviv, in January 2002, Benjamin Fine and Martin Trench P.I. made their way back to the airport. Fine knew that the British media would be initially wary, but he was now confident that he was close to achieving his main purpose of damaging Howson's career. Little did he know that present-day events back at Cranford were ingredients for a much more devastating scandal of their own.

Chapter Twenty Three
A NEW WORLD

'You must plough your furrow alone – before you reach the end of the furrow, you may have company.'
Lord Rosebery

News travels fast in communities and the story of the Carol Service intruder had spread like wildfire through both the school and, consequently, staff family and acquaintances in the local town. Benjamin was told about the incident by Sarah, the school secretary, as they resumed their weekly bridge session early in the New Year.

'The incident was quite extraordinary, some Rastafarian interrupting the exodus of the various dignitaries as they left the chapel,' explained Sarah, 'quite what he thought he was doing or what he wanted, no one seemed to know; the impertinence of it. I think he must've been high on drugs or something.'

'The only possible explanation was that he was intent on robbing somebody,' suggested Benjamin.

'Rumour has it that he knows somebody,' added Sarah.

'On the Board of Governors? Seems highly unlikely somehow, Sarah,' Fine said, chuckling.

There was a pause as Benjamin glanced over to the playing room, adjacent to the refreshment lounge, where the two friends both liked to drink coffee prior to the first 'hand'. He attempted to consider possible reasons for such an unexpected turn of events.

'Who was it in the party that the intruder seemed to be interested in?' enquired Benjamin.

'Well, strangely, the only person he approached seemed to have been the Head,' continued Sarah. 'That's what I was told.'

'The Head? Now, there's a surprise,' said Benjamin with a heavy hint of sarcasm.

'What do you mean by that comment?'

A voice called from the far side of the room.

'Ben, Sarah, are you ready to make up a game?'

Staring at her bridge partner enquiringly, the two made their way over to the table to begin the evening's play.

Both enjoyed the session as much as ever, although Fine couldn't stop his mind from going back to Sarah's comment about the Head being approached. He knew Howson was a complicated, ruthless individual, of particularly dubious parentage, but quite why he would have any connection or relationship with an ill-dressed Rastafarian was beyond even him.

He dropped Sarah off in the early hours and made his way home. Although he'd been up for some eighteen hours, he found it difficult getting to sleep, his mind focusing, as usual, on the developments of the Howson investigation, intermingled with contemplation about whether or not he should spend any time or energy trying to ascertain the identity of the mystery intruder.

'What the hell,' he said to himself, 'I have time on my hands...it might turn up something of interest.'

The following day Benjamin decided to telephone Trench, to inform him of the event.

'Do you think it's of some significance?' asked Trench.

'I really don't know, but Howson seemed to have been a party to the whole matter, so it would be worth doing some sort of checks.'

Trench didn't seem enthused:

'Well, you look into it: I'll carry on the adoptive father/fascist line.'

Benjamin hung up and decided to see if he could obtain any media interest. He dialled up the offices of the Harleybury News Group, which published a number of local daily and weekly papers and asked if he could speak to a senior reporter. He was put through to the Evening Post News Desk. A young female voice spoke:

'Julie Pettifer speaking. May I have your name?'

'Can I rely on my name not being quoted?'

'You may speak to me in confidence, of course.'

'My name is Benjamin Fine. I am a former member of the staff of Cranford College. Are you aware of the incident which took place at Cranford's Carol Service in December?'

'Sorry, Sir, what are you referring to?'

'I'm referring to the mystery intruder?'

'Oh, yes, I do believe we reported it briefly at the time. Just a moment.'

After a pause of about thirty seconds, Ms Pettifer resumed:

'The heading was *"Uninvited Guest at Cranford College"*. She continued reading. 'The annual Carol Service ceremonies at Cranford College on Sunday were interrupted by a man of Afro-Caribbean extraction. The unidentified man, said to be in his late thirties, approached the dignitaries as they were leaving the School Chapel, late on in the morning. He was believed to have approached Headmaster, Dr Joseph Howson, and spoken to him briefly. He was then seen to run towards the school exit, although no crime, other than trespass, was committed. A spokesman for Cranford College said that *"the school has been quite baffled by the incident and we're unable to shed any light on the significance of this intrusion".'*

'Oh, I'm sorry, I have been away and missed the story. Does your news desk have any interest in investigating this matter further?'

'Well, it's old news, so unless you can provide us with something of real interest, then no. As a local paper we don't have the resources to send out investigative teams to follow up every strange local occurrence. Have you any further information you wish to impart?'

'Not at the moment, but I do believe there must have been a reason for the incident and I, too, would like to find out who the intruder was.'

'No one at the school has a clue. You'll be looking for a needle in a haystack.'

'Where do you think that this sort of chap might come from?' asked Benjamin.

'Could be anywhere; however there's a fairly large Afro-Caribbean community in Harleybury, and we assumed the vicinity of the Cambridge Road, certainly on the east side of the town centre, would be the most likely.'

'Isn't that the area which is always being referred to in reports about street prostitution?'

'Basically, yes. Is that all? I don't think I can be of further assistance. Good luck and happy hunting.' She hung up.

The response was more or less as he expected. It confirmed that he was fundamentally on his own if he was to pursue this incident, which was likely to be of ultimate little interest.

Fine was not the most worldly of men. He had spent his working life resident at Cranford. His holiday interests had centred round his retreat in Cornwall, which he had purchased some twenty years previously and which he had only recently sold to move close to Cranford. He realised that in order to get any further, he was going to have to do some legwork. He would have to go out and talk to people. He was going to have to pluck up the courage to talk to the type of people he was not at all used to dealing with or, in normal circumstances, would have any desire to deal with. Ironically, he was following the path of Dr Joseph Howson in this regard.

Chapter Twenty Four
MEETING NEW FRIENDS

'People sleep peacefully in their beds at night because
rough men stand ready to do violence on their behalf.'
G. Orwell

With the new calendar year up and running at Cranford College, Joseph was doing his best to keep his thoughts on an even keel. His mind would often wander as he was delivering notes into his dictaphone. The sheer thought of what he was getting himself involved in was playing havoc with his thoughts' process. It was in the afternoon of a late January day that he read a text from Sophie on 'Doug's' phone, which he kept secreted in his study. She had located Murko and had been trying to contact Howson for some time. He immediately texted back to say that he could meet her that evening; the rendezvous was the garage where they'd first met at 8p.m.

After carrying out the necessary disguise procedure at the lodge, Howson drove into Harleybury, making sure he parked in a secluded street a good way from the centre of town. He walked the mile or so to the garage. He immediately spotted Sophie in the company of another smaller and lighter-skinned Afro-Caribbean girl. He approached the pair and offered his cigarettes.

'Hi Sophie.'

'Hi Doug. This is Michelle. Michelle meet Doug. He's a nice guy.'

'Pleased to meet you Michelle,' he said, offering his hand.

'Michelle knows Murko well.'

'Yeah, he'll be around la'er,' said Michelle. 'So you wanna meet him?'

'Yes, I'd be quite interested. How would he react to a guy like me?'

'Oh, he'll be OK with you. He's quite cool; robs dealers and does shit like that but doesn't start with straight guys. Come back in an hour or so; how much if I introduce you?'

'I'll give you a tenner for the intro.'

'Okay, that's fine but could you spare a few fags for now?'

Howson immediately obliged with a generous handful of cigarettes and gave Sophie a few as well.

'Thanks girls. See you when?'

'Give us an hour. You wait around here.'

It was more than an hour later when Michelle reappeared.

'I can take you round to see Murko. I've told him about you. He's round a friend's flat, chilling out.'

Within minutes Michelle had led Howson to a backstreet address, where she rang the front door bell. It was answered by a small and slim, but wiry, black man, who looked about late thirties.

'You must be Doug,' he said.

'Yeah. Is there somewhere we can talk privately?'

'Sure. You shoot off Michelle. I'll get rid of Donna. Hey, Doug, can you give me a tenner to sort her out?'

Howson took out two ten pound notes, gave one to Michelle and the other to Donna.'

Within a short time he and Murko were sitting together in a small living room.

'Well, what can I do for you?' asked Murko.

'Do you know Kenny?'

'Yeah, he's a fucking arsehole.'

'I want to discuss some very serious business with you. I hear you've got a bit of a reputation for tough stuff.'

'Well, I did some time for armed robbery. A pig got shot. It wasn't me, but it could've been. I would've done it. I hate the fucking lot of the bastards. I did kill someone once. That was for money. He had ten grand on him. Do you want me to do over Kenny because I can assure you it'd be a pleasure?'

'You've guessed it. I actually want the bastard dead.'

'Wanna give me a reason? None of my business, of course, but it helps to know where you're coming from.'

'Let's just say he is doing something bad to me and I've got very good reasons for having him gone.'

'Okay. Well, if you're looking for a hit job, it's gonna cost 5K for me, 2K for my partner, plus expenses.'

'How would you do it?'

'Oh, that's easy. Just shoot him in the head of course, unless you want him roughed up a bit first – that'll be extra, but my pleasure.'

Howson was quite chilled about the casual, matter-of-fact way that this Murko could talk about violence and death, as if it were all in a day's work.

'Look, Murko, I need a very professional job done and I don't want a body. I want him obliterated from the face of the earth!'

'I'm your man, Doug. Okay, let's talk business. How quickly do you want this done?'

'As soon as possible. Look, Murko, I want his girlfriend done at the same time.'

'Mary Anne?'

'Yes.'

There was a pause as Murko considered this latest request. He hated Kenny, had done so for a long time, but Mary Anne he hardly knew. In fact, he felt sorry for her, having to share her life with such a sociopath.

'Okay, I won't ask any questions, Doug. Two people will be double the price. I'll need a good 'piece': that'll cost about a monkey. I'll need to pay a driver: that'll be my mate Jason. As I say, you'll need to give me a couple of big ones for him. As for disposing of the bodies, a couple of vats of acid could be organised, I've done it before. Look, let me give it some thought. Let's exchange mobile numbers and I'll give you a call in a while; I need to work out the best way of doing this. Any chance of a small deposit now?'

'Well, I don't mind giving you a token of good faith. A hundred to go on with?'

'Hundred quid will be fine. It's just so I don't have to worry about getting a few smokes while I think about the best way of getting this done.'

'This has to be between just the three of us. If anything, I mean *anything*, gets out, the deal's off. Is this Jason discreet?'

'I can trust him like my own brother, we've done some heavy stuff before together,' retorted Murko.

Howson decided that Murko sounded convincing and was prepared to invest a few quid immediately. He could easily afford the amount asked for but would need to cover it up. This could be achieved with relative ease. All he had to do was to juggle some of their investment portfolio and in the process 'lose' £12,000 with the explanation that some of the shares had gone down in value. For this purpose, he needed to set up a 'dummy' bank account, but all these technicalities were well within his capabilities.

Their initial business concluded, Dr Joseph Howson, Headmaster of one of England's finest public schools, wasted no time in extricating himself from the area. He had much to think about and, as was his way, wanted to drive out into the country, park the car and spend some time totally alone. Murko would be coming back to him in a day or two and he needed to be absolutely sure that he wanted the deed to be done. Once he had given the hit man the green light, there'd be no turning back. Dr Howson couldn't believe the 'Mr Hyde' part of his life had adopted such a perilous path.

Chapter Twenty Five
FINE HEARTACHE
'The family, that octopus from whose tentacles we never quite escape, nor, in our innermost hearts, ever wish to.'
D. Smith

Benjamin Fine's enquiries were interrupted by a phone call, which he took from his mother, who lived in Florida.

'I've got some bad news. Dad's very sick. He collapsed yesterday and has been taken into intensive care. Some sort of heart trouble.'

Benjamin's parents had been retired, in sunny Florida, for some fifteen years. Whatever the physical distance between them, the Fines were a very close family.

'I'll get on the first available flight, Mum,' snapped Benjamin.

'I can manage but I thought you would want to know straightaway,' she replied.

Benjamin realised that his mother would put a brave face on things but he knew in reality that both parents would be comforted by his presence in such circumstances and, as he was a free agent, he had no doubt what his filial duty was.

'I'll just tie up some loose ends, get packed and prepared, and I'll be over with you.'

In spite of his obsession with the investigation of Howson, Benjamin was not the sort of man to neglect familial responsibilities. Mum and Dad definitely came first. They had been devoted and loving parents. In their own ways, they had both been brilliant people. His father had enjoyed a career in banking, while his mother had been superwife, supermum, and also had an impressive career of her own as a writer of children's books.

Benjamin thought that this interlude in his enquiries may well be an opportune time to discuss things with his mother who, at a distance, had been somewhat concerned about the circumstances of her only son's premature retirement. So, a couple of days later, armed with dollars, travellers cheques, Earl Grey tea and an array of very English delicacies not easily found in Florida, Benjamin set forth to his destination. Before leaving, he put in a courtesy call to Trench, gave him contact details and explained that he wasn't sure how long he would be away, but that he was happy to be called in Florida if there was any progress to be reported.

Rachel Fine, Benjamin's mother, was at the airport to greet him and, on seeing each other, tears of mixed emotions ran down the cheeks of both mother and son. Both of Ben's parents were in their early-eighties: father Fine, Edmund, had been in ill-health for some time; mother, Rachel, was slim, sprightly, comparatively mentally and physically unusually fit. By the time he had arrived in the USA, Ben's father's condition had stabilised and his spirits were raised significantly when his beloved son appeared at his bedside. His mother had expressed delight at the arrival of both her son and of all the highly English comestibles which accompanied him, such things not generally to be found on the heavily-stacked shelves of the local supermarkets.

Inevitably, as mother and son left the hospital on Ben's first evening, the conversation turned to Cranford. Rachel was very wise. She had no doubt that her son had been treated appallingly but her advice to him was to get on with his life and to leave Cranford and Howson behind. Of course she was shocked to hear about Howson's background, but she told him that she had always had doubts about his survival in a very gentile environment, given his Jewish origins. When Ben was growing up, the Fines were already an anglicised couple and had certainly not been at all involved in mainstream Jewish life, but his mother had warned him that, although he had converted to Anglicanism, he would never be fully accepted in the circles into which he had chosen to move. She accepted, without reservation, his view that Howson and his *modus operandi* were rotten but that he himself would be unlikely to secure any benefit from his campaign, other than some possible personal satisfaction. She warned him that people like Howson could be very dangerous and that he should watch his step.

During the ensuing few weeks, after an initial slight improvement, Edmund Fine's condition worsened and as mother and son stood either side of his bed, he slid into a deep coma, from which he failed to awake. In many ways it was Benjamin who found it harder to control his deep grief, his stoical mother remaining, albeit ostensibly, strong. In Ben's eyes, and indeed in the eyes of everyone who knew him, Edmund Fine had been a paradigm of integrity, of honesty, of love and commitment (he and Rachel had been married for nearly sixty years), of goodness and fair play. In spite of his obvious innate intellectual acumen, he had not had the professional career that such a robust mind deserved. He had not gone to university after school because he'd had to find work in order to help financially support his own family. He had subsequently completed a part-time correspondence course to secure his Bachelor's Degree in English. He had worked hard all of his life, he had been the model father and husband in a most unostentatious way. Now he was gone forever.

Mother Rachel had made a life for herself on the East Coast; she and her husband had originally emigrated from the pluvial climes of England because the dampness was exacerbating the arthritic conditions which had beset her husband as he approached retirement. She hadn't wanted to go but, such was the mutual compatibility of husband and wife, she had not given any indication that she was anything other than ecstatic about the ensuing life change. Eight years later she felt totally ensconced and settled in her adoptive country and sometimes wondered how she and Edmund had managed to survive the cold and the wet of Blighty for so long.

Benjamin made every effort to persuade his mother to accompany him back to England as he booked his return flight for mid-March.

'Mum, there's plenty of room for us both; it'll be great, just like old times, and, to be frank, I could do with your help and company.'

'I know, darling; it's just, well, I don't want any more upheavals. I have so many friends here now. I'm just not ready to change homes once again. I'll see how I feel in a year or two.'

Benjamin was disappointed about not having been able to persuade his mother to join him back at Cranford Village. He felt certain it would be to their mutual benefit. However, his mother was not for turning and so, two weeks after his father's funeral, Ben waved goodbye to his mother at the airport. He had made it very clear that if ever she decided she *did* want to come back, she was to ring immediately and he would make the necessary arrangements. If she needed him there, alternatively, he would take the next flight out.

As the aeroplane touched down at Heathrow, Benjamin Fine found tears still streaming down his face, a feeling of emptiness that he'd never felt before. He hadn't seen much of his beloved parents during his adult years – hardly at all since they had emigrated – but they were there if he needed them or they needed him. Now only his mother remained; the thought was overwhelming for him, not only because of his own sadness but also because of his anxiety for his mother, who, for the first time in her life, was living alone. Oughtn't he to give up this obsessive quest to pursue Joseph Howson, and do his duty by moving out to Florida? What surprised him was the overpowering desire to carry on his mission. As much as he loved his mother, nothing, but nothing, was going to distract him from the pursuit of what he believed to be right and proper, to correct the injustice of his departure from Cranford College and to show the world that, to coin that age-old phrase, books should *never* be judged by their covers, no matter how convincing they seemed.

Chapter Twenty Six
FAIT ACCOMPLI
'Three may keep a secret if two of them are dead.'
B. Franklin

Joseph Howson had just finished interviewing a couple of prospective parents when his mobile phone vibrated. Closing his study door, which led to his secretary's adjacent office, he answered: it had to be Murko, contacting him unannounced.

'Doug, it's Murko, can we meet to finalise details? Can you get round here a.s.a.p.?'

It certainly wasn't convenient for Howson but he was frightened of irritating his co-conspirator – hit men are not easy to find, particularly in the mostly well-to-do county of Surrey. He apologised to Sarah, his secretary, asking her to re-arrange the last two meetings of the day. She'd have to contact the members of staff concerned and ask them to come to see him on the following day, if possible.

Howson followed his set routine of going over to the lodge, changing, applying his disguise and driving to the outskirts of Harleybury and parking his car in the usual secluded road. He walked to the arranged place of rendezvous. The meeting with Murko was intense. Murko gave 'Doug' a run-down of the arrangements: the drugging, the covering of the bodies to avoid leaving any forensic clues, the actual execution and body disposal. There was then a discussion of how much it was all going to cost:

'Roughly 6K for me, 2K for Jay; a monkey for the piece, say a monkey for the acid and stuff. Probably another K for general expenses, the body bags, the nicking of the car, etc, you know, burning it out afterwards; so, around 10K all together, less the hundred you've given me. It's more than I originally said 'cos you want *two* people dead. You'll need to pay half up front. Oh, yeah, I nearly forgot, on top of all this, it'll be a further 2K for disposing of the bodies.'

Howson gulped. Although he could afford to pay the amount asked for, he would have to make up a good excuse to explain away £12,000 to Marie-Christine, in the event of her catching on.

'Okay, I agree on the amount, but there must be no hiccups.'

Howson was impressed with Murko's plan. He had clearly thought of all the angles and was obviously bright by local standards. He was also fearless and palpably a man with very few scruples.

During the short journey home, Dr Joseph Howson thought about his almost blameless and well-controlled life, right up until the growing sexual frustration caused by his wife's pregnancy and subsequent depression. Now within the space of less than two years he had lost that control, putting it into the hands of two ne'er-do-wells. Suddenly he found himself at the centre of a murder plot. Perhaps he was born evil and had managed to keep his true nature under wraps on account of his privileged upbringing. Possibly he had spent his entire life denying his true nature. Whatever the case, he was now in a situation entirely of his own making. He had been left with a stark choice: the destruction of his good name, his high-flying career and his marriage on the one hand, involvement in a double murder on the other; this was Howson's choice.

He had thought for a brief period that he'd managed to eradicate the human cancer, Mary Anne Marshall, from his privileged life but the cancer had returned with a vengeance and in a double, virulent form. If he didn't destroy this cancer, it would destroy him. Like his ancestors, he was a ruthless survivor and would fight fearlessly, now cornered.

So, the arrangements were in place: Howson had gone over all of them with Murko in precise detail, the slightest slip and Murko would not be receiving the balance of his money – there were to be no slip-ups.

On the day set, Howson would go about his daily routine as normal. If he manifested any change to his usual manner of behaviour, if he seemed unduly tense, distracted, quiet, anxious, pensive, this could be commented upon. In case any enquiries led back to him, he must make absolutely certain that no one at all had any suspicion that Thursday 14th March was anything other than a normal, run-of-the-mill school day. He had a number of lessons to teach on a Thursday and, as he delved into the poetry of Catullus with the Upper Sixth, explaining, ironically, how the poet had become unwisely infatuated with 'his little sparrow', Lesbia; as he lectured the Lower Sixth, ironically, on the growth of the fascist Lepenist Party in France, delivering lessons in his usual ebullient, entertaining manner, he proved himself, once again, to be a consummate thespian, his mind darting to the macabre goings-on that he had prompted less than five miles from where he was standing, as he continued to enrapture his 6th form sets with his compelling, absorbing, entertaining mode of teaching delivery: a delivery which never faltered, his flow not once interrupted. He went into the Staff Common Room at break time and ensured that everyone present recognised the fact that he was in buoyant mood – just in case, just in case the events down the road did not go to plan: no one would believe a man could behave in this way, if ever it were alleged that he was linked in some way to a callous double-killing in the local town.

The whole morning was a characteristic *tour de force*. Even Marie-Christine detected nothing unusual in her husband's behaviour or manner, as he popped home at lunchtime, as he often did, if his diary allowed.

Five miles away, in Harleybury, on the same morning, Jason drove Murko to a back street adjacent to, but out of sight of, the flat in Manchester Street, where Kenny and Mary Anne would be in a deep sleep after a heavy night's drugs' party, which Murko had hosted the previous day. With a powerful cocktail of assorted drugs, prepared by his own hand, he had ensured that the doomed couple would be comatose during the following day. He himself had been careful not to do anything other than some light cannabis smoking. He had to be certain that he was clear-minded this morning and also that his two targets were soundly asleep at their own home, to where Murko had driven them back late the previous evening. Now, he and Jason, each carrying two woven-plastic bags, made their way round to the flat and, using the key Murko had surreptitiously taken from Mary Anne's bag when dropping the two drug-fuelled addicts off (such was their state, he could have ransacked the entire flat and neither would have noticed), Murko quietly opened the front door. Both individuals were sprawled out on the double bed, exactly the positions they were in when they had been dumped on the spacious bed some nine hours earlier.

It would have been simple to shoot them then but Howson had insisted it had to be at a time when he himself was in school, in everyone's gaze. Murko knew that both victims would be in a coma-like state. Just to be on the safe side, Murko administered a rag saturated with the fluid chloroform over the nose and mouth of each target in succession, whereupon both infiltrators proceeded to put one bag over the head and upper torso of each of the sleepers, followed by the other bag over the lower part of the respective bodies. Gaffer tape was used to connect the separate bags. Jason took care of Mary-Anne, Murko her boyfriend. Neither of the two drugs and chloroform-saturated targets even stirred during this clinical operation.

With both bodies now hermetically sealed, Murko held his 9mm Glock pistol between the eyes of Kenny and, with the aid of a fitted silencer, fired two shots into his brain, from a six- inch distance. He then walked round to the other side of the bed and followed an identical execution on Mary Anne. Both bodies jolted on impact, but, save the extensive blood spattering on the inside of the bags, no trace of what had happened was left on or around the bed.

Both men made their way hurriedly back to the car, the plan being to collect the bodies after nightfall. Howson had arranged with Murko that once the deed had been done, Murko was to double-lock the front door, so, in the unlikely event of anybody calling that day, he or she would presume the pair were sleeping off their latest drugs' orgy, which was not an unusual occurrence. The bodies would be collected after dark and be delivered to the lodge, where they would be kept under the cellar flagstones until Murko had finalised the arrangements for the disposal of the corpses. Indeed, Murko had wanted to complete the whole job in one go and had asked Howson to wait a month or two for the execution, but his paymaster wanted the murders carried out immediately, before the blackmailers had any more opportunities of bleeding hundreds more from his already-besieged family bank account or, worse still, of disclosing what had been going on between the local illustrious Headmaster and his young, vulnerable call girl.

That evening Murko and Jason drove round to No.5 Manchester Street, loaded the brace of body bags into the boot of an ageing Vauxhall Astra, which Jason had managed to 'borrow', and they made their way round to the school lodge.

On cue, Howson opened the rear school-gates, the car sweeping right and parking at the south side of the lodge, thus out of sight of the main school buildings. The two bags were removed from the boot, carried through the kitchen and down some steep stone steps into the musty cellar. Howson had worked hard during the previous week to prepare two suitable graves. As Murko followed Howson into the pitch-black, Jason arrived moments later. Howson gestured to the pair to place the bags into the shallow holes provided. Even these two hard-nosed criminals found the fetid air of the cellar eerie and uninviting. Jason, in particular, wasted no time in remounting the steps, leaving Howson and

Murko the task of filling in the foot-deep makeshift graves, finally carefully replacing the flagstones onto the smooth earth.

Howson handed over the balance of the money to Murko, bar a couple of grand, which would be handed over when the bodies were finally disposed of.

'Let me know when you want us to collect the bodies. I reckon I'll have all the stuff in place within a month,' said Murko, while washing his hands at the kitchen sink.

'Thanks,' said Doug, 'you'll get the remaining amount when the job is complete.'

Murko nodded, waved a hand at his sidekick and the two got back into the battered Vauxhall and sped off into the dark, no doubt both looking forward to spending some of their ill gotten gains that very night.

For his part, Howson locked the front door of the lodge, closed and padlocked the rear school gates and made his way back across the tree-lined lawn, which stretched up to the main building. As he walked quickly under the trees he saw a light approaching him, coming from the opposite direction. It was a tallish figure, accompanied by a large dog.

'Who's that?' the figure called.

'It's me, Stuart, Joseph Howson,' shouted the Head, a feeling of anxiety and relief permeating his adrenalin-filled head. Stuart was Head of Security at Cranford.

'Sorry, Sir, it's just I received a call from one of the house staff that they'd seen the rear gates open as they'd driven past on their way back from town. I see you've locked it.'

'Yes, so sorry, Stuart, my fault.'

'Very good, Sir.'

With this, he disappeared back towards his own house, adjacent to the main gates at the front of the school.

After returning to his study to turn off the lights and lock the door, Howson made his way home. As he embraced his wife, there was nothing to suggest he had, within the previous twelve hours, involved himself in the most heinous of all crimes. In Howson's mind he had done what he had had to do, no more, no less.

Chapter Twenty Seven
A TANGLED WEB
'What a tangled web we weave, when at first we practise to deceive.'
W. Shakespeare

In the ensuing period until the disposal of the bodies, Howson attempted to put the macabre events of that Thursday as far to the back of his mind as possible. He was uncomfortable about the fact that the two corpses were lying in the lodge cellar and, in the cold light of day, he did wonder whether Murko had been correct in his original suggestion that the whole matter should be administered in one fell swoop. After all, Murko was the pro. On the other hand, what worried Howson was the fact that if he had delayed the assassination for a month or two, apart from the fact that the greedy pair's demands were becoming increasingly more regular, he felt that perhaps he himself would lose his nerve or Murko might change his mind.

He knew that the two's disappearance would take a while to be noticed in the streets: it was not unusual for street people to 'up and off' suddenly and, life being so unpredictable among this kind of people, individuals frequently did disappear. It was rare for anyone to become so concerned that they would alert the authorities: besides which, many viewed the police as the enemy and the thought of sharing with them any concerns they might have for one of their 'folk' was somewhat alien to them. Many of this social group lived an almost invisible life as far as the authorities were concerned; not listed on any community register; they didn't pay tax; a lot paid cash to their landlord; they drove cars with neither tax nor insurance. If ever they were stopped by the enemy, they were taken to court, paid their fine or spent a short time behind bars and then duly returned to their usual way of life.

It was Kenny's brother who owned the studio flat where the now deceased pair had been living. The former was in the middle of an eight-year prison stretch for armed robbery, the accommodation bought originally out of his own criminally acquired gains.

So, other than occasional encounters with the police, Kenny and Mary Anne had nothing to do with any agency or company and were, to all intents and purposes, practically anonymous. Mary Anne had been sacked by *Paradise Babes* and Howson felt that the only people who would even notice their absence were their regular drug suppliers. The latter were hardly likely to report their disappearance!

Life at Cranford continued much as before for its 'esteemed leader'. The College was prospering in so many areas – academically it was close to the forefront of education in Britain, its hockey sides were building a strong reputation – Howson was particularly keen on this quintessentially public school sport – drama in the school had never been stronger and serious disciplinary issues were rare. As the Lent term made way to the Trinity term, Joseph Howson managed to re-find some of his *joie de vivre*. His only worry was the setting of a time for the disposal of the corpses still in the lodge cellar. Murko had rung him to say he had secured the acid, had found a location and that he would await 'Doug's' instructions. The whole matter of the killings had had a disquieting effect on Howson's psyche, ruthless as he was, and he felt he needed a few months before returning to the dank cellar and once again touching the two body bags.

He realised that he needed to continue to use the lodge – the Bursar knew he had access to it. The Head had told him that he was penning a detailed diary and that the lodge offered him an opportunity to be on his own, in complete tranquillity, bar the passing of the odd motor vehicle on the road outside. If he were to alter any habit, it might be commented upon – he must continue life exactly as before.

It was eerie for Howson sitting at the desk in the lounge of the lodge, putting pen to paper about his life, knowing directly underneath lay two dead bodies.

It had now been two months since the murders and, with another school year coming to its close, Howson had his head full of matters appertaining to Cranford, including the CCF Annual Inspection weekend, just before the May half term, and the simultaneous opening of the newly completed Performing Arts Centre. With HRH the Duke of York coming as Guest of Honour, there were detailed arrangements to finalise. One aspect which had to be carefully considered was the pre-arrival security checks, which involved a team of police officers and the bomb squad coming down to the school on the previous day to carry out a thorough inspection of all areas of the school. The police had requested a place for their team of eight to reside for the night of the eve of the ceremony.

'I should like to suggest the gymnasium,' said Howson at the weekly school Coordinating Committee meeting.

James Hardcastle, the Director of PE intervened:

'It would mean having to cancel our gymnastics' display.'

'What about the Wilcox Room?' suggested Peter Compton, the Director of Music.

'No running water in the vicinity, I'm afraid,' said the Bursar. 'I suggest, with your permission, Headmaster, that we use the lodge.'

Howson had little time to react. What could his reasons possibly be to stand in the way of such an obvious suggestion? He had the authority to veto anything, particularly something as mundane as what they were now discussing, but he didn't want to appear too concerned.

'I'm not entirely convinced that the lodge is in an adequate decorative condition,' said the Head, 'we must have something better to offer.'

There was a pause and all sitting around the conference table remained silent. The Bursar,Bob Crickman, broke the silence:

'I could arrange for Property Services to move in one day next week, give it a magnolia once-over. I have to say, as you are aware, Sir, it was painted when old Wilson, the gardener, moved out two years ago. We really must consider utilising the house whenever possible; it seems such a waste for it to be standing empty for weeks at a time, other than for your own visits there, of course.'

There were general murmurs of agreement from those assembled and Howson knew immediately that he had no alternative but at least to seem to go along with the proposal.

With the meeting concluded, Howson immediately beckoned to Crickman to follow him to his study.

'Are you certain there is nowhere else for these people to stay? I have a lot of my diary materials lying around and I don't want PC Plod messing about with them. Pages'll get lost, mixed up, even read, you know the score.'

Howson didn't want to sound too anxious or be too overbearing, which would surely appear rather odd behaviour.

'I'll look into it, Headmaster.'

'Thank you, Bob.'

Howson heard no more about the matter until the following Wednesday, now less than forty-eight hours before the security team was due to arrive.

'Mr Crickman to see you, Headmaster,' said his secretary, Sarah.

'Ah, yes, come in, Bob.'

'Good afternoon, Headmaster; sorry to say, try as we may, there is nowhere in school available for such a large number of visitors, so the only alternative to the lodge was a local hotel. I've checked with everyone in the vicinity, but due to the fact so many parents are descending upon us for CCF Inspection and the Arts' Centre unveiling, there is absolutely nothing available. The nearest hotel I could find is as far away as Hinton.'

Still Howson was resistant, trying at the same time not to appear anxious.

'I cannot understand why Hardcastle is unable to have the gymnastics' display out on the quad.'

'I think it's because he's already set up the equipment and, if it rains, he'd have to cancel the whole event.'

'Of course,' replied Howson, beads of perspiration now unavoidably gathering above his eyebrows. 'If needs must, it'll have to be the lodge, I suppose, but I'm not particularly happy about it. I would like you to carry on searching for an alternative.'

Howson had been more assertive in his tone than he had wanted to be. Crickman had certainly noticed the discomfort in his voice.

'Very good, Headmaster,' said the Bursar, who took his leave, knowing he had already pretty much exhausted all possibilities of alternative accommodation.

Howson realised that he now had another problem to address, a problem which had to be considered without delay. He had a choice either to remove the bodies and dispose of them within the next twenty-four hours or to leave them where they were, keep the cellar door locked and carry on much as before, hoping the team did not ask for access to the cellar. After reflection, Howson settled for the latter: it would be foolhardy to start undertaking such manoeuvres with the imminent arrival of the security force and, besides, he had so much to attend to before the Duke of York's Saturday morning arrival and, even if they did go down into the cellar, they would certainly not be looking for buried bodies. They would use sniffer dogs, of course, but the dogs would be trained to search for explosives, not rotting corpses. He knew that these dogs were specialised to uncover a specific target. He felt confident that, with a thick bag, a foot of earth and heavy flagstones covering the corpses, a human nose wouldn't be able to pick up any smell of decomposition. Indeed, he had gone down into the cellar the previous day, had stood over the graves and was unable to pick up any hint that rotting flesh lay directly below him.

The team duly arrived late on Friday afternoon. As Howson sat at his desk, he witnessed a convoy of a half a dozen vehicles coming up the drive, halting side-by-side right outside the main doors. He saw Crickman emerging from the main building to greet them. Howson had decided that it was he himself who would take them down to the lodge, prior to their security search of the school.

After the initial introductions and pleasantries, Howson led them down to where they were staying, a residence complete with two dead bodies. As he gave them a brief tour of the bungalow, he saw that Property Services had installed four sets of double bunks, one in each of the three bedrooms and one in the lounge. Foodstuffs had been left in the kitchen, towels in the bathroom. Inevitably, one of the team tried to open the cellar door; Howson was quick to inform him that the door was kept permanently locked and that the key was back in his study.

'We'll need to check the cellar,' said one of the officers, 'but no hurry, it's just routine.'

'Of course,' replied Howson, 'I'll pop back in due course.'

'No need, we can come and collect it.'

The words were spoken forcibly and Howson realised that, even if they hadn't been residing at the lodge, they would nevertheless have insisted on a full inspection of each of the buildings. Surprisingly, no one came to collect the key on that Friday evening.

It was now within one hour of the Duke's arrival; precisely 8.30a.m on Saturday morning and Howson was preparing to conduct the weekly Headmaster's Assembly; just as he was about to enter the assembly hall's front doors, a police security officer intercepted him.

'Good morning, Sir, we have carried out a full inspection of the premises and, bar one problem, we are satisfied all is well.'

'A problem?' enquired Howson.

'Yes, Sir.'

'Look, I'm sorry to be curt, but my school is waiting for me. I shall speak to you after assembly.'

Howson then swept past him, gown billowing behind, as he disappeared into the hall.

As he emerged fifteen minutes later, the detective had gone. Howson wondered whether the unavailability of the cellar key was the problem. The Head was never more glad to see a member of the Royal Family, as HRH the Duke of York's helicopter landed on the school parade square (an area where the school army cadet force would, in due course, be carrying out its military parade).

As Howson approached to shake the Duke's hand, as the school band played, as the military Guard marched, the pilot once again took his "whirlybird" up into the sky, to re-land it on the Head's extensive front lawn, freeing up the square for the impending whole school march-past and salute.

The entire day was a complete success: the parade, the inspection, the opening ceremony of the Arts' Building, the speeches, the school song... As the Duke left, he told Howson it was an honour for him to have been invited to England's premier public school and that he hoped he would be invited again. As Howson watched the helicopter leave, standing on the square in the midst of his senior management team, Bob Crickman whispered into his right ear:

'Headmaster, I unlocked the cellar door on your behalf, and gave a couple of detectives a chance to make their routine check.'

'Everything okay?' asked Howson.

The Bursar paused:

'I'm afraid, Sir, there is one problem. Two detectives are waiting for you in my office.'

It took less than a couple of minutes for Howson and Crickman to reach the Bursar's office, at the centre of the Administration

Block. Howson entered nervously, to be greeted by two burly plain-clothed policemen.

'I understand there is a problem,' Howson blurted, his aggressive tone camouflaging a certain desperation, which was making his heart beat at twice the usual rate.

'Yes, Sir, it's the lodge cellar,' one replied earnestly.

Howson put his hands out to the arms of a leather armchair, which was placed just behind the door. Even thespian Howson was unable to disguise his anxiety about this turn of events.

'Would you like a glass of water, Headmaster?' enquired Crickman.

'No, no. Please tell me more,' stammered Howson.

'Dr Howson, as you know, it was our responsibility to check thoroughly all areas of the school, prior to the arrival of His Royal Highness the Duke of York. One of the areas we were obliged to verify was the lodge cellar. One of my officers was afforded access by Mr Crickman late on Friday evening and it was this officer who found this... (as he spoke the officer held out a tiny package)...underneath the cellar stairs. Mr Crickman tells me that you are the only person, other than him, who has had access to the lodge since it was vacated by your previous gardener; he left, we understand, over two years ago. This package was dropped reasonably recently.'

Howson's emotions fluctuated: utter relief that the corpses seemed not to have been discovered, while experiencing a feeling of acute anxiety as to how he was going to explain the presence of Mary Anne's heroin, for heroin he knew to be the contents of the package. (She had repeatedly asked him if she could leave some at the lodge, a request he had repeatedly denied her. Now he realised she had done so anyway.)

'If you have no knowledge of the heroin package – it is heroin, Sir, and has been there for a matter of months – then we shall have to set up an enquiry at the earliest convenience. Hard drugs found on a school campus is particularly serious, as I am sure you are aware.'

'No enquiry will be necessary, officer. It was I who put the package there,' said Howson.

Bob Crickman looked incredulously at the Head.

'I found it one evening on the path behind the lodge and, fearing adverse publicity for the school, I picked it up and decided to throw it into the lodge cellar. It was foolish, I know. I am so sorry.'

'You realise I shall have to ask you to accompany me to the local station, where you will be required to write a statement.'

'I understand. Obviously, I am keen to avoid any publicity, which was my original reason for behaving so stupidly.'

'I doubt the CPS will want to proceed with this and the press will not be alerted. However, I can offer no absolute assurances of them not finding out.'

'I presume you will not need to handcuff me,' said Howson, trying to lighten matters.

Both officers ignored his attempt at humour.

Howson spoke briefly to Crickman, imploring him not to mention his *faux pas*, as he termed it, to anyone. He was then escorted to an unmarked car parked at the front of the school and taken to Harleybury Police Station, where he was detained for nearly an hour.

On returning to school, Howson knew he would have to explain what had happened to Marie-Christine, sooner rather than later, and, when the time was right, to Lord Harris, the Chairman of Governors. He told his wife that very evening. She was, as usual, totally supportive and assured him his decision to conceal the illegal wrapping was totally understandable. Anthony Harris, Howson knew, would be more difficult to convince, but inform him, at some stage, he would have to.

Chapter Twenty Eight
SUPER SALESMAN

'No matter what their class, some people are loathsome and some are delightful.'

N. Mead

Benjamin had been back in England for less than 24 hours when he started ringing Trench. He was repeatedly put through to the answering service and, over a period of days, he left no fewer than five messages for Trench to call him back. A week later, the detective finally got in touch.

'Sorry, Ben, for not returning your calls, I've been up to my neck in another case, following a wayward husband. Once again, sorry about dad, how's mum?'

'Not too good. I begged her to come back over here with me, but she's a stubborn old bird. Nothing further on Howson?'

'To tell you the truth, I've not had that much time since you've been away. I made some enquiries about that intruder at the school, but not much joy, so far.'

'In that case, I think I'll make some enquiries of my own. Anywhere you suggest?'

'Has to be the east side of town, where most of the immigrants live. That'll be a good starting point. Let me know how you get on.'

The following day, Benjamin had a light lunch and, as it was a beautifully sunny day, he decided he would take the opportunity to go on a brief reconnaissance of the Cambridge Road area, to the east side of the town centre, as Trench had suggested. Quite what he was expecting to discover he wasn't sure, but he'd go nevertheless.

So, when the tall, well-spoken patrician figure of Benjamin Fine hit the Cambridge Road, it conjured up a scenario of *A Connecticut Yankee in King Arthur's Court*. It was about 10a.m when he parked his car in an adjacent multi-storey car park; he then ventured forth into the town centre. Being a typically obsessively organised schoolmaster, Benjamin had already purchased a street map of the town and he walked directly towards the start of the Cambridge Road. There was plenty of hustle and bustle of shoppers and people going about their business and the first few hundred yards of the long road were dominated by every kind of shop and business: there were stores, restaurants, legal firms, dentists, doctors, garages, drive-ins, a public swimming pool and a snooker hall. As he progressed, Benjamin became aware of the multi-ethnic life of this highly populated county town. Further on still, he encountered a few rows of terraced houses and the like interspersed among the shops and other businesses. The density of pedestrians gradually thinned as he left the town centre behind him. It was a particularly long road and, after about forty-five minutes' walking, he realised that wherever the street life was meant to be, he must either have passed it by or have started looking too early. Not being at all *au fait* with this sort of scene, he was unaware that the life cycle of your average street person doesn't tend to begin until late afternoon at the earliest and the presence of working girls did not proliferate until after dark. As he would soon discover, there were peak periods. One of those was when the pubs closed at the end of the evening and inebriated men tended to pour out, some of whom were ready for more entertainment, before returning home. Another peak time was after 2a.m when the large number of town-centre Harleybury nightclubs disgorged their late night throngs. Twenty-four hour opening hadn't made much impact on the hospitality industry routines in this part of town.

After retracing his steps, he took the opportunity to look at some of the new shops in the recently opened mall in the centre of Harleybury. Shopping was not one of Benjamin's principal interests, so, after a brief period of looking into windows, he decided to return home and try again that evening.

It was about 8p.m when he set out again for Harleybury. This time he made his way directly to the Cambridge Road and parked his car in one of the many side streets, close to the town centre. He decided to walk the same route. The atmosphere now was very different. For a start, the density of the road's pedestrian life had thinned considerably and most of the shops and businesses had closed. Nevertheless, for a basically urban road, it was still unusually lively for this time of day. As he walked away from the town centre, he was aware of the presence of groups of young males of a variety of ethnic types. There seemed to be quite a few young people hanging around in the vicinity of the Snooker Hall, some seated on its front steps. Occasionally, there were small congregations of people at various street corners. Eventually, he spotted a young woman who was standing alone. She was of mixed race, slightly plump, about early thirties. She was wearing very casual clothes and didn't look like she was dressed up to go out clubbing: leggings, dirty trainers and a rather grubby tunic seemed to be the order of the day. She had short brown hair and was facing the road. Not at all alluring, her complexion looked somewhat pasty and unwholesome. He wondered whether this was his first sighting of a working girl. He had expected to see leggy, painted tarts, obvious 'hooker types', as portrayed in various television documentaries and films. She certainly didn't reflect this image. He nervously strolled towards the young woman, watching for any sign of behaviour which could confirm his suspicion. As he approached, she glanced towards him. He slowed down but was far too nervous to acknowledge the glance. He stopped momentarily about ten yards from her. She looked at him again and made a small beckoning movement with her head. This time he managed a nervous smile. In a low voice, she spoke:

'You looking for business?'

Fine's knee-jerk reaction was to smile.

'Thank you for your kind offer but no, not really.'

She now gave him a strange look, barking:

'Then, what the fuck you staring at me for – are you some kind of pervert?'

Quite embarrassed, Fine muttered an apology and moved on. It occurred to him that one would, indeed, have to be pretty perverted to want to pay, or even have a free close encounter with, this particular creature. Once he was at a safe distance, he kept glancing round and decided to keep an eye on her from afar. Within a short time, she was talking to some other man and he noticed that both of them disappeared down a side street, adjacent to the corner on which she'd been standing. Obviously, there was a market for whatever dubious delights she had on offer. Benjamin Fine continued on his way. Coming towards him the other way was a tall, bearded, somewhat dirty-looking Afro-Caribbean man, wearing a tunic, blue trousers and the ubiquitous dirty trainers.

He had a frightening demeanour. Looking at Fine, he blurted:

'Can you spare some change?'

Benjamin resisted his instinct to ignore the request. At some point he was going to have to break the ice and converse with these characters. There were still a sufficient number of people around, passing vehicles, frequent marked police cars, for Benjamin to feel reasonably safe. He stopped and began to rummage around in his pockets. Before he had even produced any change, the character continued:

'You look like a real gentleman. I'm very pleased to meet you. My name is Dogger. Well, not my real name. Actually it's Keith, but everyone knows me as Dogger. He offered Benjamin a clammy hand, which the latter nervously accepted. There was a faint unpleasant odour, which strongly suggested that it was some time since his new acquaintance had had a shower.

'What you looking for? Girls? Gear? I can get you girls – some real nice ones – really sweet – won't cost you much. I can also get brown, white, weed – whatever you want. To be honest, I'm starving. I haven't eaten or slept for two days. I'll do anything for a few quid. I haven't seen you before round here. Are you new to this area?'

By this time Benjamin was starting to feel a little more at ease. Maybe this character could be of some use to him, he certainly wasn't in any way shy. He was obviously some kind of street hustler but not in any way intimidating; rather 'in your face', without any air of physical aggression, in spite of his height, which must have been about the same as Benjamin's, a couple of inches in excess of six feet.

Dogger was of indeterminate age. He could have been anything from late thirties to late forties. Benjamin decided to engage him in further conversation.

'Actually, I'm looking for someone.'

'I'll help. I know everyone around here,' he said eagerly. 'Can you spare a couple of fags, blud?'

Benjamin was a non-smoker and about to learn his first lesson in the golden rules of street life: the cheapest way of buying an instant friend in the street-scene was to be free and easy with cigarettes. Benjamin was not slow in adapting.

'I'm sorry, I don't smoke but I'm happy to get you some cigarettes.'

'Cheers. The nearest place is the twenty-four-hour store across the road.'

Dogger immediately bounded across the road, beckoning Benjamin to follow. In the shop he pointed to a cheap brand.

'Can I 'ave a packet of them?'

Benjamin asked for ten, paid and handed them over to his new associate, who lost no time in producing a lighter and, as they left the store, he lit one up and took a deep drag on it, as if he were a drowning man coming up for a gasp of air.

'So, who you looking for, blud?'

'I don't know his name. Actually, he looks a little like you, Dogger. Could be of a similar age, tall, bearded, but his face is pockmarked and he has a lot of tattoos.'

'Quite a few like that around 'ere, mate. Why on earth would a gentleman like you be looking for someone like us?'

'Well, to tell you the truth, did you hear about the black guy who turned up at Cranford College a few weeks ago? It was reported in the local paper.'

'No, I never read the papers. I'm not too good at reading. Turned up where?'

'Cranford College – the big school in Cranford. Someone caused a bit of a fuss there. I'm trying to find out who it was.'

'Be careful about asking questions, mate. There are some nasty shits, sorry, blokes around 'ere. I'd be careful if I was you. I'm just an honest hustler. Okay, I do a bit of shoplifting sometimes but I never get involved in any violence. I can get you anything you want from the shops.'

'No thanks, I just need to find out who this man is.'

'So, what did this guy do?'

'Cranford was having its annual Carol Service. There were many important people coming out of the chapel after the service – Headmaster, Governors, a Bishop, Judge, Major General, etc, and a man answering the description I've given you appeared, made a nuisance of himself, and then ran off.'

'Don't sound like a big deal – pretty fancy school, this Cranford?'

'Yes, it's a famous boarding school, public school, if you like.'

'Not the sort of thing a street-nobody like me would know anything about. Do you work there?'

'I used to but left a few months ago.'

'Well, you look and sound like a proper gentleman. Look, if you want me to help you find this bloke, I just need a bit more change for some grub.'

Dogger took out all the coins in his pocket and added them up.

'Can you spare another six quid, blud?'

Benjamin obliged.

Dogger continued:

'Look, I need to get something to eat. Wait here, I'll be back in a minute.'

With that, he bounded off towards the town-centre direction and was out of sight within seconds. Benjamin wondered if he had been conned. Indeed, after about ten minutes, Dogger still hadn't returned, so Benjamin was beginning to think he would never see him again. He kept his eyes firmly on the spot where his acquaintance had left him. After a further ten to fifteen minutes, a breathless Dogger appeared, running towards him.

'Sorry to keep you waiting, blud.'

Had Benjamin possessed any experience of the drugs' fraternity lifestyle, he might have realised that when Dogger was counting up his coins, he was trying to achieve the magic total of ten. In the Cambridge Road you could buy chicken and chips for less than two pounds, a large doner kebab for three pounds. However, the road's magic figure involved units of ten pounds because that was the minimum price for a bag of heroin (or brown) or a stone of crack cocaine (or white). When Dogger had stated that he needed to get something to eat, it was near enough the truth, as drugs were often referred to as 'food' and 'hunger' was used to describe the need for drugs. Dogger had in fact scored with the ten pounds he had managed to put together and was genuinely grateful to his new acquaintance. He now had his mind on earning his next score from this polite gentleman from another world.

'Well, I can think of Kevin Sangster – he fits the description you said but I can't imagine what the fuck he'd be doing in a place like that. Then there's Kenny. He gets around quite a lot. Has a nice motor. Don't know where he got the money from. It's usually parked near his yard. Probably no money for petrol most of the time.'

'Yard? Does he live in a yard?'

'No. Don't be funny man. Yard is what we call a guy's home, if he's lucky enough to have one.'

'Anyone else you can think of?'

'Well there's a dealer called Moses, but I wouldn't think it was him. He keeps a low profile, usually uses others to serve up.'

'Tell me more about this Kenny.'

'Look, I don't mean to be rude but could you spare another tenner 'cos I'm absolutely skint?'

Benjamin, who was not accustomed to being that free and easy with his cash, realised that Dogger was providing far too valuable a service for the price to be bargained over:

'That's a lot of money, and I don't want you disappearing again for half an hour. Will you wait until we've finished and I promise I'll give you ten pounds?'

'Don't you trust me? Look, make it a fiver now and then you can give me another fiver when we've finished talking.'

Benjamin settled for the compromise. Dogger obviously needed to be fed with dollops of cash, a bit like a short-time parking metre or slot machine: Benjamin had no alternative but to go with the flow. If Dogger could identify his target for twenty or thirty quid, he would be very satisfied with the result.

'Kenny's a nasty bit of work. I don't have much to do with him. He hasn't got too many friends on the scene; in fact, fuck all. He knocks around with a girl called Mary Anne. She's a real darling – I love her, I'd like her for a girlfriend – no chance of that – sometimes I smoke with her but Kenny gets really jealous. Don't know what she sees in him. He's a real piece of shit.'

'Smoke? You mean share fags with her?'

'Not exactly – I mean a pipe.'

Benjamin was learning a lot of new concepts. It gradually dawned on him that Dogger was referring to some drug or other.

'Drugs?'

'Yeah, crack – we all smoke crack around here, blud.'

'So, where could I find this Kenny?'

'He lives quite near. Come to think of it, I haven't seen either of them for ages. Normally bump into one or the other or both quite often, like every few days, but haven't seen them for a couple of weeks.'

'Would you be willing to tell me where they live?'

'I'll do better than that. If you let me get another couple of smokes, I'll go round there with you. I wouldn't go up there on your own – it's a dangerous area, you could easily get mugged and Kenny won't be very friendly with a guy like you – probably try and rob you. Just give me the other fiver, allow me twenty minutes and I'll trust you to give me another tenner later. You're a real nice guy. I'm not just doing this for the money. I wouldn't want you to get robbed or hurt. You need protection, honest to God.'

Dogger was again somewhat economical with the truth. The money was flowing and, in such a situation, he was like the proverbial bee sticking to the honey pot. Nevertheless, in spite of being a bit of a freeloader, he was always prepared to help anyone on the street if he could, especially in return for a 'pipe', the major street barter currency, probably worth about two to three quid – (you could get three or four pipes out of a ten stone of white).

So, Fine was led up through the back streets, turning left, right, left, until they reached a small residential side street with a lot of fairly old-looking, tall terraced houses, in poor external decorative order.

'Here it is. Number 5 Manchester Street. It's the basement flat. Leave it to me.'

Dogger bounded down a few wrought-iron steps and approached the basement door.

Within a few minutes, he was back again.

'No sign of life – no lights on, no one in. Sorry mate.'

Benjamin accepted that Dogger had certainly earned the extra tenner and, as they walked back, he said:

'Look, thanks, Dogger, I'm really grateful. Here's the money. Do you have a mobile?'

'I normally have one but I had to sell it, but it's easy to find me, blud. I'm always up and down the Cambridge Road. Just talk to the girls. They can usually track me down. Really nice to meet a true gentleman like you around these parts. Would it be possible to ask you for just a couple of quid for some more fags?'

By now Benjamin had realised that tenners were for crack and that small change was for food and fags and that Dogger, in his own street-style, would push things to the limit and milk the maximum from any chance meeting. Benjamin parted with some more change, concluding with:

'And a pleasure to meet you too, Dogger.'

With that, the two parted company. It was quite late by Benjamin's standards and he felt that it was time to return home. As he walked back to his car, he was aware that there were more poorly dressed girls hanging around on street corners: quite a contrast with the younger, heavily made-up clubbers, who he sensed were part of normal local nightlife. What a desperate state to get to whereby you had to sell your body to stay on an even keel, mused Fine. He had so often told the pupils in his charge over the years that one *never* stops learning, whatever one's age – today had certainly been an education for him.

Chapter Twenty Nine
The Life Cycle of Mayflies
'Keep asking and you'll find the answers.'
J. Canfield

It had certainly been another one of those very long, exhausting days and, as Fine drove back to Cranford, he felt cautiously confident that there was a chance that he may have been lucky and hit on the right person. Of course, the intruder may not have even come from Harleybury, but he was confident that if he did, then Dogger would have known him and that, so far, this Kenny, who apparently had transport, was the most likely candidate. Even if it wasn't Kenny, he would surely be a good source of information. It took some time for Benjamin to get to sleep that night, as he turned over in his mind how he was going to proceed. One thing for sure was that next time he paid a visit to Harleybury it was going to be after dark.

So, at about 10.30p.m, the following evening, fortified with a good meal and armed with plenty of cash, including loose change and a few packets of cigarettes, Benjamin set off for the centre of Harleybury, some three miles away.

It was not long before he was patrolling the Cambridge Road. This time he approached the first available working girl type and when he was regaled by quite a pretty twenty-something brunette, with the ubiquitous invitation to do business, he replied:

'I could be interested,' and offered the girl a cigarette, which she accepted with alacrity.

'My name is Laura. I can give you a nice blow job for twenty. Do you have somewhere to go? Or do you have a car?'

'Well, wait a moment. I'm not sure yet, but can you spare a few minutes to chat?' asked Benjamin.

'Sure,' she said, 'but not here and I really need to earn some money.'

Laura was a little more polite than the street girl he had encountered on the previous night. The cigarette freely offered may well have helped.

'Look, how about a tenner just to have a brief talk? If it goes on for more than ten minutes, I'll give you more,' Fine suggested.

Laura was obviously delighted to do a small 'chat job' for a tenner. It was normally just a bit of dirty talk while the punter masturbated in an alleyway. However, she was not sure that this well-spoken gent was looking for that sort of relief. In any case, Laura invited him along a side street, to one of Harleybury's many nooks, and Fine quickly got to the point.

'Do you know Mary Anne?'

'Sure, she's a nice girl, sort of one of us, but she don't really work the streets. She's got a boyfriend called Kenny. Actually, haven't seen either of them around for quite a while.'

'I suppose people come and go.'

'Yeah, but when they go it's usually because they've been banged up by the Pigs. They usually come back after they've done their time. Most of us have been around for years. Kenny and Mary Anne are quite well known – Kenny's a big crack-head and Mary Anne's also a brown-head. Maybe Kenny smokes some brown too, but Mary Anne bangs up.'

That was the second time this phrase had been used, but obviously with a different meaning. He inferred from the context that this meant that Mary Anne injected heroin, as opposed to merely smoking the stuff. Laura asked for another cigarette.

'Do you know Kenny's surname?'

'People don't tend to use surnames around here. I'm sure I've heard it but I can't remember.'

'Is Mary Anne a friend of yours then?'

'Not specially. As I said, she's a nice girl but she don't hang around the streets that much. I think Kenny does the scoring for both of them.'

'What is Kenny like?'

'Not my type. He's got a bad reputation, but luckily I've never had any trouble with him. I try to keep myself to myself as much as possible. You'd be best off talking to someone like Nadine – she's a big black girl, who seems to know everyone. Come to think of it, I've sometimes seen Mary Anne with a girl called Shelley.'

'Does she work the streets?'

'Oh yeah, but not every day.'

'What does she look like?'

'Slim, blonde, average height, about my sort of age – also quite a nice girl. Seems to do well when she *does* work.'

'Do you know, Dogger?'

'Sure, everyone knows Dogger. He's a bit off-putting at first, but actually he's quite harmless, although I'd watch your wallet when he's around.'

'Any chance you could help me find Dogger again?'

'Oh, you know him. Well, can you give me another tenner? I'll ask around and see if I can find him for you.'

There was more parting of money, more hanging around, as Laura went off to find Dogger. It wasn't long before the two came, arm in arm, along the side street.

After a brief hello, Fine came straight to the point:

'Dogger, do you know a girl called Shelley?'

'Sure I do. She's not out every day.'

'Could you keep a lookout for her for me? Here's a tenner. Phone me on my mobile number, which I'll give you in a moment. It's worth your while. I'll give you twenty if you can arrange a meeting for me.'

'Good choice – she's another nice one – very attractive, not quite in Mary Anne's class, but you'll like her. I'll need some loose change for the phone call.'

Benjamin handed Dogger some change and desisted from reminding the small-time crook that he really wasn't interested in sampling the goods.

'By the way, have you heard anything more about Kenny and Mary Anne?' enquired Benjamin.

'Nah, I've asked loads of people about them. No one seems to have seen them for a few weeks.'

In street terms, a week is an age. People on the street-scene seem rapidly to lose track of time. Most of them seem to live a mayfly existence – twenty-four hours is the normal life cycle and each day they start afresh in their scramble for money, drugs and food, an almost animal-like existence in the more hardened cases. In some cases, the life cycle extends to forty-eight hours, or even more on the occasions they haven't managed to get any sleep.

Benjamin gave Dogger a piece of paper on which he'd written his mobile number.

'Don't show this to anyone else. If you do, no more readies.'

As Dogger nodded approval, Benjamin decided to return home. It wasn't long before his mobile rang. It was Dogger in a state of excitement.

'Hi, it's Dogger here. Look, can you get down here quickly? I've got Shelley with me. If you're quick, she'll wait around – you'll need to give her about twenty.'

'That's very quick. Where shall we meet?'

'Outside the garage.'

'Okay, I'm on the way.'

Fortunately for Fine, there was a dearth of traffic as he raced back to Harleybury. When he arrived, some fifteen minutes later, Dogger was waiting for him but there was no sign of any girl.

'Hi, man, sorry, Shelley won't be a minute. I think she's talking to a regular punter.'

A minute turned into ten, which then extended into another twenty. Benjamin was beginning to learn that punctuality and reliability in this opportunistic environment were not important

238

concepts. Street people invariably follow the immediately available cash. He chatted to Dogger, who kept saying:

'I'm really pissed off, man – I go and earn her twenty quid and she fucks off. I'm really sorry. I'm sure she'll be back soon.'

After a further few minutes, a breathless and rather attractive blonde-haired girl suddenly appeared.

'Oh, I'm sorry. It was one of my regulars. He's normally very quick but tonight he took ages to cum; probably drunk too much. So you're looking for my friend Mary Anne?'

'Yes.'

'Well, I haven't seen her for two or three weeks. To tell you the truth, I've started to get a bit worried about her.'

'Is she a close friend?'

'Not really close. I've only known her a few months but we get on and sometimes smoke together. She's mostly with a guy called Kenny but sometimes she's able to get a little time away from him and seems pleased to have a girlfriend to chat to.'

'Does she ever talk about her life or about Kenny?'

'Not really. She often complains about Kenny, saying he's a useless, stupid twat.'

'Do you know how she makes her money?'

'Not really. She doesn't like talking about things like that. She always seems to have what she needs, although when I'm with her she never seems to have much on her, but then, none of us do.'

'Do you know Kenny?'

'Not well. He's a loud-mouthed, dirty man. If Mary Anne isn't there, he's always trying to talk me into a free shag, but I wouldn't go with him if he'd pay me double the going rate.'

'Does Mary Anne know he's propositioned you?'

'What?'

'That he's asked you for sex?'

'Don't think so. She might suspect but I don't want to make any trouble between them, so I say nought. Sometimes she talks about the dirty bitches that Kenny smokes with and she's convinced that he does things with some of them, but then she says she doesn't care a fuck. I don't think she loves him. She's scared of him alright and I get the impression that, in some ways, he's got his uses.'

'Why do you think they've disappeared?'

'Oh, people sometimes disappear. Kenny might have upset one of the dealers, like maybe he owes someone money and has had to go into hiding – it's not good if you have the yardies after you. They can hurt people.'

It seemed that he had exhausted Shelley's usefulness. He felt he ought to pay a return visit to Manchester Street, preferably with Dogger, but it was a bit late now for what he had in mind. He thanked Dogger and Shelley, handed £20 to each of them and then asked Dogger to meet him at 6p.m on the following day, when he would earn some more money. Dogger didn't hesitate:

'You can rely on me. I'm your man. Six tomorrow, same place, okay?'

With that, Benjamin returned home, pretty content with the progress he had made. He spent the next day dealing with personal admin: laundry and the like, and then drove to Harleybury for his meeting. On this occasion, Dogger was waiting for him and ready for action. The two unlikely comrades made their way to Manchester Street, at the far end of the Cambridge Road. On arrival, Dogger made a routine visit to the basement of No.5 and confirmed, as expected, that there was still no sign of life. Benjamin suggested he rang each of the flat buzzers in turn. Dogger was not endowed with too many inhibitions and went straight for the panel of numbers at the side of the main door of the narrow, four-storey house, which had been converted into eight flats. He tried the lowest number first, which was 2. After a couple of unsuccessful attempts, he tried number 3. After a few minutes, they were aware of movement. Someone was coming down the stairs and, within moments, a suspicious-sounding male voice from the other side of the main door asked: 'Who is it?'

Dogger replied:

'Sorry to trouble you, mate, but I'm looking for Kenny, who lives in the basement flat.'

'Don't know the guy. Never speak to him. Haven't seen him around for a while. Sorry, can't help you.'

'What about his partner? Have you seen his girl?'

'They keep themselves to themselves. Never spoken to her. Sorry, can't help.'

Dogger's next effort, at flat 4, was equally unsuccessful. After he had exhausted all the buzzers, the only thing that both men had learned was that the one person who had bothered to answer hadn't seen either of the occupants of the basement flat for a significant time.

Dogger started on the adjacent terraced house, to the right. He walked down the steps and knocked on the door of that basement flat. After a few moments, a female voice asked over the intercom:

'Who is it?'

'Sorry to trouble you, but I'm looking for Kenny and Mary Anne, who live next door. Do you know them?'

This time the response was more interesting.

'Sure, I know Mary Anne but I haven't seen her for a while. I think she must've gone away.'

At this point, Benjamin indicated to Dogger to move away and he interposed. He took the not unreasonable view that *he* was more likely to gain the confidence of the occupant. The youngish-sounding woman was suddenly regaled with a very different accent:

'My name is Benjamin Fine. I am the person looking for Kenny and Mary Anne. I don't actually know them in person, but I'm trying to contact them on a matter of importance.'

'Can you come back tomorrow about 6? Just *you* please. I'll speak to you then. I should be back from work by that time.'

'Sure, that's very kind of you. Look forward to meeting you. Bye for now.'

Benjamin suspected that the young woman was alone and was not going to risk opening the door to two male strangers at that time of night. He was pleased with this latest turn of events and thanked Dogger for his help.

'Okay, I can handle this on my own now. I think I'll call it a night.'

With that, he deposited Dogger as rapidly as possible where he had picked him up, handed him twenty pounds and made his way back home.

Chapter Thirty
CONCERNED FRIENDS
*'Be generous with kindly words, especially about those who
are absent.'*
J. Goethe

Benjamin made sure he was punctually back at Manchester Street.
The voice asked him if he was alone, which he confirmed. This time
the main door was electronically opened and Benjamin made his
way to the front door of the basement flat. An attractive young
woman, he guessed in her late twenties, was standing at the door.
She had long brown hair and was dressed in a blouse and slacks.

'My name's Pat. Come in.'

Benjamin was immediately led into a small lounge, where a
neatly dressed blonde of a similar age was seated.

'This is Emma. She also knows Mary Anne.'

After introductory pleasantries had been completed, Pat started
proceedings:

'Look, as it happens, we're both worried about Mary Anne. I
don't know her that well but sometimes she'd appear at my door,
usually upset, and she'd come in for a chat. Emma knows her
better than I do.'

Emma interposed:

'Mary Anne isn't a close friend but she's a nice girl, who I see
sometimes for a coffee and girlie talk. To be honest, Pat called me
last night and asked me to come over because you'd come looking
for Mary Anne and she's been worried about her too. Neither of
us've seen her for a few weeks. If she was going away, she'd
definitely've told me. The last time she disappeared it was because
her bastard boyfriend had hit her black and blue. When she got
back she told me she wouldn't just disappear again without telling
me. I'd been right worried and I told her so. She's got a bad drug
habit and lives with a guy called Kenny. She isn't at all happy with

him. They're always having rows. I think Mary Anne is a sort of working girl, if you know what I mean.'

'And what about you two? What do you girls do?'

Pat was the first to answer.

'Oh, I work as a receptionist, nine to five-type job, broke up with my boyfriend about three months ago, live alone, don't do drugs, sometimes have a few drinks – no boyfriends at the moment.'

She glanced over to Emma.

'I used to be a working girl, but managed to get off the gear and now I've got a part-time cleaning job, sometimes have a smoke, but I can take it or leave it. Sometimes have a pipe with Mary Anne. We've become pretty good friends.'

Both girls were surprisingly well spoken.

'Do you have any theories?' asked Benjamin.

It was Emma who replied:

'Not really. If Mary Anne had disappeared and Kenny was around, I would've been very suspicious, but they both seem to have disappeared at the same time. It seems odd because I had the feeling that if Kenny had gone off somewhere, Mary Anne would've used the opportunity to get rid of him. She's always talked about leaving him. As I said, she went off for a few weeks at the end of last year – didn't she Pat? – but she seems to be too frightened of him to stay away for long. She's very young, only about twenty. I offered to take her in with me once but she said that Kenny'd find her and probably beat us both up.'

'How much do you know about Mary Anne's life? How does she make her money? Does she work the Cambridge Road?'

After glancing at Pat, Emma continued:

'She doesn't talk about it very much but she did say that she'd been an escort girl but that was some time ago. She certainly wasn't one of the regular girls. There was a period when she seemed to have loads of money and was very generous with me; would always share a pipe, buy me drinks and stuff. I could never match her; I used to feel rather guilty. More recently she complained of being very short of money and her appearance really deteriorated: come to think of it, a little while back, when she seemed loaded, she used to disappear for a day or two at a time, saying that she had a big job to do. I had the feeling that she may have had a sugar daddy, but she'd never speak about that sort of thing.'

Pat interrupted:

'Do you mind me asking who exactly you are? I mean, what is your interest in a girl like Mary Anne? You aren't the police by any chance?'

'Oh no, to be frank, I used to be a teacher at Cranford College. Do you remember the news about an intruder appearing there some weeks ago. He seemed to resemble this fellow Kenny and I'm trying to find out the surrounding circumstances.'

'So you're investigating this on behalf of the College?'

'No, not exactly. When a man involved in drugs turns up at a place like Cranford and approaches the Head teacher in front of all the Governors and then runs off, it's natural for a lot of people to ask questions. I have personal reasons for wanting to find answers.'

'And just why do you want to get these answers?'

'Well, I am, of course, asking you to respect my confidence but I'm not exactly a friend of the Head and I believe that he's been up to no good.'

'Sounds very interesting,' said Pat. 'So you think the Head has somehow been associating with people like Kenny for some reason?'

'Possibly.'

'Do you think that their disappearance is somehow connected with all this?' enquired Pat.

'I haven't a clue, but there are certainly some strange and worrying matters here. I need to find out more about Mary Anne. Do you know the name of the escort agency she worked for?'

'No idea. Mary Anne would often talk about her background and the way she got involved in the drug scene but she was rather embarrassed about her involvement in prostitution and didn't like talking about it. It is a bit of a stigma, you understand. Not many of us are exactly proud about lying on our backs for money. I don't do it anymore. Anyway, I'd be too frightened to do it again. You never know who you are dealing with these days. It's a horrible way to make money.'

'How do you think I could find out more about Mary Anne?'

'Well, the only woman I can think of who may be able to help is Helen. She still works the streets, but she used to be known as the 'Queen of the Crack Houses'. She knows everyone on the street scene. She was once very attractive but getting on a bit; she's well connected and into everything: drugs, guns, robberies, but can be very kind, if she likes you. Very outgoing, friendly woman, unless you get on the wrong side of her – then she can be a nasty cow.'

'How can I find her?'

'Very easy, she's always around during the evening, looking for punters. Just ask. They all know her.'

'Look, I'm really grateful to both of you. Let's keep in touch.'

'Sure thing. Will you let us know if you find out anything? We'd like to know that Mary Anne's okay.'

After mobile numbers were exchanged, Benjamin reminded the girls of the need for discretion and keeping his involvement confidential. Farewells were then exchanged and Fine decided to make a beeline for the red light area, to see if he could track down this Helen.

In spite of the fact that it was only early evening, he proceeded with his enquiries, confident that he could now distinguish between so-called street people and normal locals, who were going about their business. Sometimes the distinctions could be blurred; indeed there were those who had their feet in both camps, but Benjamin had grown in confidence in this adjacent world. Head dipped, he made his way up to Western Oaks, which seemed to be a favourite haunt of working girls. En route, he put in a mobile call to Dogger. This yielded an immediate answer.

'Do you know a girl called Helen?'

'Sure, everyone knows Helen. She's usually around. Do you want me to find her for you?'

Dogger was always available as an intermediary. Of course, Fine's costs went up using him as a middle man, but he did garner quick results.

'Are you anywhere near me? I'm just coming up to the corner of Western Oaks and Cambridge Road,' enquired Benjamin.

'I'm never too far from Western Oaks. See you in a couple of minutes.'

As Benjamin had learned, a couple of minutes meant that Dogger was probably on the other side of town and that he'd be about a half an hour. On this occasion, he was wrong. Five minutes later, the bouncy figure of Dogger, in his grubby tunic, tracksuit bottoms and dirty trainers, appeared from the direction of the town centre.

'Hi, blud. Look, you couldn't do me a big favour could you? I haven't had a smoke all day. I only need six quid. Please, I beg you, could you help me out? Then I'm all yours.'

Fine was not surprised by the immediate request; he was just pleased that the charge on this occasion was only six pounds.

There was more hanging about while his 'agent' went about his business and some forty minutes later a breathless Dogger returned.

'Come with me, I've found Helen. I've promised her you'd give her a fat twenty bit.'

'No doubt you're in for a cut of that.'

By this time, Benjamin was becoming wise to the ways of the street: Dogger obviously took his commissions from both sides of every deal, whenever possible.

'Well, you know, a man's gotta eat. She'll only give me one pipe out of it.'

'All right, Dogger, I don't mind. Just like you to know that I'm well aware of your entrepreneurial skills.'

Benjamin surprised himself with his growing confidence in this alien environment.

Dogger led him into one of the many side streets off the Cambridge Road, to yet another shabby terraced house, and Benjamin soon found himself in a long lounge-cum-kitchen, occupied by a disparate collection of people who all, except one, seemed to be engaged in the use of drugs. The kitchen was well fitted and tidy. A slim, middle-aged, white man was introduced as Dave, the flat owner. At a circular, white table there were two men of about thirty; one was a tall, bearded gentleman of Rastafarian appearance, the other a nondescript, lightly built, white man. Seated on stools, both were occupied with small inverted bottles, which were obviously crack pipes. Another young white man was sitting on a cushion by the hearth, smoking some brown substance, off a piece of metal foil. Fine assumed that this was heroin.

A fairly well built woman in her late thirties was sitting on the couch and was also fiddling around with a crack pipe. The atmosphere was mellow, not in any way hostile or menacing, but Fine's impression was that this was a desultory collection of individuals, each occupied in a solo activity, with very few words exchanged between the assembled company.

Dogger whispered to Benjamin to hand him his fee, which the former duly passed on to Dave. He, in turn, produced a tiny, plastic-wrapped ball. As Dogger unwrapped the goodies, the woman on the couch looked up at Benjamin, smiled and said:

'I'm Helen. What's a guy like you doing in a place like this, with us druggies?'

'Well, certainly not to join you,' said Benjamin with a charming smile.

'Well, I'm sure I could show you a *very* good time doing something else,' Helen replied with a seductive smile.

'I've little doubt of that,' said Benjamin, 'but forgive me, I'm only here to talk about a girl called Mary Anne.'

'Oh, you're looking for her. Well, of course, she's much younger than me and very pretty.'

'I'm really not looking for her personal services,' said Fine, 'I'm more concerned about her whereabouts.'

'Haven't seen or heard of her for a while,' said Helen. 'Don't know her very well but she's a nice girl, not your usual type, a few cuts above the rest of most of the bitches and scammers out there, although I've heard that, in recent times, she and her man, Kenny, have pulled a few stunts. He would've put her up to them. Kenny's filth; doesn't dare mess with me – with my connections, he wouldn't dare; not that I wouldn't hit him myself if I had to, but he robs a lot of the girls. Used to hide in a tree, outside a dealer's, and would wait for any girl to appear and, as she was about to score, he'd jump down and rob her. Fuckin' robbin' bastard.'

'What do you know about Mary Anne?'

'She's not a regular working girl, but used to be an escort. I don't know where she gets her money. They used to have loads and had a really nice motor until recently. I think they ran out of money and sold it.'

'Do you know the name of the agency she used to work for?'

'Not a clue, but I know the names of some of them agencies. I used to work for *The Girlfriend Experience* – specialised in going a lot further than the girls from the other places – then there's *Champagne Companions*, er, let me see... Fuck, what were they? Oh, yeah, *Elegant Escorts* and *Party Princesses*, usual stuff, you know. There was one other place for the really loaded punters, called *Paradise Babes*.

Benjamin produced a notepad and pen.

'Do you mind if I write those down?'

'Sure, be my guest.'

'Do you have a mobile?'

'Yeah, I do,' said Helen. 'Now, before you go, you sure you don't want some light relief?'

'Helen, you're a most charming and attractive young woman and, in different circumstances, I may've been tempted, but I must really focus on the reason why I'm here in Harleybury. I'm eager to ascertain Mary Anne and Kenny's whereabouts. They do seem to have disappeared into thin air.'

'People do,' said Helen. 'They might've robbed the wrong people. In our world you can easily end up in an unmarked grave. They've probably had to do a runner.'

'Or maybe they've upset the wrong guy and are already in that grave,' suggested Dave, amidst a cloud of smoke.

'Oh well, that's possible, but I think I'd have heard if there'd been a contract out,' said Helen. 'I know all the bad guys in this town – word gets around about these things.'

Benjamin felt that if he had not outstayed his welcome, he had certainly spent sufficient time in this crack den for his own particular liking. He decided to thank the assembled company, handed a twenty pound note to Helen and turned to Dogger, who had just inhaled a full pipe of thick white smoke, suggesting it was time to go.

'Just give me a little while, I've just got one more bat and then we can be off.'

'Okay,' said Benjamin, 'I'll wait outside.'

Dogger wanted to make sure he got his cut from Helen, who dutifully broke off a piece and handed it to him.

'Shit, that's really small,' he said.

'That's all you're getting; I did the work and you've already been paid off.'

Benjamin physically distanced himself from this little spat, which was obviously a not uncommon squabble about divvying up the precious white substance. For Fine it was comparable to children battling over their share of a bag of sweeties. He wondered what was so exciting about the white smoke but decided that his curiosity was far from sufficient to engage in any first-hand research.

As Fine emerged once more into the evening's fresh air, he was pleased to be relieved of the increasing feeling of claustrophobia, which the fetid atmosphere of the tawdry den had engendered.

Chapter Thirty One
A NICE JOB FOR DOGGER
'An Englishman's home is his repeatedly burgled castle' |
Anon

Following the information which he had gleaned from the voluble Helen, Fine returned home, exhausted but somewhat elated. He decided to try and get some sleep but his brain was still very active. What was the explanation for all he had learned? There was little doubt in his mind that Kenny had been the intruder at Cranford. The description matched in all details: some facial hair, pockmarked, tattoos, height, age. Maybe he could obtain a photo of Kenny, as it was important to be sure before he went any further. Then there was the question of the purpose of Kenny's visit. The public nature of the intrusion suggested that Kenny wanted to make some sort of point. But what possible connection could he have with one of the dignitaries of Cranford College? Then the thought crossed Benjamin's mind that a possible explanation for the unscheduled school visit could involve some sort of threat, although this did seem far-fetched. He would have to gain access to Kenny's flat; he'd need help for this.

The following morning he put in a call to Dogger and arranged to meet at 11a.m at the corner of Western Oaks. Before departure, Fine prepared a short document on his computer and printed it out. He then drove off for his meeting. Dogger was waiting for him; Benjamin duly ferried him to a quiet side street, where both men could speak without being too conspicuous.

'Dogger, how would you like to earn some really good money?'

'You know me, man, anything to earn an honest sort o' crust.'

'Well, what I want to ask of you is, in fact, not all that honest. I assume you're no stranger to house-breaking?'

'Well, I've done a few burglaries in my time, I've got to admit.'

'I want you to break into Kenny's flat.'

'No problem. Easy as pie. Not likely to be anything there worth taking.'

'Dogger, I want you to break in and look for information. I'm really interested in you finding any photos of Kenny.'

'Well, let's say, five hundred for the break-in and a further two hundred for each photo,' said Dogger.

'I can't afford that kind of money. What about two hundred for getting in and a hundred for each photo – maximum four hundred. Take it or leave it. I can find someone else.'

Dogger knew that there were others on the street who would have done the whole job for much less. 'Okay, but a hundred in advance.'

'Fifty in advance,' said Fine, 'you'll have to trust me if you want the job. Furthermore, you're to promise me that you won't steal anything else.'

'Oh come on, blud, you expect me to take all that risk and make fuck all on the side. There may be a TV, DVDs and stuff, all useful to me.'

'I am not aiding and abetting theft for profit. If this is in your mind, the deal's off. In fact, there's another condition.'

'What?'

'I'd like you to sign and date this.'

I, Keith Johnson, otherwise known as "Dogger" of Harleybury, have been asked by Benjamin Fine to enter the unoccupied premises of the basement flat, 5 Manchester Street, Harleybury, for the sole purpose of obtaining photos of the occupants. The motivation for this is that Mr Fine is very eager to establish the identity of the man who turned up uninvited at Cranford College's Carol Service Ceremony last year, as reported in the local press. He strongly believes this to be a person he knows to be called Kenny, who resides at this address and who has seemingly disappeared with his girlfriend, Mary Anne

Signed.................... date 15th April 2002.

Benjamin was aware that what he was proposing was of dubious legality and that the outcome could be embarrassing if Dogger were to have his collar felt over the incident, nevertheless pragmatism insisted that an organised burglary was imperative under the circumstances.

Dogger read the short statement slowly. 'You're tying me up in knots.'

'No, I'm protecting you. If by any chance you get caught, give me a call and I'll go to the police and show them this piece of paper. I'm willing to take the chance that there'll be no prosecution in the circumstances. I'm placing myself at risk in order to protect you. It would be very embarrassing if you were caught. I'm not interested in any real criminality. What I am asking you to do is technically criminal but I intend to find a way of compensating the owner if you do any damage to the lock.'

'I can pick the lock. No need to do any damage,' said Dogger with a smile.

'Okay, will you sign please?' said Fine, offering Dogger a pen.

'Okay, blud. It's as good as done.'

Benjamin took the signed document and produced the promised fifty pounds and Dogger immediately bounded off, no doubt desperate to score.

Benjamin was woken up at 2a.m by his ringing mobile. It was a breathless-sounding Dogger.

'I've got it; a photo of Kenny, probably when he was a few years younger.'

'Any sign of the two?'

'Nothing; mouldy food in the fridge. I think they've fucked off. I did find something you'll be interested in. Can you meet me?'

Benjamin was sufficiently intrigued that he agreed to meet Dogger straight away.

So, at 2.30a.m, Benjamin collected Dogger from outside the Snooker Hall and within a few minutes was driving him off to a quiet location on the outskirts of town.

'Well?'

'Money first, man,' said Dogger.

'I'll pay you in full. I'll show you the cash, but I'm not parting with a penny until I see what you have.'

'Another fifty and I'll show you,' said Dogger.

Benjamin impatiently thrust five £10 notes into Dogger's outstretched hand.

Dogger then unzipped his tunic and retrieved a couple of items which looked ideal. One was a small, framed photo which was of a family group of Afro-Caribbeans, obviously taken outdoors. It was a cheerful picture of six people. There was an elderly woman, a middle-aged couple, two young men and a very young woman. Dogger pointed to the older of the two young men and said:

'That's Kenny.'

On the back of the photo, all the names had been written – The Churchill family - Mom, Wayne and Pearl, me, Joe and family friend Mary Anne.

The man in the picture looked early thirties. There was no sign of any tattoos or facial hair. The other item was an A5-sized thin booklet, which had the name of **"St Michael's School"** on the front and a crest, which obviously related to the school. There was also a sub-heading:

LOWER 6ᵀᴴ, 1998 LEAVERS' BALL.

Benjamin flicked through the small number of pages: a letter from the Headmaster a few photographs, a number of short stories, written by some of the leavers about amusing incidents which they had experienced during their time at St Mike's. The one interesting thing was that it contained a list of names of those leaving, with a brief one-line description of their achievements at school. It did not take Benjamin long to find the name of one *Mary Anne Marshall*: *actress – house play "The Crucible",*

Autumn 1997; dancer – "Pure Dance" Summer 1998. Benjamin was convinced that if the two had really decided to leave of their own volition, it was this kind of memento which a girl like Mary Anne would surely have taken with her.

He did not know whether this little publication would, in itself, prove to be of interest. However, it also indicated that Dogger was not running a scam. He had obviously done the job genuinely and, although it hurt him a little, Benjamin was content to hand over the promised additional £200, plus an extra twenty for the booklet.

'Is that all? Can't you make it fifty? That was the hardest thing of all to find. I had to search through a box of cards, letters and papers for it,' said Dogger.

'Don't be greedy. You're doing very well out of me. I'm grateful but I'm not a rich man and this has already cost me a small fortune and, ultimately, I'm not going to make a penny out of it!' said Fine, feeling that he had already overpaid for what must have been less than an hour's work in Dogger's usual line of business.

'Okay, blud, fair play; you know how to find me if you've got any more work.'

With this, Benjamin dropped Dogger back at the snooker hall, from where he once again disappeared into the night.

The next morning Benjamin started to attend to his next task. He produced the list of escort agencies and proceeded to use Directory Enquiries to find the telephone numbers. Two were not listed. The three which were listed were *Elegant Escorts, Paradise Babes* and *Champagne Companions.*

He called 'Elegant Escorts'. There was no reply. He tried 'Paradise Babes' and a well-spoken female voice answered.

'Are you Paradise Babes?' enquired Benjamin.

'Yes. My name is Fiona. Are you looking for company, Sir?'

'Yes.'

'Can I have your name, please?'

Benjamin obliged.

'When do you require company?'

'Actually, I'm looking for a particular girl.'

'I don't have any record of you as a regular customer.'

'No, I have used you before but, to be honest, I used a false name.'

'So Benjamin Fine isn't your real name?'

'Actually it is. I'm sorry for the earlier deception. It was my first time and I was a bit nervous about revealing my identity. Now I know that you are a proper organisation, I feel safe in giving you my real name.'

The voice at the other end sounded sceptical.

'Just who is it that you'd like to see?'

'I really like them young. My favourite is Mary Anne Marshall.'

There was a pause.

'No one of that name on my list.'

'Are you sure?'

'Give me a few minutes; can you call back?'

After a good five minutes, Benjamin rang.

The receptionist's tone was somewhat curt. 'I'm sorry, I'm new here, I've just checked up and Mary Anne no longer works for us. She hasn't been with us for months, but we have a very pretty brunette of only twenty-one. Are you interested?'

'Not just at the moment, but I'm really grateful for your trouble. I'll be in touch if I change my mind. Oh, you don't happen to have Mary Anne's number?'

'Sorry, Sir. We never provide personal details.'

Benjamin knew he was going to have to be patient if he was to stand a chance of ascertaining the reason for Kenny's visit to Cranford and for his and Mary Anne's subsequent disappearance. What buoyed him was the fact that he seemed to be edging inexorably closer in his quest.

Chapter Thirty Two
UNCOMFORTABLE REVELATIONS
'The scholar does not consider gold to be the most precious treasure, but loyalty.'
Confucius

Benjamin Fine kept Martin Trench in daily contact about all the information that had come his way about the Carol Service intruder. The investigator was in no way convinced that this had anything to do with Joseph Howson, considering it rather as some random act which, although not immediately explicable, should not be over-concerning Fine.

'Ben, you are putting a lot of effort into all these enquiries and, thanks to your doggedness, we seem to be on to a great deal about Howson's background, but there's a danger you'll see a possible area of concern whenever you're considering anything with which he is vaguely connected. You must avoid becoming obsessed.'

'I take your point,' replied Benjamin, 'it's just... well, the whole matter was so odd and this Kenny bloke seemed to focus primarily on Howson; well, I have a feeling Howson may have done something to initiate it all. I can't be certain, of course, time will tell. I'm certainly not going to get bogged down by this, but I can't help trying to get to the bottom of it all.'

'Let me know if you discover anything further but, Ben, you be careful. These drug dealers don't like being spied on and they're not to be trusted. They talk to each other; on the face of it they'll seem to be your helper, while at the same time passing information on to each other. They can be complete bastards. This Kenny sounds pretty unsavoury, I can't imagine Howson striking up any sort of relationship with someone like that. For what purpose? Unless, of course, you're suggesting the man's some sort of clandestine drug trafficker. You can tell he's not a user.'

'I know the whole thing seems ridiculous but, I'm telling you, nothing would surprise me about Howson. He finished my career like someone swatting a fly; he did it with hardly a second thought. So, I know firsthand the man can be a heartless, cunning rogue; no one will convince me otherwise. He will brook no opponents; he wipes them aside without a by-your-leave.'

Trench had a certain admiration for his friend's (for that is what the two had become) single-mindedness and courage. Most individuals would not dare to have taken up cudgels against a man of Howson's reputation and contacts. They would have accepted their fate as unfortunate, banking the generous severance pay, realising there was little else that could be done under the circumstances. This course of action would have been so easy for Benjamin. He was comfortable financially; he had time on his hands to pursue his favourite leisure activities, denied to him over the years by the relentless pressures of working in a seven-day-a-week boarding school; he now had the opportunity to travel throughout the world, something that he had always wanted to do. He was in his fifties, still enjoying good health. Wasn't his departure from Cranford in some ways opportune? Trench thought that even *he himself* would have reluctantly accepted matters and got on with his life. Then he reflected for a moment and thought perhaps no, he might possibly have done exactly the same as his friend. Trench was a thoroughbred detective; he had an investigator's mind, rarely taking things at face value. He did consider that, after all this was done and dusted, he might just offer Benjamin a job at his agency, if the latter was interested.

For his part, Benjamin decided to give Sarah a ring. The two had been close friends ever since she had joined the school eight years previously. Their first point of contact was their weekly bridge evenings and neither of them had missed barely a single meeting throughout the whole of that time: that is, until Benjamin's departure. Suddenly, Sarah started making excuses as to why she couldn't make it: she still attended on occasions but was absent more often than not. The two close friends, who had immediately hit it off, felt a strain in their relationship for the very first time.

'Sarah, it's Ben. Look, I was hoping to see you at some point. I need a heart-to-heart chat; you're one of the few people at Cranford I can trust.'

Sarah fleetingly wished that her former bridge partner could *not* trust her. She was employed by Cranford, Howson was her boss and she was well aware that her responsibility, her duty, was to it and to him. Although she treasured Benjamin as a friend, she felt reluctant about being dragged into his personal enquiries and suspicions about this intruder-figure, which she feared was Fine's focus.

'I'm not sure I can help you, Ben. If it's about that Caribbean fellow, I think you're making a mountain out of a molehill. I think it prudent you should drop the matter, Ben, before you make a fool of yourself or cause embarrassment to the school.'

'It's not just this incident. I need to talk to you about... there are other things. Just hear me out. It's important I paint you the entire picture.'

'Come for coffee on Saturday morning, if you want. But don't tell anyone to do with the school. You know what Howson is like; if he were to find out we were seeing each other socially, outside the bridge club, I'd be out the door!'

'Yes, I know what Howson is like. Look, can you come over here, say 11 o'clock?'

'Just this one time, Ben, but if I feel too uncomfortable about what you're saying, I shan't stay long!'

'Trust me, Sarah, you'll want to hear the developments of my enquiries.'

Sarah was always punctual and Benjamin knew that she would arrive right on time. He had already boiled the kettle and some fresh cakes had been placed on the dining room table.

Sarah was a spinster in her late thirties, who possessed a certain attractiveness but could hardly be described as a 'man's woman'. She always dressed in an immaculate and business-like manner, was of medium height, slim, with short dark hair. She wore spectacles and was usually only lightly made up. She was not beautiful in the conventional manner, however she had a certain class and femininity, which some men found alluring. As a woman, she seemed unapproachable and the few men who were particularly attracted to her invariably felt that she had erected a barrier, which would be difficult to overcome. The only person who had come close to surmounting this wall was Fine himself.

Both exchanged pleasantries, bringing each other up-to-date about personal events and reminiscing about one or two amusing bridge hands, which they recalled from their regular club days. After some twenty minutes, placing an empty coffee cup on an adjacent table, Benjamin suddenly said:

'I need to talk to you about something really serious, Sarah. I don't want to compromise you professionally in any way and I'm not going to ask you for any information, but firstly I feel that you should know I was fitted up over the Jeremy Majors incident.'

'You know I can't comment on that, Ben, but I certainly understand how you feel.'

'I've discovered that at Dr Howson's previous school, a large number of long-standing staff left very soon after his appointment. Some were good teachers, but were manoeuvred out because they had the temerity to challenge Howson's swingeing changes.'

'Ben, you know as well as I do that it was a failing school and he had to take drastic steps to rescue the situation.'

'True, but, as a fellow Christian, I have to tell you that it's my perception that all is not right with Dr Howson. Are you aware that he was adopted as a child?'

'Ben, you know I can't get involved in gossip about my employer's family background and character.'

'Please, at least listen to what I have to say, Sarah. I think I should tell you that I've done some research into Howson's background. His real father was a high ranking SS Officer, a highly intelligent but ruthless individual, and, furthermore, as a young man, his adoptive father was one of Mosley's Blackshirts.

Sarah visibly blanched at these extraordinary revelations. Ben continued unabated.

'Although I wouldn't wish to suggest that his childhood circumstances reflect too badly on him in any sense, I think you should know that his genetic origins are also particularly questionable and, while possibly providing an explanation for his obvious academic brilliance, could also give some indication that he may himself be ruthless and also possess a tendency towards racial prejudice.'

'I think Dr Howson must be judged on his career and record. If what you say has some truth in it, it's still not his fault that he happened to have the misfortune to've been born to a father like that or to've been brought up by an equally distasteful adoptive father. In any case, how do you know about this adoptive father?'

'I visited his parents and saw a photograph of him decked out in an obvious Blackshirt uniform.'

'You mean they showed you such a thing?'

'Not exactly – let's just say that I'm observant.'

'You mean you were snooping. Even if that's true, it was a long time ago, probably long before Dr Howson was born; lots of people do silly things in their youth.'

'Not all of them get arrested and charged with murder!'

'What do you mean?'

'Here are copies of the two newspaper reports.'

Fine produced both from his jacket pocket.

Sarah read them thoughtfully and then sat for a while, seemingly perplexed.

'Are you sure that this Howson is the Headmaster's adoptive father?'

'Of course, I've had everything checked out; likewise details of his real father.'

With this, Fine thrust an A4 sheet of paper in front of Sarah, listing the various ranks that Howson's real father had held in the SS movement.

'If any of this information got into journalists' hands, it would be disastrous for Cranford,' said Sarah.

'I very much doubt anyone'd touch it. The adoptive father was arrested, yes, but never charged through lack of evidence; never even got near a Court; laws of libel, you know. His father's activities would stir things up, however.'

'In any event, it's nothing to do with the Head. So his non-biological father had an embarrassing interview with the police, I presume years before he was born. Howson's probably unaware of the whole matter and was too young to remember his real father.'

'This is correct and, in many respects, it's to his credit that he's done so well, coming from such a background. Nevertheless, Sarah, I believe that he is deficient of two important human qualities: one is compassion and, dare I say it, the other is basic morality and it's my belief he was born devoid of these qualities.'

'I'm not prepared to have an argument with you, Ben, about the concept of original sin, suffice to say you may express your opinions and you know I have great respect for your intelligence, your insights and your own good heart. However, *I* cannot possibly comment on all these sinister allegations. Dr Howson has always treated me with the utmost respect and kindness. Besides which, there's certainly no proven automatic link between one's genetic forefathers and one's own basic morality, as you put it.'

'Sarah, you prepare his correspondence. You're there in the background and witness many secrets. I cannot believe that you're totally comfortable about his *modus operandi*. For example, what about the Simon Cohen incident.'

'As his secretary, it's not my business to judge him. I've no knowledge of anything immoral or corrupt. If I had, I'd resign.'

'Come on, Sarah. Simon Cohen was one of the outstanding pupils of his year. Not only was he a clear choice as Head of House but many would have considered him as a possible choice for Head of College. But Howson changed the rules in order to veto him. It was the only choice he did veto.'

'Ben, I'm a professional secretary, not a schoolmistress. I knew Simon well. He had something obviously superior about him, in the nicest possible way. The whole community admired him and I do know that he's excelling on his Classics course at Cambridge. Dr Howson simply felt that he wouldn't fit into his prefectorial team. You have to agree, Simon was hardly one of the hearty types that Heads usually prefer as prefects. I dealt with all the Head's correspondence on this whole matter and certainly noticed nothing untoward.'

'I'm surprised by that, Sarah; that's all I can say. Do you think that his treatment of me was correct?'

'I've had no reason to believe it was incorrect. You know that, on a personal level, I'm not comfortable about what happened but that's because of our friendship. As I've stated, if I were made aware of anything which could establish that he'd behaved incorrectly or immorally, you know I'd resign. It'd be a big step for me because I enjoy living in the area and I find the job interesting and, to a certain degree, challenging. I don't know how easy it would be for me to obtain suitable, alternative employment. In any case, I've always loved Cranford. I have a long association with the college. I attend functions whenever possible and I love the atmosphere and the children. I'm proud to have my job and to contribute, in my own small way, to the success of the school. But, be sure, as I said, if I thought for a moment that the Head was in any way corrupt and he was being allowed to get away with something untoward or immoral, I'd resign immediately.'

Sarah surprised herself with this robust rejoinder. For his part, Benjamin had never witnessed his friend voicing a personal opinion with such passion.

After a pause, with both sitting face to face in silence, Ben continued:

'Sarah, you know he was uncomfortable about our weekly bridge sessions.'

Sarah looked down at the floor.

'Yes, I know...'

'You know that he regards you as a possession, just like his wife. He is the reason why you've been avoiding me, me, one of your closest friends in the world-in fact, the closest.'

He stared at Sarah and as she lowered her eyes. She knew exactly what Ben meant.

After a pause, that seemed an age to Sarah, Fine continued:

'He wants to choose your friends, veto or approve your associations. The man's a megalomaniac. He disliked me from the moment I challenged him at a staff meeting soon after he arrived. That's a pretty clear indication of his true character.'

'He's never told me to stop seeing you.'

'Of course, he wouldn't have dared but he must sometimes have made you feel uncomfortable. As you've admitted, he'd hit the roof if he thought we were meeting together now.'

'I'm a grown woman. I can handle him.'

Fine was now on a roll.

'And what about this black guy who turned up at the Carol Service procession?'

'No one seems to have a clue who he was or what he was doing,' said Sarah, as she took a sip of coffee.

'Come on, Sarah... you're a highly intelligent woman; you surely don't believe that was a random occurrence! What kind of association could Dr Howson have with a character like this?' With that, he thrust out the photo of Kenny with his family. Pointing at Kenny himself, he asked Sarah, 'Do you recognise this character?'

Sarah stared at the photo for a few moments.

'Can you prompt me?'

'I'm talking about the Carol Service. Do you remember the intruder?'

'Oh yes, now you mention it, that's the fellow - looks a bit younger but it's definitely him.'

'Would you be interested in knowing what sort of man he is? He is a piece of drugged up lowlife! What possible connection could such a person have with Howson?'

'Look, Ben, I'm not in the business of engaging in speculation about matters which I'm completely ignorant of... I'm starting to feel really uncomfortable about this conversation; I knew I would. I'd better go now. Perhaps I shouldn't have come in the first place.'

Sarah put down her cup of coffee.

Fine stood up, approached Sarah and, placing his hands gently on her shoulders, said very quietly:

'Sarah, you know how much I care for you and I also know that deep down you really care for me.'

Sarah looked down at the floor again and, after a few moments, spoke in a strained manner, as if she was trying to fight back tears:

'I'm really sorry... but I must leave now.'

With that, she stood up slowly and gently planted a kiss on his cheek. Then she picked up her handbag and took her leave.

Fine stood in the doorway as Sarah made her way to the car, looking at her sadly and longingly. He felt for her like for no other human being and he was confident that she felt similarly about him, while fully understanding the difficult dilemma in which she presently found herself.

For her part, Sarah drove home with a decidedly uncomfortable feeling in her stomach. Ought the Governors to know the details about Howson's real and adoptive fathers? Was it her place to tell them? They would want to know how she came by the information. They would question Howson. It would all come back to her. She would never be able to keep her job. She decided to sleep on it, except, that night, such was Sarah's disquiet, she found sleep particularly elusive.

Chapter Thirty Three
A BURDEN LIFTED
'Sharing a story can be endlessly healing.'
B. Vereen

After a fretful night's sleep, Sarah, having been woken by her alarm at 6.30a.m, began her early morning ritual of at first a cup of tea, ablutions, dressing and then sitting down to her customary bowl of cereal, yoghurt, with fresh banana chopped in, and a glass of freshly-made fruit juice.

She had been quite disturbed by her meeting with Benjamin. On the one hand, as far as the shortcomings of her boss were concerned, she had admiration and sympathy for her dear friend but, on the other hand, she wondered whether it was fair of him to drag her into his battles. The problem was that she now knew things; she had information which she felt could not be ignored. It was not so much that she felt that it was her place to make judgements about her boss's parentage. The problem was that she was aware that the revelations contained a potential threat to Howson, and thereby to the school. Although she would never admit it, she had her doubts about Howson. She was not too comfortable about his character: there was something cold and unfeeling about him. Benjamin's comment about prejudice confirmed her own suspicions, kept at the back of her mind, that Howson did not favour Jewish, Chinese or Asian pupils at the school. As with most modern public schools, an increasing proportion of pupils at Cranford came from abroad or ethnic minority backgrounds. Economic factors dictated that the school could not afford to turn away such pupils. They were often extremely bright, highly motivated and from very affluent backgrounds. Many of the parents of such pupils were extremely generous and responded well to the school's various appeals. Furthermore, they helped to keep the school high in the league tables. Jewish pupils were well known for their academic prowess and their parents were often extremely generous. In fact, the retailing billionaire father of one Jewish Cranfordian had funded an entire new dormitory block, although the school did have to name the block accordingly, some years before Howson's appointment. So it was that Cranford boasted the 'Sternberg' block, a designation which may not have lived well alongside that of the great British historical military and political names normally used for the boarding houses. For their part, the Chinese pupils tended to produce a very high number of A grades at Mathematics, Further Mathematics, Physics and Computer Science at A2 level, even if they did not figure high on the list of budding classicists. Not all foreigners lost out under Howson. Sarah was aware that one foreign pupil, Alex Wittner, had recently been appointed as a College prefect. He came from Austria and didn't seem to be an obvious choice, although he was academically bright and was an outstanding footballer.

As Sarah slowly progressed through her very healthy breakfast, she realised that she was probably duty-bound to apprise the Chairman of Governors of the information she had gleaned. By doing so she would inevitably put herself at risk but she was firmly resolved not to reveal the source of the information. She could not be required to do so. She certainly didn't want to do anything to hurt or betray Benjamin. She decided that she would have to make a delicate approach to the Chairman of Governors.

Later that day she found a quiet moment when she was alone in the school office and gingerly dialled the Chairman's number. She didn't expect for one moment that she would get straight through to Lord Justice Harris and, as expected, she was put through to the Judge's secretary.

Sarah immediately gave her name and explained that she needed to see Lord Harris, if possible, concerning a very confidential matter to do with Cranford and, if it would be possible, to have an audience with His Honour at the earliest opportunity.

The response was that Lord Harris was very busy in Court for at least a couple of days but might be free on the following Friday. Sarah asked the Secretary if her strict personal confidence could be respected and proffered her mobile number for future contact. The secretary confirmed that all information would, indeed, be treated with the strictest confidence.

At 7pm that same evening, Sarah was surprised to receive a direct call from Lord Harris. She had met him on a number of occasions, but always in formal contexts, such as governors' meetings or special school occasions. His telephone manner was warm and he soon put Sarah at ease:

'Hello, Sarah. This is Anthony Harris. I have heard the most marvellous things about you from the Headmaster.'

She was quite taken aback by the warmth and informality of the esteemed man's approach. 'Now, what can I do for you?'

'Lord Harris, it is a delicate matter and I would rather not talk about it on the telephone.'

'Sarah, I know you live close to the school. I am dining at home and am probably only about forty minutes away from you. Would it be impertinent of me to suggest that I call round to see you at your home at about 8.30pm? That is, if this suits you?'

'You must be a very busy man, I'm quite happy to drive round to you.'

'I wouldn't dream of putting you out – in any case, it's no effort for me. I have a chauffeur. What is your address?'

To her amazement, a chauffeured Rolls pulled up outside her small house on the dot of 8.30, Lord Harris emerging in casual, country attire. Sarah had been on the lookout, so she was already at the door, with a nervous smile, to welcome her guest, as he made his way up the garden path. He followed her into the lounge and she offered him a drink. He tactfully looked at her drinks cabinet.

'I'll settle for a small brandy, if I may. It's such a relief not to be in Court, or on public display. Please call me Tony.'

Sarah was warming to this charming and charismatic man. He was elegant, well spoken and obviously doing everything he could to gain her confidence.

'Well, maybe what I have to tell you is something you probably cannot do anything about, but it may have some bearing on the interests of the school. Either way, I don't want to have the information on my conscience or be criticised at a later date for keeping it to myself.'

The Judge, as would be expected, was extremely perceptive.

'It must be something to do with the Headmaster and you cannot tell him.'

Sarah lowered her eyes.

'I expected something of this sort. Let me give you an assurance that you have nothing to fear. It is quite right of you to have contacted me,' said Lord Harris reassuringly.

'I have come by a piece of information concerning Dr Howson's background, which I have no reason to believe reflects badly on him personally, but could possibly be embarrassing for Cranford, if it came to light. I don't know whether you or the Governors are aware that Dr Howson was adopted.'

'Yes, I am personally aware that he was adopted, but I doubt if many of my colleagues are. Dr Howson has never concealed that from me.'

'I have good reason to believe that Dr Howson's adoptive father was a member of Mosley's Blackshirts in his youth and that his real father who died when Dr Howson was a young boy, was a high-ranking Officer in the Nazi Party.'

There was a pause as Lord Harris did his very best to seem unfazed by this extraordinary information.

'Sarah, these are very serious statements. Do you have any evidence for your beliefs?'

Sarah opened her handbag and produced copies of the two newspaper reports and the A4 sheet, which Ben had handed her. He read them quickly, with a slight frown on his face.

'Are you sure that the Michael Howson mentioned in these reports was indeed the adoptive father of Dr Joseph Howson?'

'Quite sure. I am privy to the circumstances in which this information was obtained and I believe there is also hard evidence appertaining to Dr Howson's real father's connection to the Nazi Party.'

'Are you able to reveal your sources?'

'I acquired the information from a friend whom I trust. I did not seek it. I had no part whatsoever in unearthing it. I have no grudge against Dr Howson, as he's always treated me correctly and with kindness.'

'Do you have any further copies? May I keep these?' asked the Judge.

'I don't possess any further copies but I've no need whatsoever to keep them. I only accepted them when they were offered to me so I could pass them on to the proper authorities.'

'Did your source expect or want you to do anything with them?'

'My source is a person of integrity, who has the interests of Cranford at heart. He placed no restrictions upon me. Obviously, that person knew that I was likely to share the information with the appropriate parties. I haven't told anyone else and have no intention of doing so. Frankly, I'm relieved to have passed on the responsibility. There are some things that perhaps one would rather not know.'

'Do you think that the person who provided this information is likely to proliferate it?'

'I don't really know. I think that investigations may continue and there is the possibility of more being unearthed. That is part of the reason why I felt absolutely bound to keep you informed. I don't intend to fish for any more information, but if anything happens to come my way, I assume you'd like me to call your secretary?'

The Judge produced a business card with contact information and wrote a number on the card.

'I've also given you my home number, Sarah; you are welcome to call me at any time. You have done the right thing. I am very grateful to you for having the courage and sense of duty to bring this to my attention. I don't know what consequences will follow from these revelations, if any, but you have certainly given me something upon which to reflect. Let me assure you that whatever happens, Dr Howson will never know that *you* have provided any information about him or his background. Now, I won't take up any more of your valuable free time. I am sure your job is just as demanding as mine and that you probably get up even earlier in the morning than I do and, furthermore, have to drive your own car!'

Polishing off his brandy, the judge stood up, shook Sarah's hand and walked towards the door. Sarah saw him out and returned to her sitting room with a sense of great relief that the esteemed Lord Harris had taken her approach so well and had taken a lot of trouble to put her at her ease. The meeting had certainly taken a weight off her anxious mind.

Chapter Thirty Four
HOWSON DINES ON HUMBLE PIE
'If you think your teacher is tough, wait until you get a boss.'
F. Zappa

Eight days after his statement at Harleybury Police Station, Howson telephoned his boss.

'Good afternoon, Tony. I need to come up to see you at your London offices as soon as possible.'

Lord Harris detected immediately some disquiet in Howson's voice.

'It's fortuitous that you've rung because I need to speak to you, too.'

Howson was taken aback somewhat, more by the tone of Lord Harris' voice, rather than by what he said.

'Come over to mine this evening and we'll pop out for dinner; Mrs Harris has had to go down to her mother's in Hampshire,' he added.

Howson's drive to Lord Harris' home was unpleasant: poor weather, heavy traffic and an anxious state of mind all combined to set off an ache in Howson's chest. It was an ache which he had experienced shortly after the now infamous Carol Service incident of the previous year. On that occasion it had thankfully disappeared the following day, as quickly as it had come. Howson had now to face one of his most testing interviews since assuming the Headship of Cranford.

Harris met Howson at the front door and told him he had booked a table at a restaurant on the other side of the park – the chauffeur was waiting.

When dining with Lord Harris, as Howson had done on a number of occasions, only the best food and the best wine were acceptable: *pâté de foie gras*, *game pie*, the *plateau de fromage*, followed by *crème brulée*, all washed down with a half bottle of

Veuve Clicquot champagne. As the beleaguered Head was tucking into his first mouthful of *entrée*, the general state of play at Cranford having been fully discussed, with Lord Harris waxing lyrical about yet another superb Speech Day, the latter paused for a moment, put down his knife and fork and wiped his mouth slowly with his serviette.

'I need to ask you a few questions first, Joe, and I hope you don't find my enquiries either intrusive or impertinent.'

Howson looked Harris straight in the eye.

'Ask what you want, I will always be open with you, Tony,' replied Howson confidently, camouflaging a smouldering inner anxiety.

'Certain pieces of information with regard to your familial background have come my way and, for the sake of the school and its history, I feel I should be made aware of the full, true picture. We are both well aware how information and misinformation are passed around.'

Howson was taken completely by surprise by this sudden line of questioning. Didn't he have enough on his mind at present without having to ward off an attack – because he was certain that this was what it was going to be – on his familial roots?

'What information, in particular, has come your way, Tony?' asked Howson with a hint of irritation in his voice.

'Look, Joe, I'm not here to grill you about the life of your father and adoptive father and thereby judge you... I want only what is the best for Cranford. If I am armed with all the necessary facts, if a journalist were to approach the school at any stage, I should be able to protect you to the hilt.'

'All I know is that my real name is Engelmann and that my father was killed during the sixties while attempting to defend himself against an Israeli gunman. Dad – sorry – my adoptive father, told me he was shot by government thugs in a case of misidentification. It was always an emotive topic in my family and I tried not to ask too many questions, for fear of upsetting my parents. I never knew him, as I was only a baby when he died. I fail to see how any of this has any bearing upon me; for God's sake, I was a mere babe in arms.'

'Look, Joe, there have been a number of enquiries into all this recently by someone who seems to have an inordinate interest.'

'Who?' asked Howson, while staring intently into Lord Harris' eyes.

'I honestly don't know. As I said, I just need to know the facts to avoid any possible future embarrassment for our school. What about your adoptive father?'

At this point Howson's eyes moistened. There was a long pause as both men picked at the food on their plates.

'I can tell you that Dad was the most wonderful parent any child could've hoped for. Nothing was too much trouble for him. He did tell me that he was a Blackshirt during his youth, but, hey, he was young, ambitious and desperate to forge a successful life for himself. He never did anything which he hadn't been ordered to do. He was one of hundreds of young men who were proud of their roots and were fiercely loyal. God, this was over sixty years ago; I wasn't even on the planet, how could this be seen as of interest today? It was a whole world away, for God's sake. Am I to be held to account for stuff that happened in the thirties?'

'Joe, I have always believed in your integrity and I see no reason to question it now. I would very much like to speak to the person concerned to establish a motive as to why he is so interested in your background. Is there anything specific you know of that could be of interest to the press?'

'The only thing I could see as of possible interest is that he was arrested – among others, I hasten to add – in connection with the murder of a Jewish shopkeeper in the thirties. But there was so much hysteria about the Jews and how they were being persecuted from all areas in those days, people like Michael were fair game. He wasn't even charged, so if the press were to print details of any of this over sixty years later, quite honestly, it would look pretty spiteful.'

Lord Harris placed his knife and fork neatly on his plate.

'Is the person a journalist, do you think?' asked Howson, breaking the silence.

Lord Harris appeared not to be listening.

'Sorry, Joe; a journalist? I don't think so. We'd have read something by now, if it were. Now, you did say you had something to say to me.'

Joseph, in an uncharacteristically nervous manner, gave Lord Harris a full account of what had happened during the previous twenty-four hours. The latter sat back, astounded. When Howson had finished, Harris leaned forward and looked straight into his eyes.

'Joe, are you in your right mind? This is an extraordinary tale. This behaviour is so uncharacteristic of you. I appreciate that you were trying to protect the school, but to take such a risk. I mean, I can understand you throwing it over a country hedge in the middle of nowhere, but to leave it in a school house, for God's sake – what on earth made you do that?'

'I panicked, I suppose.'

'Just imagine if the press got hold of this. Coupled with this other business and, boy, you are history. It wouldn't reflect well on the school, certainly.'

Howson looked down, unable to receive Lord Harris's glare. He knew he'd be angry but it still didn't make the interview any the easier. Howson now fully appreciated how senior pupils felt when being admonished by he himself.

'I shall have to convene a meeting of the Governors before next term and it could be we recommend that you consider taking a sabbatical year, to allow you to get back into the right frame of mind.'

'No, Tony, please... please don't suggest that. I'm quite capable of seeing this through. I've turned this school round, just as I promised you, Sir Marcus and the rest of the Board. You needed me then and now I need you. I refuse to run away, even for a year.'

'I take your point, it's just that my experience tells me that once things start unravelling, it usually gets worse before it gets better. You have the summer months to review the situation and I shall speak to you again before we convene. Whatever the outcome, Joe, we very much appreciate the superb job you've done and continue to do at our beloved Cranford and you can, of course, count on our full support.'

With this, Lord Harris stretched out his arm and patted Howson warmly on the shoulder. 'Let's just hope this is all a storm in a teacup.'

As Joseph made his way back to Cranford, he felt besieged, something he had never before experienced. 'Full support' – he'd heard football Chairmen using this phrase about their club manager, only for the poor guy to be sacked within weeks.

As he had dealt with one serious problem, so another had reared its ugly head. He was tired, both physically and emotionally. Perhaps Lord Harris was right – he'd had to deal with, and may have to again in the near future, serious personal problems and, while these were at the forefront of his mind, he may need to take his eye off the successful running of the school. How many Heads did he know who had become diverted from the task at hand, or had become arrogantly complacent, with the result they experienced a speedy downturn of fortunes at their school? It was the same as running a business, managing a football team: you have to maintain focus, beware of complacency, as success can quickly change into failure. During that journey home, Dr Joseph Howson seriously considered taking Lord Harris' suggestion of a year's sabbatical leave.

Chapter Thirty Five
A NEEDLE IN A HAYSTACK
'The right to be heard does not automatically include the right to be taken seriously.'
H. Humphrey

With the continuing dissemination of information re Howson's biological background and, more recently, the vanished school intruder, Benjamin Fine was becoming commensurately more convinced that his erstwhile Headmaster had much to hide. After much consideration of all the facts at hand, Fine had convinced himself that, somehow, this Caribbean intruder, Kenny, had discovered the Nazi connection and was intent on blackmailing Howson. There could be no other explanation for the sinister incident after the Carol Service, now seven months previous. He had, in all likelihood, been paid to 'disappear'. He had to find Kenny.

Since his interview with Sarah and Emma, Benjamin had been telephoning Dogger day after day, asking him to go round to Kenny's flat to see if the two had returned. After a week had passed, Benjamin decided to pay another visit himself. He pressed the buzzer but, as expected, there was no answer. He proceeded to press each of the other seven on the plate. No response. He rang Dogger.

'Any news from Shelley or any of the others?' he enquired.

'Absolutely fuck all. Everyone's convinced that they've both upped sticks and fucked off for good. Probably 'cos of Kenny; Mary Anne would have to go with 'im.'

'Look, Dogger, you must do some more digging for me. I *must* find out what's happened. One of them must have said something, or someone must know if they had any pressing debts.'

'The last anyone saw of them was at Murko's party, about three weeks ago. One of the girls was there too and she was surprised to see Kenny, as he and Murko never got on. I think Murko had bad-mouthed him at some point and Kenny had promised revenge.'

'Where does this Murko live?'

'Anywhere and everywhere. You can never tie him down. He's not been seen for weeks either, but that's not unusual. Whenever he's into any sort of money he pisses off to London until it's run out. He must've done a big job for someone.'

'Big job?' enquired Benjamin.

'Varies. Use your imagination. Hey, gotta go. I'll ring if I find anything.'

With this, Dogger hung up.

Benjamin Fine's mind went into overdrive. Perhaps Murko had a part in all this. A 'big job' had been mentioned – Benjamin could only imagine that this was a street euphemism for a big drugs job or even foul play. These people were robbing each other on a daily basis, so this would hardly be referred to as a 'big job'. It occurred to him that he couldn't possibly carry out investigations alone, as the bigger the crime, the more complicated the investigation. He'd need either Trench's help or perhaps, if Kenny and Mary Anne had met a possible untimely death at the hands of some fellow street lowlife, he should now consider informing the police.

Early the next day, Fine put in a call to the Harleybury police and asked if he could speak to a senior CID officer. When asked for further information, he indicated that he was concerned about the apparent disappearance of two persons and his suspicion was that foul play could possibly be involved. He stressed he had no firm evidence. It was a couple of hours before he was called back.

'Am I speaking to Benjamin Fine?'

'Yes.'

'I am Sergeant Corbett, of the Harleybury Crime Squad. Can I be of assistance?'

'It's a matter concerning the disappearance of two people. I don't want to discuss this on the phone.'

'Would you like to meet here at the police station? I should be free at 2p.m.'

'That will be fine, Sergeant.'

Corbett was a tall, smartly dressed man of forty-something. He was wearing a silk tie and sported a folded white handkerchief in the breast pocket of his suit, rendering Fine somewhat sartorially challenged. Corbett invited Fine into an interview room and opened proceedings by asking for the names of the two people who had allegedly disappeared. Fine asked if the discussion could remain highly confidential and was given such an assurance, with the provision that any information appertaining to a serious crime would be used. However, Fine himself would be protected as an information source.

'Okay, I believe that Kenny Churchill and Mary Anne Marshall of 5, Manchester Street, Harleybury, are missing.'

'They are both known to me,' responded Corbett.

'I believe they've been abducted or possibly murdered.'

'Start from the beginning and tell me how you've formed this opinion.'

'Are you aware of the incident last December when there was a Caribbean intruder at Cranford College, who met the Carol Service processional party?'

'Vaguely.'

'That intruder was Kenny Churchill and he made a bee-line for the school's Headmaster, Dr Joseph Howson.'

'How do you know it was this Churchill guy?'

'I obtained a photo of Churchill, with the help of one of his drug associates, and someone at the school, who saw the intruder, identified him from that photo.'

'What's the significance of all this? Why are you interested in this matter? How come someone like you is involved with these sorts of people?'

'I used to work at Cranford, as Head of Physics and Housemaster of one of the major houses. Let's say that the Headmaster and I did not see eye to eye and I felt obliged to take early retirement.'

'That doesn't explain why you seem to have been consorting with crack addicts and robbers.'

'I can assure you, Sergeant, that I've never used any illegal substances.'

'So what's all this about?'

'I believe that there was a sinister reason for Churchill's intrusion on that day. He might have something on the Headmaster.'

The Detective laughed, almost mockingly.

'Are you suggesting Dr Howson dabbles in hard drugs?

'No, but I can tell you he is the adopted son of a former Blackshirt, who was once suspected in the slaying of a Jewish shopkeeper. Furthermore, his real father was a member of the Nazi Secret Service, who was assassinated by Israeli agents in the early sixties.'

'And how did you come by this information?'

'With a little detective work and the assistance of a private agency. I do have proof. Do you want to see it?'

'Does it have any bearing on your current concerns, as I'm finding it difficult to marry the two issues?'

'Not really, except that Joseph Howson is not all that he appears.'

'What have you found out about the whereabouts of Mary Anne and Kenny?'

'Simply that they disappeared about three or four weeks ago and that no one has the faintest idea why or where.'

'People like that are always vanishing. They'll turn up, like bad pennies do. They may well have got into trouble with one of the drug dealers. It happens all the time.'

284

'But when that happens, street people normally know. Information travels like bushfire in Harleybury.'

'True, but if you want to report them missing, I am willing to file a report but I would need something more concrete to justify allocating an officer to the job. We're very hard pressed in Harleybury. I could use another twenty in my department alone and still not get on top of every drunken rage, street robbery, shoplifting expedition, or GBH case in town.'

'Sergeant Corbett, please respect me. I am an intelligent man. I suspect that Howson was being blackmailed and could possibly be connected to the disappearance of these two.'

'And what do you think Howson was being blackmailed about?'

'I'm not entirely sure. His background, perhaps? Mary Anne used to work for a high-class escort agency called *Paradise Babes*. He might've had relations with her. Can't you do some investigations there?'

'Sounds far-fetched to me. Anyway, they wouldn't give us any information, I'd need a warrant. I've no grounds to justify such an application. Even then, it wouldn't force the owners to give us any information, only allow us to seize and search such records as we could find, and, in my experience, that is unlikely to amount to anything.'

'Has no one else reported them missing?' enquired Benjamin.

'I can assure you that we've had no concerns raised by any friends or relatives of either of them.'

'Would that make a difference, because I do know of one or two people who are concerned?'

'Not really. Unless someone can come up with more solid information, we'd be looking for a needle in a haystack. I'll file a report and personally mention the situation to a senior officer and also the prostitution liaison officer, Susan Hopkins. She has a special responsibility for the welfare of prostitutes and I will ask her and her colleagues to keep their eyes and ears open but, at this stage, I can't do any more than that. If you find out anything else, don't hesitate to let me know. Sorry I am unable to be of further assistance at this time.'

'Aren't you concerned by what I've told you?'

'I accept that there may be something in your theories but you must appreciate that I deal only in facts. What is more, I must advise you to tread carefully. You're obviously taking great risks. These are not the sort of people that someone like you should be messing about with. They'll rip your throat out for a ten stone of crack.'

'What am I supposed to do, Sergeant? I believe that something untoward might've happened to these two people. I also believe that Dr Howson could be implicated. You, a representative of law and order, seem not really interested. My conscience dictates that I have no alternative but to continue to probe.'

'No, I *am* interested but am constrained with prioritisation criteria. If you insist on continuing to investigate, that's your prerogative. This isn't a game for amateurs, although I can see that you're no one's fool. I'm simply warning you of the risks. Please take care. We certainly don't want another disappearance on our hands.'

With that, Fine thanked Corbett for his time and left Harleybury 'nick', feeling somewhat deflated. He appreciated the Sergeant's reluctance even to contemplate murder, no matter who was involved. After all, it could be the case that the pair had simply upped sticks. On the other hand, if a man like Howson had disappeared and there was the faintest suspicion that someone like Churchill was involved, Harleybury would be gridlocked with 'paddy wagons': one rule for the great and good; another for the hoi polloi. Fine resolved that his next line of enquiry would involve *Paradise Babes*. Someone there must have knowledge of Mary Anne's outcalls to clients. The question was how he was going to get at that information.

Chapter Thirty Six
THE NET BEGINS TO CLOSE
'I shall not be visiting the massage parlour – the pleasure is momentary, the position uncomfortable, the expense damnable.'
E. Waugh

The next day Fine plucked up courage and called *Paradise Babes*. He identified himself as having called earlier and asked if the telephone receptionist could recommend someone, preferably one of their experienced escorts. Having established that the charge by the agency per booking was fifty pounds an hour, with a minimum charge of seventy-five pounds, Fine reconciled himself to the fact that he might need to invest a fair amount of money in his forthcoming quest.

'Can you give me an idea of your preferences, Sir?'

'Someone well-spoken and friendly.'

'I have a lovely girl called Shireen. She's a beautiful Iranian, twenty-eight years of age, but could pass for much younger. We've always had very satisfied clients with her. I am sure she won't disappoint you.'

'That sounds excellent. I only need an hour with her. When will she be available?'

'I'll call you back.'

Five minutes later, Fine's mobile rang and he was informed that Shireen could be with him in an hour's time. He provided his address and waited with a good deal of uncertainty.

When the elegantly attired, young beauty arrived, Fine handed over seventy-five pounds to the driver and invited the girl into his home.

'My name is Ben. Would you like a drink?'

'I'd love one, thanks. Just a coffee'd be fine.'

'Do sit down. Do you mind if we just chat for the time being?'

'Of course, I'd be delighted to talk.'

Fine duly produced two coffees before explaining:

'Look, I know you are here to earn some good money, but I really only want to chat. How much do you want for your time?'

'Depends on how long you want to talk for. I would normally charge £100-£150 for an hour of sex, depending on what you wanted. Do you want to talk dirty?'

'No, no. Please forgive me, but I'm not looking for sexual services of any kind, although I must admit you're an extremely beautiful girl. I'm trying to find out something about a previous escort, called Mary Anne. Do you know her?'

'Why are you asking?'

'It'd take me a long time to explain, but let me tell you that Mary Anne's disappeared and I'm endeavouring to find out where she is.'

'Why are you asking? Are you police?'

'No. I'm simply a retired teacher. I assure you I have Mary Anne's best interests at heart.'

There was a pause before Shireen continued:

'I know of her but I didn't really get to know her, as such, if you see what I mean. We girls don't really mix much but we usually go out together at Christmas and I can remember meeting Mary Anne last time. She's very pretty, very sweet. She's a nice girl.'

'What do you know about her life?'

'Not much, except that she seemed to spend most of her time with another young girl called Tracy. Look, I don't mean to be mercenary but I could be earning good money. How much do you propose to pay me?'

'Will a hundred be okay?'

Shireen was slightly taken aback.

'That'll be great. If you change your mind and want to do something a little more intimate, I'm sure I could make you feel very good, for just a little extra!'

'That's very sweet of you but I couldn't possibly use you in that way.'

'I understand. Sorry to be pushy, it's just I haven't done very well this last couple o' days and I need to pay my rent urgently.'

'Well, if you give me a good lead, I could possibly go above a hundred. Tell me about Tracy.'

'Oh, she's left. I think she now works in the Cambridge Road *Pussy Cats Massage Parlour*. She'll be easy to find.'

'What does she look like?'

'Oh, very pretty, long blonde hair, slim, lovely breasts, only early twenties at the most.'

'Look, I'm really grateful.'

Fine produced two fifty pound notes and handed them to Shireen.

'You're a really sweet man. I hope you find her. Do you need to know anything else?'

'No that's fine, Shireen. I'd appreciate it if you kept our conversation under wraps. You can call your driver now.'

'Oh, he'll be waiting for me, as this was only a short call-out. You can rely on me – I won't say a word. Thanks again; it was nice to meet you.'

With that, the sultry Iranian made her way to the door and Fine saw her out.

'You're a real gent, Sir,' said Shireen, giving Fine a tender kiss on the cheek and promptly descending the steps to her awaiting car.

As the taxi pulled away, Fine lost no time in making his way to Harleybury. He was aware of the *Pussy Cats* parlour at no.550 Cambridge Road. Within a short time, he was making enquiries as to the presence of a blonde called Tracy. The receptionist informed him that Tracy worked only at weekends and advised Fine to return on the following Saturday evening.

Fine waited impatiently for the weekend to arrive and duly turned up at 9p.m. The duty receptionist informed him that Tracy was busy with a customer but would be free within about half an hour.

He opted for the minimum service, which was an hour's massage, priced at fifty pounds. He correctly assumed that there were additional charges for such extras, as could be negotiated in the massage room.

Within a short time, a pretty blonde girl appeared and invited Ben to accompany her. He was not sure whether to go through with the charade of a massage or to get straight down to the real purpose of his visit. As soon as they were alone Tracy told Ben to take a shower and call her when he had finished. He decided to continue with the process and within a short time, clad in his Y-fronts, he called Tracy, who appeared through a neighbouring door.

'Lie down and take your underpants off.'

'I'd rather not, if you don't mind, Tracy.'

'Up to you, mate.'

Tracy, who was wearing a very short skirt and white blouse, then routinely asked Ben to lie on his stomach and she proceeded to massage his back slowly and gently. After a few minutes, she transferred her attention to his shins and then slowly worked her way up the back of his legs. Ben's impression was that, although Tracy was giving him a very relaxing and pleasant experience, her range of technique would have hardly earned her a masseuse's certificate.

As her little hands started to probe the area where the back of the legs joins the buttocks, Ben started to experience a distinct stirring in his loins. It occurred to him that there would be few red-blooded heterosexual males who would be able to resist the titillating intentions of this sweet and gentle young girl. Indeed, the inevitable 'would you like any extras?' soon emerged from her lips. Tracy was well spoken, certainly not from Harleybury's ubiquitous underclass.

This was only about ten minutes into the hour, for which he had already paid. Ben was all too aware that Tracy's income would be generated principally by the extras and that there was no way that she was going to continue to rub him down chastely for the remaining fifty minutes.

At that point, Ben sat up.

'That was very pleasant, Tracy. Look, I don't want any extras, but I will give you a generous tip, if you'd be so good as to answer a few questions.

'Are you police?' Tracy blanched at this surprise development.

'No, I assure you, I'm not a policeman. It's just that a girl called Mary Anne has apparently disappeared and I've been told that you knew her at the *Paradise Babes* agency.'

Ben was getting slightly tired of having to prove his credentials each time.

'What's it got to do with you, if she's disappeared? You a client of hers?'

'No. Look, I can't go into the full details, suffice to say I'm keen to locate her. I know it sounds far-fetched but I think that Mary Anne and her boyfriend, Kenny, may have some important information to share or they could even have come to some harm as a result. I'm trying to find out where they are or what's happened to them.'

'But if you're not a policeman, what concern is it of yours?'

'I'm an honest do-gooder. I'm a retired schoolmaster and I suspect that one of my former colleagues had something to do with Mary Anne and I just want to find out what's happened to her.'

'Sounds very odd to me. Do you actually know Mary Anne?'

'No. I've never met her. Look, you're really not in any trouble yourself, Tracy, I promise. You've done nothing wrong in here, just given me a very nice massage. Even if I were a policeman, nothing illegal's taken place.'

'Okay, I'll trust you, but it all sounds really weird. Yes, I did know Mary Anne. We were working partners. When a client wanted a threesome, I worked with Mary Anne. I haven't seen her for ages.'

'Did you know anything about her clients?'

'Not really. Sometimes she'd say she'd just been with a real dickhead and sometimes she'd say she met someone really nice. Come to think of it, she did have one special bloke for a short while, who she often talked about.'

'What can you tell me about him?'

'Only that he was really handsome, clever and charming; also very generous. I think she really liked him. I know she went on an all-nighter with him.'

'Can you remember any other details? Did she mention his name?'

'Can't remember if she did or not.'

'Can you please try and remember the name? I'll pay you fifty pounds if you can.'

Tracy detected an unusual amount of emotion in her client's tone. She remained silent for what seemed, to Benjamin, like an age. Her eventual response was well worth the wait. Indeed, he was not prepared for the bombshell that was about to be dropped. When Tracy produced her next utterance, he experienced a frisson of instant excitement, more enjoyable than the type of thrill which Tracy had been trying to sell him.

'Mack...Matt....maybe Max, no, no. I know, I remember now, it was Maxim – I'm sure it was Maxim because I remember thinking that the name sounded foreign- I asked her if he was a foreign bloke and she said no he was as English as they come.

'Maxim', of course! – this was surely more than a coincidence. Had Howson used his real father's name as a pseudonym? Maxim Engelmann. Surely Corbett was not going to dismiss this morsel of information out of hand.

'Look, Tracy, you don't know how helpful you've been. I'm really grateful for this'.

'You'd better pay up and leave now,' said Tracy curtly.' I'm not too happy about this conversation'. She bowed her head.

'I'm sorry if I've upset you in any way,' apologised Benjamin. With this, he reluctantly re-clad himself, handed over the promised amount of money, gave Tracy a peck on the cheek and took his leave.

Chapter Thirty Seven
FINE OFFERS TO DO 'BUSINESS'
'Goodness speaks in a whisper, evil shouts.'
Tibetan proverb

Fine left the parlour excited about the revelation of the mysterious Maxim but still feeling he had a number of questions that he should have put to Tracy. He needed to speak to her again and decided he would have to question her away from work, without the pressure she obviously felt about discussing her trade and former employees.

If these escorts went on outcalls, they would surely have regular drivers. Tracy would, therefore, be able to shed light on the *modus operandi* of the agency and she might even be able to lead him to find a driver who had actually delivered Mary Anne to Howson, for, in his own mind, Maxim was surely Howson.

Ben decided to wait around and keep an eye on the parlour entrance. It seemed an inordinately long wait. There were various comings and goings, Saturday night always being quite busy. Eventually Tracy emerged and started walking towards the town centre. Ben caught up with her and called her name.

She immediately turned to face him.

'Look, I can't talk to you. I'm likely to get the sack if I'm seen with you, especially outside the parlour.'

She carried on walking fast. Ben needed to think quickly. Following slightly behind her, he tried a gambit:

'Tracy, I swear I'm not a policeman but I have reason to believe that Mary Anne's been harmed by Maxim and I know his real identity. I need you to help me nail him. Here's my mobile number.'

He thrust a small piece of paper, enveloped in a £10 note, into her hand.

This statement was enough to stop Tracy in her tracks. The Cambridge Road was, fortunately, quite busy. She once again turned to him.

'Look, I can't speak to you here, but I'll phone you in a few minutes. Please go away now.'

'Of course. I'm really grateful for what you've told me already. Anything extra'll be a bonus.'

Ben returned to his car and, after another interminable wait, his mobile phone rang.

'Hi, it's Tracy. Now, tell me what this is all about.'

'I'll tell you the whole story if you promise to keep it to yourself.'

'Okay, but be quick because someone's waiting for me.'

Ben decided to risk everything and he explained the entire scenario. Every so often she interrupted to ask questions. When he had come to the end, Tracy said:

'How do I know that you haven't made the whole thing up?'

'Why would I? Look, I'm prepared to meet you in the presence of a solicitor of your choosing and I'll pay the bill.'

'I'm really nervous about this whole thing, I just know I'm going to end up losing my job. I'll be wanted as a witness and everyone's going to know about the kind of work I do. I really don't want to get involved.'

'But do you want Mary Anne's abductor – possible murderer – to get away with his crime?'

'Murder? Look, I want to help, if I can, but I need to think about this. I'll call you again, I promise.'

It was not until Tuesday late morning when Ben next heard from Tracy.

'Hi, it's Tracy. I've checked you out.'

'How did you do that?'

'I rang Cranford College and asked to speak to you. They told me that you no longer worked there.'

Ben was impressed with the girl's intelligence.

'So you know I am who I claim to be. Can we meet again then, in a safe place?'

'Do you know the French café, *Le Croque Monsieur*, in Montefiore Street?'

Ben, not being a local *bon viveur*, had not heard of the said establishment, but replied that he would find it.

'One o'clock okay?' she said.

'I'll be there,' said Ben.

So, it was over coffee and quiche Lorraine that he was able to engage Tracy in further discussion.

'How much would you like me to pay you for your time?' enquired Benjamin.

'I'm not here for the money,' said Tracy, 'I may be a working girl but I'm still a human being. You can pay for lunch.'

She smiled ever so sweetly.

'You're a very good man, I can see that. Most people wouldn't care if one of us was burned at a stake. You're taking very big risks, Ben, especially if you think Mary Anne might've been knocked off. There are some very nasty people around in Harleybury.'

'Well, you're a brave girl, too,' said Ben, 'or you wouldn't be here with me.'

'Thank you,' said Tracy with another one of her heart-melting smiles.

'I wanted to ask you about transport arrangements for your outcalls at *Paradise Babes*.'

'The agency had arrangements with a group of minicab drivers who acted as drivers, collectors and security. The way it works is that the agency arranges everything. We didn't get to choose the drivers, although if someone had a particular favourite, the agency would do its best to provide you with your choice.'

'Have you any idea which drivers might've been involved in taking Mary Anne on outcalls?'

'Not really. It could've been any one. Let me see... there was Rob, Dave, Monty and an Irish guy, called Seamus. They were the main ones. I liked Seamus because he had a real sense of humour and was bloody tough. You felt safe with him around.'

'What about the boss? Who ran the agency?'

'It's run by a retired escort called Cathy. She's very nice actually; won't stand any nonsense and personally trains all the girls; any complaints from clients and you aren't likely to get a second chance. She's very bright, actually has a heart of gold; looked after all of us, if we had any problems; organised wicked parties.'

'Why did you leave?'

'Agency work is not as lucrative as people think. You don't get clients every day and often only get one for an evening. A lot of them will want to take you out for dinner but very few will pay more than £150 for sex. You have to be dressed and made up and it's quite hard work. I enjoyed it because I met a lot of very nice gentlemen but the massage parlour where I work now is a much better earner. I do one long day there and usually take home about £400-£500. I don't work the rest of the week, except for one or two private regulars.'

'Forgive me for being curious, but you're an intelligent, beautiful girl. How on earth did you get into this?'

Not for the first time, Ben heard a sad tale of a broken home, absent father, wrong company and the inevitable tale of involvement with class A drugs.

'I'm basically a crackhead. I don't use as much as some people - don't have a smoke every day, but I do like my pipes. Luckily, I've never got involved with heroin, but I use about £30 a day worth of crack, on average. I also smoke weed, which helps bring me down from the highs. But weed only costs me about thirty/forty a week.'

'Do you have a boyfriend?'

'Yeah, but I'm not happy with him. He's a junkie and is always pestering me for money.'

'So why do you stay with him?'

'Good question. I feel guilty. I throw him out every so often but he always pleads to come back and I take pity on him.'

Ben could never understand why these sweet young girls became involved with such men. He knew only that the tale had a familiar ring to it.

'Do you think Cathy will cooperate with the police?'

'I am sure that, if she knows the truth, she'll help in any way she can. I'm still on friendly terms with her. I can speak to her, if you want.'

'That's very good of you, Tracy. I'm going to try to keep you out of this as much as possible. If I can have your number, I'll call you if I need further help but let me try the police again and see if I can move them to some action.'

'It's a pity I can't move *you* into some action,' retorted Tracy provocatively, stroking the back of Ben's right hand.

With lunch over, Benjamin bade his farewell. As he put his arm around his new associate's shoulder, for the first time since his investigations had begun, the ageing bachelor thought seriously about a little bit of 'action'. He looked into the deep blue eyes of this alluring specimen of femininity and proceeded to kiss her gently on the cheek.

Chapter Thirty Eight
MIXED FORTUNES FOR FINE
'It's not that I'm so smart, it's just that I stay with problems longer.'
A. Einstein

Ben Fine wasted no time in contacting Sergeant Corbett, strongly requesting another meeting, which the latter assented to after lengthy persuasion. At the police station on the following day, after Ben had taken a somewhat impatient detective through his entire story in one of the vacant interview rooms, Corbett replied:

'So, what you're saying is that Dr Howson gets a strange and inappropriate visit from a black guy. Then the same bloke and his girlfriend, who are known drug addicts and petty criminals, leave their home address and their whereabouts are now unknown. Your ex-colleague identifies Kenny from an old family photo but could be mistaken. You then produce some hearsay that Kenny's girlfriend had a punter called Maxim and coincidentally your man Howson had a real father, whose name also happened to be Maxim.'

'On the face of it, it sounds like a series of coincidences,' said Ben, 'but we are talking about suspicion of possible blackmail here. *I* wouldn't rule out murder.'

'Frankly, Mr Fine, I think you're paranoid. You've a grudge against Joseph Howson because he pushed you out of your post. I think your imagination's been working overtime. Are you expecting me to believe that such a high profile public figure as Dr Howson is a party to drug-fuelled blackmailers or, even more preposterous, is some 'Joseph the Ripper', chopping up the local whores and their boyfriends? If I passed this on to a senior officer for consideration, he'd think I'd lost all sense of judgement.'

'Howson may be an ostensible charmer, witty, intelligent, good looking, with a perfect head of wavy blond hair, he's nevertheless also a ruthless, evil man, whose biological father was an assassin and was brought up by a fascist, who, in all probability, was also involved in murder. These sorts of traits run in families.'

'Look, Mr Fine, you've been reading too many thrillers. Real life isn't like an airport novel. Although there's quite a lot of crime in Harleybury, there are very few murders. You're talking about, on the one hand, a reputable Headmaster of a top school and, on the other, two missing persons, both known drug-addicted ne'er-do-wells. You make it seem as if two corpses, both from regular backgrounds, had been found hidden in Howson's home! You're on a vendetta, Mr Fine. I really cannot allocate any more valuable police time to this matter. You'll need to come up with some hard evidence, if you expect us to take action.'

'I disagree, Sergeant, I'm going to deposit all the evidence I have with a solicitor. If I turn out to be proved right, I'll arrange for the dated evidence to be released.'

'Look, I understand how strongly you feel, but I'm afraid that the police cannot be pressured in this manner. We have a duty to deal with reported crimes, not vague suspicions. At the end of the day, you've not reported a single crime, only filed a report about two missing persons, neither of whom is even known to you personally and who, in all probability, have decided to leave the area of their own accord.'

'I've given you all the information you need to establish whether or not Mary Anne Marshall was linked to Howson. You're telling me that you have no intention of checking it out.'

'If I approached this escort agency woman, I'd probably get a solicitor shoved up my backside. Even if I could establish that Howson had been seeing the girl, I'm not convinced we'd be able to go any further. Even if I was to buy your theory that Howson has been blackmailed, don't you think it more likely that he'd've paid the two of them off to get out of town?'

'I don't think Howson woul've trusted them,' retorted Benjamin, 'he'd never've been able to stop them coming back to him for more. You know what blackmailers are like. An über-intelligent guy like

Howson would certainly have worked out the slippery slope of committing himself to blackmail. Anyway, I'm obviously flogging a dead horse. Thanks, once again, for your time.'

'And, once again, I have to warn you of the risks you're taking. I'll be recording the fact that I've given you clear advice to stay out of this,' said Corbett, deliberately forcefully.

'I've no intention of dropping this matter. Having already come this far, I intend to bring Howson to justice, with or without the police's assistance.'

With that, Benjamin Fine stood up and made his way towards the door of the interview room.

On leaving the police station, he put in a mobile phone call to Tracy.

'Can you please contact Cathy and see if you can persuade her to speak to me?'

'I can try but can't give you any guarantees. Can I give her your number?'

'Of course; I'd be delighted to hear from her. Please reassure her that any discussion will be in complete confidence and I'll not get her into any trouble.'

Fine then returned home and decided to wait. He was confident that he had convinced Tracy of his theories, even if he'd failed to move the sergeant. He prayed that she'd be able to persuade her former employer.

He also realised that he would need a good photo of Howson. That was easy to acquire. All he needed was a Cranford College prospectus, freely available to prospective parents, on demand. With a little cotton wool in his cheek to alter his voice, he telephoned the school office, withholding his own number and an innocent clerical worker was soon awaiting a taxi driver, who was due to collect two prospectuses on behalf of a **"Dr Stanley Ford"**, interested in sending his twin sons to Cranford. As Fine well knew, a glorious A4 sized photo of the smiling Howson adorned the prospectus, alongside the ubiquitous trumpeting of the school's educational benefits.

It was a couple of days before Fine received the hoped-for contact from Cathy. It was a Wednesday morning at 10a.m.

'Tracy's told me all about the disappearance of Mary Anne. She was a lovely girl. I was sorry to lose her but she had too big a habit to sustain it on our kind of irregular work. I'm told you know *The Croque Monsieur*. Can you make it there at 12?'

'I certainly can. Look forward to meeting you.'

'I'm about 45, short black hair and rather larger than I'd like to be. I'll be wearing a blue skirt and red jacket.'

Indeed, when Fine saw a plump, heavily made-up, middle-aged woman enter the café, attired as described, he realised that Cathy, if anything, had understated the full extent of her girth. This was definitely not the sort of lady he would want to have either a high speed collision with or indeed, in another sense, a low speed one.

Within a short time, the two were ensconced over steaming mugs of café latte, sharing a plate of almond croissants. Cathy asked Ben to go through his story again, as she wanted to hear it from the proverbial horse's mouth. Benjamin obliged.

'What makes you so confident in your beliefs?'

'In my experience, when there's a series of strange occurrences, the explanation for them is often the simplest one available: high profile public figure resorts to services of escort; it happens all the time; remember Sir Alan Green, the Director of Public Prosecutions, who was caught kerb-crawling in London's Kings Cross area, pursuing the services of a scrawny junkie? You must know about members of parliament consorting with prostitutes: the married Lib-Dem MP Michael Oaten and his association with a London rent boy, a case in point?'

Cathy laughed as she interrupted:

'You'd be amazed at the number of policemen and lawyers I have as clients: such hypocrites. In court, the pillars of respectability, but between the sheets with my girls, wild animals, I can tell you. I once had full sex with a judge, who liked wearing his wig in the bedroom and would sentence me to spankings and other little 'punishments' – right kinky old sod. I used to visit some city big wig, who told me he was a descendant of Queen Victoria. He had a beautiful house in Berkshire, near Newbury, swimming pool, the fucking lot. He was into all that smacking lark. He was about as kinky as it gets. He used to suck my toes as he pleasured himself to climax. He was married with two daughters, he took pleasure in showing me their photos: such a hypocrite.'

Cathy took another sip of coffee before lighting up a menthol cigarette.

'Actually, now I think about it, Mary Anne and I did have a run-in just before she left. It was after I accused her of seeing a client privately. She denied it but I've worked in this business long enough to recognise these things when they happen.'

'That would have been Howson, no doubt in my mind, the pieces fit perfectly. He was probably incognito at the time, but somehow Mary Anne finds out his true identity, tells the boyfriend and the blackmail starts. There would be no end to their demands, if the two were junkies who needed daily supplies of drugs. Howson is a ruthless man, who comes from a pretty terrifying biological background. I can just see him considering it safer and cheaper to have these two scumbags, as he would consider them, removed totally.'

Cathy bowed her head, obviously uncomfortable having to listen to this man-on-a-mission. Hardly without drawing breath, as he took a sip of hot coffee, Fine continued:

'Kenny and Mary Anne disappear suddenly. It doesn't appear that there've been any significant removals from the flat; nothing packed; dirty dishes in the sink; no word on the street about dangerous people after either of them; no warrants out for them by the police; not a word said by either to any of Mary Anne's local friends.'

'Look, I might be able to help you. For obvious reasons, we don't keep written records of outcall details but I have a vague recollection of sending someone out to Cranford a good few months ago; if you can give me a photo of this person, I'll check to see if any of my regular drivers recognise his face.'

With that, Fine produced the prospectus photo, which he had cut out, while he continued to make general conversation on the subject of the rights of prostitutes to ply their trade, and indeed the risks associated with the oldest profession. He looked straight into Cathy's eyes.

'Would you be willing to share anything we discover with the police?'

'I don't see why not. We haven't done anything wrong. I operate within the law. In any case, the police know what I do. They prefer my organised business to the public nuisance on the Cambridge Road.'

'Thanks, Cathy, I'm really grateful.'

Benjamin's spirits were considerably lifted as he made his way home. He knew that if he could make a direct connection between Mary Anne and Howson, a reason for the police to investigate would be compelling. However, he also appreciated how reluctant they'd be to start investigating a local public figure without some hard evidence upon which they could firmly rely. At least the fact that a witness could tie in Howson with Mary Anne would be sufficient for them to start taking his allegations seriously. Fine's mood was almost elated when he took a call from Cathy that afternoon.

'Ben, I've got something for you.'

'Good or bad news?' asked Fine.

'As good as it gets,' retorted Cathy, 'best for you to come to my home rather than discuss it over the phone. I have someone you'll be interested in meeting.'

Cathy gave the address of her fifth floor flat in Ditcham, a small town about twenty miles away.

As he made the journey, every cautious driver who caused Benjamin Fine to slow up irritated him disproportionately; every red light he encountered seemed to exceed its allotted time; every roundabout caused him an almost unbearable delay.

On arrival at Cathy's surprisingly smart block of flats, rather than take the lift, belying his fifty-two years, Benjamin ascended the eight staircases with the energy of a teenager. As he arrived at her flat door, he was greeted by the smiling face of his recently found acquaintance and by the presence of a short, balding, middle-aged man of greasy complexion and narrow eyes. He was dressed in an ill-fitting blazer and blue jeans.

'Ben, this is Rob Mercer. Rob, Benjamin Fine.'

'How do you do?' said Benjamin.

'Ben, Rob is the driver who more than once took Mary Anne to the lodge bungalow at Cranford College. What's more, he'd return later to bring her back.'

'The lodge? Did you see the person she was visiting?' interrupted Benjamin.

Cathy raised her hand:

'Ben, allow us to tell you what we know. I showed this photo of Joseph Howson to Rob but, unfortunately, he was unable to identify him. He never saw the person who Mary Anne was visiting, but she did say things on her journey back which suggested the man she'd been to see was a real gentleman, even though he was only a school gardener.'

'I don't ever say nothing about who I take where, Mr Fine, it's company policy. If I'd said a thing, Cathy would drop me straight away,' said Mercer, 'but when Cathy showed me the article in the local paper about her goin' missing, well, I had to speak about what Mary Anne used to say. I liked her, I did. She's a sweet girl, unlike the others, hard, brazen tarts, most of them – sorry Cathy. She was always nice to me, never aggressive, like some o' them.'

'How often did you take her to Cranford?' asked Benjamin.

'Two or three times, I suppose.'

'But you never saw or met who she was visiting?'

'Never, Sir, but, like I say, she liked him so much she couldn't help saying things about him in the back of my car. Gorgeous, he was, she said, tall and blond – just her type. It's unusual for any of these girls to say anything about who they've been with.'

Cathy coughed, indicating that she felt that Rob had said as much as she wanted him to.

As the meeting in Cathy's well-maintained flat drew to a close, Benjamin Fine experienced a feeling of elation that his (and his friend, Trench's) endeavours were at last bearing fruit. The only person using the lodge on a regular basis had been Howson – it *had* to be him. He could envisage the net closing in on the ostensible golden-boy. One day, Benjamin felt, he would bring this man his just desserts and that afternoon's meeting in Cathy's flat seemed to be bringing that day inexorably closer.

Ben thanked both Cathy and Rob profusely for their help and took his leave, descending the smartly decorated stairwell as athletically and enthusiastically as he had come up.

Chapter Thirty Nine
COLD BLOODED BODY DISPOSAL
'Maybe this world is another planet's hell.'
A. Huxley

Unbeknown to both Sergeant Corbett and Benjamin Fine, Joseph Howson had visited Harleybury Police Station the previous week, on account of the discovery of a Class A drug found at the school lodge, for which Howson had taken responsibility. The Sergeant in charge of the matter decided he would press no charges, as Howson's drug test had come back negative. He did not consider for a moment that a man of such standing could possibly have any connection with the desultory world of drugs.

For his part, Howson now knew he could not risk leaving the bodies any longer in their shallow cellar grave. He had originally told Murko that the lodge was a temporary 'resting place' for the corpses but, for obvious reasons, they could not be left long-term. Murko was asleep when Howson rang him from his study early the following morning.

'Murko, it's Doug. Look, we'll need to dispose of these bodies a.s.a.p. You've got it all sorted?'

'I told you, man, it's all in hand. I keep telling you, just give me the word and it'll be done,' said Murko reassuringly, albeit with irritation at having been awoken so early. 'When do you have in mind?'

'The weekend?'

'Saturday, late, okay?'

'Fine,' said Howson, 'You've got transport all worked out?'

'I told you, man, we've been ready for weeks: have the money ready. Meet you at midnight, on the dot.'

Joseph Howson was able to continue his day's work at Cranford in a slightly more relaxed frame of mind, although the strain of the past week was beginning to take its toll. Even though the pupils had left for their summer holidays, Headmaster Howson had at least a couple of weeks' administration to complete, including writing over seven hundred reports. As usual, he locked himself away in his study for days on end with a **DO NOT DISTURB** notice on his study door. The only interruption he allowed was his secretary, Sarah, to bring him spasmodic refreshment or to buzz when an urgent call came through.

Marie-Christine and his son were due to fly out to the Val de la Loire on the first Friday of the holiday, but such was her concern for her husband's state of mind, following his visit to the police station, she offered to postpone the trip.

'Joe, I can easily re-schedule the flights.'

'Certainly not. You must go as planned. Mum and Dad are expecting you. I'll be okay. I've got lots to attend to here, but once it's all done, I'll take the first flight over to join you.'

'If you're sure,' replied Marie-Christine.

'Chérie, comme je t'aime,' was her husband's reply, as he put his arms around her and kissed her tenderly on the lips.

Marie-Christine was not used to receiving overt affection from her husband. She knew he loved her dearly, but he was not a natural when it came to showing signs of his feelings.

'Moi, non plus,' was her response, as she stood on tiptoes to receive her husband's embrace.

So it was that on that Friday Joseph drove his wife and son to Heathrow. As both waved to him, as they made their way through the appropriate gate, Joseph Howson's feelings were a mixture of sadness, witnessing his beloved family's departure, and of relief, that he could now put his mind firmly on what he considered was the last piece of the jigsaw, the disposal of the bodies: once these were out of his life, he could resume some sort of emotional equilibrium. Every time he visited the lodge, which had become increasingly less frequent, he had a strange feeling of the macabre,

310

knowing that two corpses lay below him; it was a good job he gave no credence to the supernatural.

Howson was standing at the kitchen window of the lodge as Murko and his sidekick Jason pulled up on the gravel path to the south of the residence, out of view of the main school campus. He was holding an envelope in which there was a series of crisp £50 notes, amounting to the agreed £2,000, which Howson was to hand over to the pair for this final task. He had told Marie-Christine that he was putting money aside for extra pensions' contributions but, following the domestic hiatus which took place last time she questioned her husband about substantial withdrawals, she was determined never again to broach family account details. Knowing he was going to have to fork out a couple of large payments to his two accomplices, he felt it prudent to warn her well in advance.

'Darling, you must do whatever you feel necessary,' Marie-Christine had said, 'I know you will always act in our interests.'

With this, she pointedly turned on her heels and left the room. It was clear she wanted no further discussions about the family's bank account withdrawals. Nevertheless, the whole business had created a certain tension between them.

As is always the case with hit men, the money had to be handed over first, before any business commenced.

Faces masked, all three descended the stone cellar steps. As the flagstones were removed and the graves uncovered, they were hit by a putrid smell from the rotting corpses. The bagged -body remains were put into two fresh body bags and Murko and Jason carried them up the stairs, through the kitchen and into the back of a Saab estate, which Jason had managed to 'acquire'. Howson replaced the stones, filled in both graves, smoothed the surfaces and the whole area looked untouched. He then joined the others, the three men setting off for the arranged location.

It took ten minutes to reach a roundabout on the main road leading out of Harleybury, going to the east. There was a signpost to the left, which read **Sunflower Industrial Estate**. Considering the fact that this was an area of heavy industry, dominated by quarries, chemical factories and a sewage plant, the name chosen by the local worthies responsible for nomenclature was particularly ironic.

Jason, the driver, took a left turn down a muddy track, which led down to a network of grassy land and waterways. There was a tunnel, which crossed underneath the dual carriageway, through which they drove. They were now making their way alongside a waterway on the left and a sewage disposal plant on the right. The whole area was desolate and deserted. The three men were now aware of another distinctly unpleasant odour. As they reached a muddy bank, with plenty of trees and foliage adjacent, Murko told Jason to stop the car. The two hired hands alighted from the Saab and, donning complete body suits, adding masks once again to cover their faces, they opened the boot, removed the bodies simultaneously and ferried them across to two waiting vats of acid. Howson found the scene gruesome and sickening. He had to get out of the car and make his way over to a nearby clump of foliage, into which he started to retch.

As Murko stood at the drum, watching the acid gradually doing its work, he smiled as he saw the distraught Howson on his knees throwing up the remains of his evening meal of king prawn risotto, which Marie-Christine had prepared for him before she left.

'Not got the stomach for it, eh, Dougie?' taunted Murko, 'Why don't you come and have a look at the bodies dissolving? It's real cool.'

As Howson convulsed even more, Jason beamed.

The wait seemed interminable as the two bodies were slowly, but inexorably, consumed by the acid. The stench was dreadful; the sights and sounds were worse than anything from a horror movie. Murko and Jason waited impassively, occasionally sharing a joke, unmoved by this sickening tableau of rotting corpses. More than once they called to Howson to give him an update on the continuing disintegration. The latter decided to return to the car, convinced there was no more food in his stomach to discharge. The whole macabre scene was of Guignol proportions. The infamous murderers and grave robbers, Burke and Hare, would have felt at home here in this secluded wasteland.

It was a good hour before Murko decided that the multicoloured sludge was sufficiently amorphous for it to be ready for disposal. It was quite a job gingerly moving the drums and their contents to the edge of the stagnant pond. Covered from head to toe, for fear of any splash of acid, Murko and Jason managed to manoeuvre the whole horrific mass into the muddy quagmire. Immediately both men returned to the car, congratulating each other on a job well done.

'Job done, maestro. Your problems are over,' said Murko chillingly, as he removed his body suit, 'if you need anything else done, you know where to come. Fancy something to eat?'

Murko and Jason roared with laughter; unsurprisingly, Dr Joseph Howson failed to detect even a smidgen of humour in the whole macabre, stomach-churning event.

Chapter Forty
UNDER CLOSE SCRUTINY
'Honesty is a good thing, provided it is kept under control.'
D. Marquis

At Harleybury Police Station D.I. Latham and his senior team of officers arrived for their usual Friday morning meeting in early July. One of the items on this particular morning's agenda was Benjamin Fine's allegations of misconduct on the part of Dr Joseph Howson, of which the D.I. had been appraised. Allegations were rarely brought up at such meetings but in view of the fact that it involved a local 'celebrity' and that a connection had been made between this celebrity and a missing drug addict, Latham decided he would elicit the opinions of his senior colleagues.

'This man's obviously on a mission,' started Latham, 'he was retired early by Howson, by all accounts in dubious circumstances, and Fine's obviously very bitter. Sergeant Corbett took it initially as simply that... but, well, a link has been made between him and that prostitute, what's her name?'

'Mary Anne Marshall,' a colleague replied.

'That's it. Mary Anne Marshall. She and her boyfriend, Kenneth Churchill, disappeared over a month ago. Not unusual for these drug-types to up sticks and out, I know, but there is something vaguely odd.'

'You're not suggesting Dr Joseph Howson has had them kidnapped?' interrupted a colleague.

'Well, blackmail can push people to do extraordinary things, especially when they've a lot to lose, as we're all aware.'

'You think Howson may have had relations with this girl at some point?'

'A possibility, you'll agree. He won't be the first, or the last, public figure to become embroiled in such a matter.'

'They tend not to follow it up by kidnap.'

'As we know, Dr Joseph Howson is a very strong, domineering, proud man. One of the reasons for the success of Cranford College is his single-minded approach. He runs the school, I'm told, like an oligarch: he'll brook no opposition, in any area. He's not your typical human being, or leader, for that matter.'

D.I. Latham had laid his cards on the table. He obviously had concerns and wanted to look further into the whole affair.

'We'll look into it,' said one of his inspectors, 'Foster and me, if you want.'

Latham nodded.

'The first thing you must do is to re-interview Benjamin Fine; he seems to have all there is to know at this stage. But, make sure it's all done on the quiet at this point. I do *not* want the press alerted.'

Latham was aware that if the fact got out that the Headmaster of Cranford College was being investigated in connection with a missing prostitute and he was duly innocent, his own job would be very much on the line. The damage done to Cranford's reputation would be enormous and the potential court pay out didn't bear thinking about.

'Be careful,' he concluded, 'I don't want any cock-ups.'

He refrained from offering the obvious pun.

During a casual discussion between D.I. Latham and one of his colleagues, D.I. Robin Stewart, at lunch that day, the former mentioned the covert investigation about to be undertaken of Dr Joseph Howson, distinguished Headmaster of one of the country's foremost schools. Stewart's response took Latham completely by surprise:

'He's just been carpeted for handling a Class A drug.'

Stewart proceeded to fill Latham in on the saga of the heroin discovery.

'This gets weirder by the moment,' retorted Latham. 'Perhaps this Benjamin Fine is not as loopy as we first imagined. Look, I think this should come upstairs to us. Could you let the team know? We're going to have to proceed extremely carefully on this one.'

The wheels were now in motion. The police were going to undertake an investigation of Ben Fine's allegations. There were a number of coincidences, and Latham, who had risen through the ranks thanks to his meticulous detective work, was not going to give anyone the opportunity of accusing him of negligence. He still had serious doubts in his own mind that Dr Joseph Howson could have possibly involved himself, either directly or indirectly, in anything so sinister and macabre as kidnapping, or possibly even murder, but he felt compelled to ascertain if there were any links between the man of letters and accomplishment and the two ne'er-do-wells, who seemed to have vanished from the proverbial face of the earth.

D.I. Latham convened a meeting of himself, Benjamin Fine and Martin Trench on the following Thursday. He informed the pair that he would be recording what was to be said and asked them to go through all the details of the series of events, which had led to the present worrying situation.

Fine took centre stage, with Trench offering additional details from time to time, as well as giving his own account of the investigative work he had carried out on Benjamin Fine's behalf. Fine spoke of his own dismissal and the trumped-up charges laid against him; of the discoveries that both he and Trench had made about Howson's background, including specific details about both his adoptive and natural father and their links with the Nazi movement; he spoke of the latter's death and the provision made for Joseph's adoption and private education; details were given of the intruder at the Carol Service procession; of the enquiries relating to the aforementioned; of the disappearance of this intruder, Kenny, and his girlfriend Mary Anne. Fine talked of his discovery of the connection between Mary Anne and Joseph Howson, who, he believed, were having sex together; he spoke of his tracking down of the driver who had ferried Mary Anne to the school lodge, and the fact that Howson was the only member of the school community to have regularly used the lodge during the previous eighteen months. He stated that he matched the description that Mary Anne had given to the taxi driver.

Latham finally interrupted.

'I can inform you, in the strictest confidence, that Joseph Howson was arrested last week on account of there being a very small amount of a class A drug found at the school; in the school lodge, as it happens, which Howson himself claimed he had found while walking in the grounds and had hidden the substance, to avoid any scandal. We did do a drugs test on him and he came out clean. It was decided no charges would be brought.'

'Well, that strongly implies he was covering up for Mary Anne, his lover, or sex partner, or whatever their relationship was,' interrupted Fine.

'It doesn't actually do that, but we do know that Mary Anne Marshall has a drug habit and heroin is at the centre of that habit. It would seem logical to suppose that she left the substance there and Howson either forgot about it or was unaware of it: probably the latter. She more than likely had a fix in the bathroom or wherever, during their, um, sessions together.'

'Have you any clues as to where she and her boyfriend are now?' enquired Trench.

'It is my guess that they've taken a large, one-off payment from Howson and disappeared into the night, as it were – gone to live abroad, perhaps. We need to call Dr Howson in for questioning.'

'Is he at the school at present?' enquired Fine.

'Until tomorrow. I'll be calling him in to see us later today.'

It was at 8pm precisely on that Thursday evening in early August, the day prior to Joseph Howson's intended departure for France, that two police officers arrived at Cranford House. D.I. Latham had considered it prudent that an evening call would cause less fuss and would be carried out without the witness of the secretarial staff.

'Dr Howson?'

'Yes.'

'We are police officers, Sir, and we would like you to accompany us to Harleybury Police Station.'

'Is this to do with that wretched drug? I've told you all that I know.'

'If you don't mind coming to the waiting car, Sir.'

'As a matter of fact, I *do* mind. What's this all about? Will you please tell me?'

Howson felt a mixture of high anxiety and anger.

'It's to do with the disappearance of Mr Kenneth Churchill and Miss Mary Anne Marshall.'

'I have no idea whom you're talking about.'

'You can explain this at the station, Sir.'

The police officer's tone became increasingly irritable and Howson felt he should accede to the request. After going back into the house to pick up his jacket – Dr Joseph Howson went nowhere without a jacket – he made his way over to the unmarked car and took a seat in the rear. In his mind he had no idea how much the authorities knew of his relationship with Mary Anne. He would deny everything, of course. Was the drug the link? Perhaps forensics had connected it to Mary Anne? So, she had dropped it in the college grounds, what had that to do with him? He was aware that it was a possibility that either of the two might have told someone what had been going on, but why would they have done? They would effectively be cutting off their healthy earning supply. This was illogical. He would have to wait to see how much the police knew, or didn't know. Whatever the situation, Howson had to be ready to answer their questions clearly and unambiguously. He knew from his years' experience of questioning reluctant, recalcitrant youths that the best way to convince an interrogator was confidence and consistency in response.

He was led into a waiting room at Harleybury Police Station for the second time in a matter of weeks. On the previous occasion he had felt reasonably confident that the matter would all be done and dusted there and then – after all, there was no connection at all between him and either the distribution or administering of any drugs – Howson didn't even smoke cigarettes – let alone dabble in heroin and the like. This evening he was less confident and the wait seemed interminable. It was twenty minutes to be exact when a tall, good-looking man, probably no older than his late thirties, came in and introduced himself.

'Good evening, Doctor, my name is D.I. Latham and I'm heading the enquiry into the disappearance of Kenneth Churchill and Mary Anne Marshall, I believe my officers mentioned their names to you.'

'They did, but I fail to see what this has got to do with me. You're lucky I was at school. I'm flying out to France tomorrow.'

'We know, Sir. Let's hope we can complete matters this evening.'

'Matters? You people talk in riddles,' said Howson more confidently than he actually felt.

'Would you come with me, please, Sir?'

D.I. Latham led Howson into one of three interview rooms at the station and asked him to sit down. As he looked at this distinguished, successful, handsome academic, for a moment Latham doubted that such a specimen of seemingly graceful humanity could possibly have involved himself in the lives, let alone in the disappearance, of the unfortunate missing duo. However, as he knew so well, criminals come in all shapes and sizes and his own years of investigative experience had taught him to deal only in facts. As he looked at Howson, Latham's thoughts went briefly to that other distinguished, handsome, erudite scholar, Jonathan Aitken, a former MP, who had been sent to prison for dishonesty during the final days of the Major government. Neither was he the first nor the last privileged public figure to fall from a lofty height. Sometimes powerful individuals take it into their head that they are untouchable and it is this arrogance which sows the seeds of their personal destruction. As he gazed at the impressive face in front of him, D.I. Latham wondered whether Howson had adopted a mindset of invincibility. What else would explain why a man who had seemingly everything – outstanding career, devoted wife and child, wealth – would want to risk it all by associating himself with a young woman of loose living and a drug-dependent blackguard?

After explaining to Howson that he wanted to interview him formally about information which had come his way with regard to the missing two, Latham asked him whether he would like to ring for legal representation.

'Is it that serious a matter for me?'

'It could be, Sir.'

With his fingers shaking, Joseph Howson rang his lawyer friend of many years, David Janney, who said he would make his way down to Harleybury immediately and told Howson to say nothing at all until he got there.

He arrived at approximately 9.45p.m. Howson was sitting alone in the interview room.

'Joe, how great to see you, old boy. What the hell is all this about?' Janney put his arm on his long-standing friend's shoulder, a friend he had known since they were at prep school together in the late 60s.

'David, thanks for coming. I'm about to be questioned about the disappearance of two people, one of whom I've never met; presumably, the police think their disappearance may have something to do with me: crazy. I did meet one of the two on a few occasions. Info so far has been limited. The person in charge is D.I. Latham.'

'D.I.? So it's pretty serious then,' said Janney.

'I suppose.'

'Okay. Let's hear what they've got to say. Make sure you say nothing you're unsure about, without first checking with me.'

Janney went back out into the corridor to tell the waiting Sergeant that he and his client were now ready for questioning.

Howson sat in the interview room, beads of perspiration rolling along his forehead, the odd one finding its way down a cheek. He had continually to keep wiping the moisture from his jaw-line as D.I. Latham, in the company of an investigative colleague, first read Howson his legal rights, then posed a succession of questions. As one after the next was put Howson's way, he soon became aware that the authorities knew far more than he'd presumed; the whole of the initial interrogation was based around Howson's use of the lodge for his private study.

'Did you ever receive visitors at the lodge?' enquired Latham.

'From time to time, of course, but these were few and far between.'

'Were these colleagues? Friends...?'

'Look, I can't remember exactly who came when, but I presume there's no law about inviting people to one's home?' Howson realised immediately the point behind the question.

'Yes, but this isn't your home, is it? As you've said, you used the lodge to work in. If you wished to socialise, why not invite these friends to Cranford House?'

'My wife hasn't been particularly well in recent years and often she liked to go to bed rather early. Occasionally I invited friends to the lodge to enjoy a glass or two without disturbing her.'

Howson sounded more confident than he actually felt. As he was giving his answers, he simultaneously had to prepare himself to respond to the inevitable question about Mary Anne.

'Have you ever seen this young woman or this man?'

Latham produced two photographs of the missing pair.

'I *have* met this woman but I don't recognise the man.'

'Could I ask you how you know this woman?'

'I met her by chance in Harleybury some time ago, probably two years or so, and we began chatting and I told her I was writing a book. She told me that she had been educated at a private boarding school, had not taken full advantage of the opportunities which such an education had afforded her, and told me she had got herself into a hopeless situation: petty crime, living with a bully, no family, no job... the usual story of no hope. I felt sorry for her and invited her to visit me from time to time. She read some of what I'd written and asked me for advice on how to become an author. She showed me some of the short stories she'd already completed.'

'Do you still have these?'

'No, she took them with her when she went.'

'Did she ever take drugs while on the premises?'

'Not to my knowledge,' responded Howson, sweat collecting upon his upper lip.

'But you were aware she was a drug addict.'

'I inferred that she was from the way she looked sometimes and also from her mood swings.'

'So you must have seen her pretty regularly to notice inconsistency of mood?' Latham looked at Howson full in the eyes.

'As I've said, her visits were spasmodic – I saw her no more than half a dozen times in the year I knew her.'

'Dr Howson, as you are aware, a wrap of heroin was found in the cellar of the lodge by a security officer just prior to the visit of the Duke of York. You said, at the time, you picked it up in the school grounds while out for a walk one evening. Do you now stand by what you claimed?'

Howson paused, pulled a handkerchief from a trouser pocket and once again mopped his moist brow and face. David Janney sensed he was under intense pressure and asked D.I. Latham if it were possible for a brief adjournment, so that his client could have a glass of water and that he could have a short discussion with him.

Latham acceded to the request and left the room.

'Joe, before we go any further, you've got to tell me, in full, about your relationship with this girl. They're on to something here and it would be foolhardy to be economical with the truth on minor matters, if, by doing so, you jeopardise yourself in the bigger frame. If she was taking drugs in the lodge and the substance they found was hers, tell them. You've not broken the law; you cannot afford to protect her.' Janney spoke more firmly than he would have liked.

'She didn't inject or swallow or smoke drugs of any kind in the lodge, to my knowledge. She did disappear to the bathroom from time to time; I had no idea she was using heroin in there.'

Howson put his head into his hands and began to breathe heavily.

'What have I done, David? Why have I been so stupid?'

'Was your relationship with this woman purely platonic?' enquired Janney.

'Yes... No... No,' replied Howson, now on the point of complete emotional collapse.

Janney put his hand on Howson's shoulder. He couldn't believe that he, David Janney, a modest, non-games player, average academic, was comforting Head Boy, brilliant, talented Joe Howson, a boy whom he looked up to, as did virtually the entire community, throughout his school days.

'Joe, if you had sex with this girl, it's not the end of the world. Once again, you haven't broken the law. The police are obviously trying to establish a close relationship between the two of you. If you maintain something's purely platonic and they can prove something more intense, then they will try and discredit other things you say. You had nothing to do with the pair's disappearance, so why not tell them the truth?'

'You know what the police are like. The next thing they'll be suggesting is a *crime passionnel*. David, I did have sex with her but it was purely mechanical; just sex. If Marie-Christine got to know about it, about that girl, she'd go, I know she would, she'd leave.'

'If the police implicate you in the disappearance of this pair, such as you arranging their disappearance, you'll lose more than your wife, old chum. The papers would have a field day. Joe, if you are open and honest about your relationship with this Mary Anne, it'll be better for you in the long run. You can't second guess the police – if you get it wrong, this D.I.'ll eat you for breakfast.'

After a few minutes' respite, Howson indicated to his friend and solicitor that he was ready to continue the questioning. Janney went out to the waiting D.I. and his colleague. They returned to their seats in the interview room.

'Look,' Howson started, 'I've not been entirely open about Mary Anne and me. Yes, we did have sex, but only on a few occasions. For me it was purely relief, as my wife, Marie-Christine, went right off sex prior to and after the birth of our child. As soon as this girl started to become emotionally involved, I stopped seeing her. That was nearly a year ago. It's as simple as that.'

'Did you pay for the sex?' asked Latham, irritated by the lengthy pause in the evening's proceedings.

'I have to admit at this point that I initially met Mary Anne through an agency in Harleybury.'

'Paradise Babes?'

Howson looked up, surprised.

'I believe that was the agency's name,' he stuttered.

'How many times did she visit you on this 'professional' basis?' enquired Latham.

'Like I said, not many. Say five or six in all.'

'And the heroin which was found?'

'It was hers. I had no idea she was shooting up during these visits. She'd disappear for five to ten minutes – I honestly had no idea she was using heroin.'

'So what you said about finding the heroin on the school grounds was a lie?'

There was a pause as Howson got his breath back. He glanced at Janney, who nodded.

'Yes, it was a lie,' he retorted.

The questions continued, Latham asking for precise dates, as far as possible, of the visits and when their *liaison dangereuse* had ended. He moved on to the incident of Kenny Churchill's intrusion at Cranford.

'What, precisely, was that all about?'

'This fellow, whom I'd never met, presents himself in front of me and asks, sorry tells, me that I should contact Mary Anne a.s.a.p. and that he knew who I really was...I'd told the girl I was the school gardener, you see... he then ran off.'

'He said nothing else?'

'No, it was all over in a matter of seconds.'

'But if this man is her supposed boyfriend, why would he be eager for you to re-involve yourself in his partner's life? You see my point, Doctor?'

'I don't know – perhaps he realised the only way to keep her was to keep her sweet. I don't know, I've really told you all I know.'

'And you neither saw, nor heard from, the pair ever again?'

'That's correct.'

Janney interrupted. 'Look, Detective Inspector, it *is* getting late and if there are no more pressing questions, I feel it wise that you allow my client the opportunity of returning home, as he is due to take an early flight tomorrow morning.'

With the formalities concluded, David Janney drove his client back to Cranford, the latter wondering what he would do if Lord Harris or his beloved Marie-Christine found out about this latest police station grilling. What worried him as much was the local press finding out about his arrest – that would certainly bring into question the continuation of a, hitherto, golden career.

Chapter Forty One
A TEMPORARY REPRIEVE
'Ce que je rêve, c'est un art d'équilibre, de tranquilité, sans sujet inquiétant ou préoccupant.'
('What I dream of is an art of balance and serenity, devoid of trouble or worry.')
H. Matisse

Howson was relieved that no restrictions of movement had been set and thus he was able to fly to France the following morning, as had been his intention. David Janney had advised him to say nothing about the matter to anyone, not even to his wife and immediate family. Of course, it was never this proud man's intention to share the ignominy of being escorted to Harleybury Police Station for the second time within a couple of weeks with any of his fellow human beings – Howson had never been one to discuss mishaps, setbacks, errors, even with his wife. He had become used to dealing with problems on his own: such was the nature of the beast. On the other hand, God had provided him with supreme confidence and he had always managed to come up trumps from any difficult situation in which he found himself – and being questioned by the police about the disappearance of two human beings, whose execution he had stage-managed, was as difficult as it comes.

As he left Heathrow for Paris Charles de Gaulle that sunny July morning, Joseph was as depressed and anxious as he had ever been in his life. He was also dreading that telephone call from a newspaper hack – investigative journalists they called themselves – or from the local radio station – asking him about why he had been taken to Harleybury Police Station. He also didn't trust the police: a white, upper middle class scholar was not the Force's favourite interviewee; Howson felt there was a certain inverted snobbery about the police, many of whom he considered mere humble beings.

As he drove his hired car from Paris down the A10 towards Tours, Joseph Howson kept mulling over in his mind about who it was that had been so obviously active behind his back, delving into his family background, endeavouring to make connections between Kenny and Mary Anne and himself; with regard to the latter, he assumed it had been the taxi driver who had seen Mary Anne's photograph in the paper – but how could the driver possibly have considered that a few visits to Cranford Lodge to be in any way significant in a young girl's disappearance over a year later? There had to be a missing link in all this. Who was so eager to ascertain details of his familial history? Why would they even bother? He had always been extremely careful about discussing his parents; he had kept even Marie-Christine in the dark about his real father's Nazi connections. Perhaps he would ring his parents on returning to Britain. He knew that once he pulled up at his in-laws' grand mansion, nestling in the idyllic French countryside betwixt Tours and Blois, on the banks of the Loire, he was going to have to be ebullient and carefree, as is the norm for any schoolteacher throughout the months of July and August, the profession's favourite time of the year. He could not let on in any way that he possibly stood on the cusp of ruin.

Those weeks were good, indeed this sojourn was a small light in Howson's mind, as the black cloud of depression continued to engulf him. He walked for miles with his son on his shoulders, holding his beloved wife's hand, chatting beneath the uninterrupted sunshine, which caresses the Val de la Loire for so much of the summer. Halcyon daylight hours made way for relaxing soirées, sometimes at a restaurant, sometimes at home: either way, Joseph enjoyed haute cuisine and imbibed the very best local wine. Such was the holiday that he was able to keep the tornado, which was hovering off the coast of his mind, firmly at bay. He realised that with A and AS results published mid-August, he would need to return to England within a fortnight, so he determined to make the most of every moment. Occasionally he would catch his wife's perfect profile set against the light of a flickering candle – beautiful, exquisite, the visible personification of perfection, he thought. How lucky he was to be married to someone so graceful, so charming... many men would sell their soul to share their life with someone so beautiful, so intelligent, so cultured. And yet *he* had wanted more – as ever it was sex that had reared its ugly head. Howson was convinced that sex, while on the one hand so pleasurable and, of course, necessary for continued procreation, on the other hand was the province of the devil, the cause of so much unhappiness and anxiety, so often the catalyst in the ruination of relationships, in some cases the destruction of lives. It had been Howson's sexual drive which had put out its diabolic hand and led this extraordinarily intelligent individual into such an imprudent liaison; a liaison so obviously fraught with dangers. If he had been thinking clearly, a skill which he had used throughout his life to climb rapidly the ladder of life's success, he would surely have repudiated any notion of consorting with a lady of loose living. It could end only in tears: did he honestly think that a man in his position could dance with the devil and expect it to walk away once he wanted the music to stop? He'd been fooling himself; he'd been reckless; he had acted with puerile carelessness; he had allowed his heart to get very much the better of his head.

Well, the diabolic music was *not* going to stop, he wanted it to but it would not and soon he was going to have to leave his beloved wife and family and to continue dancing. Howson, on this occasion, had no choice.

Chapter Forty Two
GOOD NEWS FOR THE DOCTOR
'In examinations those who don't wish to know ask
questions of those who cannot answer.'
Sir Walter Raleigh

Public examination results were better than ever: everyone was aware that, with the Government's hands firmly in the results' pie, it was hardly likely to allow the country's exam grades to fall into decline, but this notwithstanding, Cranford College was in competition with the most successful schools in the country and this year's statistics suggested that the historic College was now the best in the land.

Languishing 'low-premier-table' when Dr Howson assumed the Headship, the school had been driven to the top within two years by the expertise, single-mindedness and industry of its leader. Now, fleetingly, the man at the top experienced a feeling of pride and contentment. It occurred to him that, if his life and career were to begin crashing down around him, at least he will have achieved what he had promised at the outset and perhaps it would end not entirely sourly.

Howson was well aware that the succeeding four to six weeks were going to decide his fate: perhaps the police would take no further action with regard to the missing drugs' duo, assuming that, in the absence of any firm evidence, the pair had simply disappeared into the night. After all, he was sure there was no proof of foul play and the police would certainly not be finding any dead bodies: it would be difficult charging someone with murder without a corpse! Neither Murko nor Jason would be revealing anything, as the result would be life sentences for them as well. Just as it had been arranged prior to the murders, Murko and Jason were now long gone.

As the Head sat alone in his study, with the late August sun disappearing behind the cricket pavilion, he considered for a moment that perhaps his worst fears would not be realised and that the whole dreadful episode in his hitherto immaculate life would go the way of Kenny and Mary Anne's bodies... into eternal oblivion.

He had no intention of speaking to Lord Harris or Sir Marcus Silver about his questioning at Harleybury Station. He was well aware that if information subsequently leaked, it would suggest he had something to hide; nevertheless, it was a chance he was prepared to risk. Volunteering information about his relationship with a missing call girl might well be the death knell of his reign at Cranford, regardless.

If details of the interview did reach the Governors' ears, they might even want to keep matters under wraps, for the sake of the school's reputation, and he would be permitted to make a dignified exit at the end of the academic year, his own good name and reputation intact, still young enough to make a new career in some area of the government's enormous education department, perhaps. It could be that, with the school experiencing such a zenith, the Governors would allow him to continue as Head, sweeping the whole matter under the proverbial carpet, then nailing the carpet firmly into place.

If it came to him going quietly, he was sure that an opportunity would come his way somewhere in the Education Department. When Tony Blair said "Education, Education, Education" in 1997, he should have said "Expansion, Expansion, Expansion", such was the growth of this particular area... so many advisory bodies, so many committees, so many quangos on the one hand, yet such a shortage of actual teachers of key subjects on the other. Or he could even have said "Intervention, Intervention, Intervention", such was the number of changes to the curriculum, such was the number of initiatives, such was the incessant governmental meddling. Howson was of the opinion that it was easier to find a modern languages advisor than a modern languages teacher. If his own career went 'belly-up', as the saying goes, there would surely be an opportunity awaiting him in the civil service, so he could join the other millions already there, all paid for by the stoic taxpayer. Howson had made up his mind that *he* wasn't offering any information about recent events.

The country's GCSE results followed the next Thursday, the last in August, and, once again, not only did over 90% of Cranford's fifth-formers secure ten grade As, most of these had a star put next to them. (Nathan Worsthorne, however, refused to call the acronym GCSE anything other than the 'General Certificate of Second Rate Education', much to some of his colleagues' irritation).

The Governors were due to meet the following Monday, ostensibly to discuss the examination results, but in Howson's absence, they would also be considering the heroin incident of the previous term. There had been no word from any source with regard to the questioning of their Head about the disappearance of Kenny and Mary Anne. For his part, Howson decided he would put all his energy and thoughts, at least as best he could, into getting the new academic year off to a good start. He hosted a pre-term drinks party for the staff on his front lawn with his customary bonhomie and charm... although the staff tended to feel nervous in his presence, none doubted his charm and wit, particularly female members of the Common Room, and wives. This Bond-like figure could charm the proverbial birds out of the trees.

With the term up and running, Howson was beginning to find some of his former enthusiasm and vigour – as well as being as ubiquitous around his thriving school as often as possible; he also asked Marie-Christine to assist him in entertaining as many staff as possible at dinner over the course of the term, an initiative which sat extremely well amongst members of the Common Room. After working twelve hour days in school, the Head was returning home a couple of times a week to spend hours at the dinner table with three or four members of staff and their spouses. After dining, the entire party would sit in his elegantly furnished, spacious lounge listening to some of their Head's favourite pieces of music, topped by Wagner's *Tristan and Isolde* overture, Howson explaining how, in his opinion, this piece was the pinnacle of all love music. Bach, Beethoven and Brahms were the supporting cast, as the Howson mansion resonated with music at its finest.

The re-found spring in the Head's step was partly due to the fact that Lord Harris had arrived unannounced at Cranford on the second morning of term to inform Howson of the Governors' deliberations.

'Joe, we talked at length about this drugs' business and it was clear that the Board of Governors feel they have never doubted your integrity and they see no reason to question it now. You were uncharacteristically foolish, but, well, we appointed a man, a human being, to run our school, not a machine. It was strongly felt that we should, um, it is our duty to support *you*, just as your commitment and expertise have been a magnificent support and inspiration to Cranford, thereby to all of us as Governors. This is the end of the matter.'

Joseph Howson could hardly think of an appropriate response, so he said simply, 'Thank you.'

Was everything back on its proper course, thought Howson, as he watched Lord Harris's chauffeured Rolls disappear out of the main front gate of the school? Had he finally managed to put his ills behind him? Dr Joseph Howson was allowing himself positive thoughts for the very first time since this whole desperate saga had begun.

Chapter Forty Three
FINE GOES IT ALONE
'When a door closes, somewhere nearby a window will open.'
R. Rogers

Benjamin Fine had spent the whole of August back in Florida with his mother. She had found it extremely difficult to settle after the death of her husband and when her son was due to return to England in early September, she had become very upset. As Fine sat in his club-class seat of the Virgin Airline, which transported him back across the Big Pond, he once again wondered whether he should let his home back in Blighty and reside in America with his mother for the remaining years of her life. He had again made efforts to coax her into returning to England with him but she was adamant that she was not prepared to make another upheaval, this time away from her new circle of friends and acquaintances.

During his sojourn in Florida Benjamin had kept in irregular contact with Martin Trench with regard to any developments in their investigations. There hadn't been much to report by Trench, as he was busying himself with an extramarital love tryst, having been hired by a wealthy businessman in West London.

As soon as Benjamin was re-ensconced, he gave Trench a ring:

'Martin, it's Ben, a call just to tell you I'm back. I don't suppose you've picked up any info since our last chat?'

'Sorry, Ben, I've been up to my eyes in another case,' replied Trench, 'as I told you over the phone, they've definitely interviewed Howson but, as yet, as far as I can gather, there's been no follow-up. Latham told me, in no uncertain terms, when I last spoke to him, that any leaking to the press could damage irreparably any case they build up. We'll just have to sit tight for the moment and see what transpires. Look, Ben, the police've now taken this whole matter on board. Best to let them get on with things; we could put Howson on his guard or even damage the case if we ask more and more questions. Be careful, whatever you do. It's over to PC Plod, now.'

Benjamin Fine hung up, Trench's words echoing in his head – perhaps the time had come to sit back and, as Trench had pointed out, to allow the police to run proceedings here onward. It seemed sensible. They had the resources and the experience in these matters; Fine had spent a vast quantity of his personal funds on this mission, even though Trench had charged him reduced fees virtually throughout. Fine had been desperate for the authorities to become interested in the story of the real Dr Howson and they now seemed to be. He decided that the most prudent course for him would be to sit and wait; the police had interviewed Howson and were now in a position to investigate further, as they saw fit.

Days turned into weeks and Fine heard nothing; even his new friend and investigative colleague Martin Trench was tardy in answering Fine's voicemail messages. Trench did phone late that August, in excited mood, to say that he had managed to ascertain the identity of the second suspect in the bagel shop killing:

'As you know, my partner, Karl Frost, has a police background and he's had an interest in that killing from the outset. He's used some of his connections within the Force to carry out some detailed research.'

'Tell me more,' said Fine.

'It wasn't difficult for Karl to ascertain the identity of the original witness to the murder; as you may recall, he was a co-worker at the bagel shop, a man by the name of Monty Greenberg. The poor bloke was approached back then by two Blackshirt thugs who told him, in no uncertain terms, that, unless he feigned a loss of memory and a general uncertainty of detail surrounding the incident, he would not only meet an unpleasant end but that end would be witnessed by his wife and children, who would then suffer the same fate. Furthermore, this didn't apply only in the short term, but as long as he was drawing breath!'

'Karl did well to find this out. Is this Greenberg still alive?'

'Oh no, he died years ago, however he did leave a letter for his oldest son, Teddy, which was to be opened only in the event of Monty's death. Karl has seen a copy of the letter. In the letter Monty poured his heart out over the matter which had blighted his life. He not only named Michael Howson as the person he had identified with absolute certainty – Howson was well known in the area – but he also named the person he believed to be Howson's accomplice.'

'How would he have known the accomplice? Was he well known, too?'

'Pretty much; everyone knew Howson and who he worked with.'

'Great stuff from Karl; these findings will be a great relief to the Lazarus family, for sure. Can there be legal steps on this matter?'

'Unlikely, any prosecution would be pointless, as the alleged accomplice is long dead and Michael Howson is senile and, for sure, would be judged unfit to stand trial. Furthermore, it's unlikely he would be convicted on the strength of a letter. The whole case would be costly and there would be little or no chance of it leading to a prosecution. At least, as you say, the Lazarus family will feel some sort of closure has been achieved.'

Fine thanked Trench and asked him to pass on his very best wishes and gratitude to Karl Frost. However, as he replaced the receiver, Fine's emotions were mixed. He was delighted that his deep suspicions about the Howson family were being proved correct but, at the same time, he felt frustrated that his investigative colleagues seemed to have made first rate progress over an incident which happened over half a century ago, yet seem paralysed about, as Fine saw it, skulduggery which had taken place within the past few months.

As September went and the mid-October half-term holiday approached, the only news appertaining to his former place of employment was how superb their examination results had been, with photographs of pupils holding their A, AS or GCSE certificates under the legend **CRANFORD PUPILS BEST IN THE COUNTRY**, etc. Week in, week out, there were photographs of the school's various rugby teams, particularly the First XV, as the college prepared itself for the annual Cranford Schools' Rugby Festival, the country's premier schools' tournament, and obviously a superb publicity opportunity for Cranford and its main man. As Joseph Howson possessed both an extremely keen intellectual acumen and film star looks, there was rarely a report without either a photograph or contribution from the great man himself. Howson was often to be seen offering erudite opinions on *BBC News 24* (latterly called the *News Channel*) and Fine found it hard to go through a week without hearing his learned tones on national radio: Howson even had his own occasional weekend slot on local radio.

With the end of October on the horizon, Benjamin Fine decided that he would contact D.I. Latham, at Harleybury police station, and request an interview; surely he would be amenable to this after all the work that Fine himself had done on the police's behalf. It took several attempts over a period of days before he was finally put through to Latham:

'Hello, Ben, good to hear from you.'

'Roger, I was wondering what progress had been made vis-à-vis all the info regarding Dr Joseph Howson.'

'I know it sounds odd, given the impetus you, yourself, have given to this enquiry, but I have to be guarded in what I say, at a professional level, but what I can tell you is that Dr Howson has been interviewed at length; he was under caution for two to three hours. Look, Ben, the man may, I say, may, be in some way involved in the disappearance of those two...' (there was a brief pause), ' uh, Mary Anne Marshall and Kenneth Churchill. He admitted to knowing her but has never met Kenneth Churchill, other than being accosted by him during the Carol Service procession. There is not one shred of evidence linking him with their disappearance. It's the general consensus here that, if he is in any way involved in their disappearance, it'll be by way of paying them to disappear, as it were. We couldn't possibly charge him with anything, as things stand.'

'Well, what are the police doing to find a link?'

'I cannot comment on this, you know that I can't.'

'In other words, you're saying to me, because those two are drugged-up low-life and Howson is something of a local and national celebrity, you're not prepared to upset the proverbial apple cart.'

'This is not what I'm saying, Ben. You know you're on an obsessed mission to get Howson back for effectively pushing you out of Cranford. I understand how bitter you are but my team and I have spent many hours on this case, far more than *I* would've normally – in fact probably, as a D.I, I wouldn't've become involved at all, had it not been for the fact that you sounded so passionate and convincing. To criticise me now is, I have to say, unfair and disrespectful. To imply that I am not proceeding with the case because I consider Joseph Howson from superior social stock to Mary Anne Marshall or Kenneth Churchill is, quite frankly, impertinent. *I* have to decide whether or not we have enough information to press charges. It is *I* who is held accountable if my station spends time and resources pursuing a line of enquiry which has no chance of resulting in a conviction for anything. On what we have so far, the CPS would laugh in my face. Not to mention the flack me and my team would take if we besmirched the name and reputation of Dr Howson without good cause. Can you imagine the reaction if we accused him of direct involvement in their disappearance and it turned out to be unfounded? Allow me to make decisions in the way I see fit, regardless whether or not they coincide with your own particular viewpoint. I'm sorry to be so curt in my tone but, no doubt, you understand why. I hope we'll have a more productive conversation next time.' With this, Latham hung up.

Fine sat in his lounge looking out across the local fields, wondering if all the work he had done during the previous year had come to precisely nothing. Martin Trench was pursuing other projects; the police seemed likely not to proceed. Was he on his own once again? Was he, truly, the only person who believed that Joseph Howson was schizophrenic, some modern day Dr Jekyll and Mr Hyde? The man had managed to keep Mr Hyde under wraps for most of his privileged life, but Fine had witnessed that Hyde; he knew of Howson's darker side and Fine was quite convinced that it was Mr Hyde who had been instrumental in the disappearance of two missing persons. Was he going to call it a day and permit Dr Jekyll to carry on enjoying his privileged existence, or was he going to expose, finally, the darker side of his persona? If the police weren't having it and Martin Trench had had his attention diverted, then Fine would have to be resourceful and carry on alone.

He kept mulling over in his mind the warning that Latham had given him – do *not* contact the media, as this would jeopardise any future case; but Latham had just all but stated that there wasn't going to be any future case and Fine knew that the longer that this went on, the less likely it would be that he could stir anyone's interest. Benjamin Fine decided there and then that he had no alternative – in spite of the clear warning, he would have to contact the national press. He knew they'd be reluctant to attempt to connect Howson with Kenny and Mary Anne's disappearance; they could use only hard facts, particularly when dealing with someone as powerful and as wealthy as prestigious Headmaster Howson. Well, he had some facts for them– the fact that both Howson's biological and adoptive fathers had interesting backgrounds and the fact that Dr Joseph Howson had admitted to having some sort of relationship with a call girl, what's more, entertaining her at the school. He could throw in the drug incident for good measure. How about all this for starters, thought Benjamin Fine? Fine was a man on a mission and although he was tired of, and frustrated by, the constant obstacles he was obliged to overcome in pursuit of justice, he felt as determined as ever to bring down his nemesis.

Chapter Forty Four
TWO OLD HEADS
'My experience of life has been drawn from life itself.'
Z. Dobson

That same evening, at about ten thirty, Benjamin made his way to 'the Crooked Billet' pub-cum-restaurant, which he knew his ex-colleague Nathan Worsthorne liked to frequent. Much to his relief, he found a slightly inebriated deputy head propping up the bar.

'Fancy bumping into you, old chap,' said Nathan. 'Can I get you a drink?'

'An orange and lemonade would be much appreciated,' responded Benjamin.

Nathan himself was halfway through a large whisky, diluted with water.

'And what brings you to this sort of den? How are you getting on these days?'

'Well, I've been pottering about, recently returned from visiting my mother in Florida. Dad died, I'm afraid.'

'I'm sorry to hear it. Things must be tough.'

'I'm certainly keeping busy.'

'And what about the bridge?' Nathan himself was a fairly keen player.

'Well, as you know, I play once a week with Sarah but, as I'm not too popular with the Head Man, she hasn't been seeing me as often as she used to. I'm a bit out of practice.'

'So why have you ventured forth to my regular haunt? Surely, old boy, you can obtain orange and lemonade more easily and certainly more cheaply from the supermarket?'

'Nathan, I want to show you something.'

'Go ahead, my dear chap; we can sit over there.'

'Let's go outside. I'd rather not make a public display of this.'

Nathan, always a curious man, agreed to accompany Fine to the pub garden. The latter walked over to his car, retrieved a framed family photo and brought it over to Nathan.

'It's a bit dark. Hold it over to that light,' said Nathan. The deputy head was wondering why he was being asked to look at a photograph of a family of Afro-Caribbeans.

After a quick perusal, Nathan announced, 'Doesn't mean anything to me, old chap. None of these is part of my regular social circle, ha-ha.'

'Look at the two young men, Nathan.'

Nathan stared at the photo for a while, 'The older-looking one seems vaguely familiar.'

'You think you might have met him?'

'I doubt it, but I feel you're going to tell me I have.'

'What about the chap who turned up after the Carol Service?'

Nathan paused for a moment.

'My God! Is that him? Yes, that's him, but somewhat younger.'

Nathan fixed Benjamin with a penetrating glare.

'Look, what are you playing at, Ben? You're putting me in an awkward position.'

'You've known me for over twenty years, Nathan. Can I trust you not to repeat any of this to the Head Man?'

'Now, you know Ben, I am duty bound to pass on any information relating to the school to Howson.'

'I understand your position, of course, but would you want to endanger my very life?'

'That sounds very dramatic to me, you've been reading too many novels in your retirement,' said Nathan.

'Nathan, can I take you into my confidence? I'm not being overly dramatic but I believe there is something fundamentally wrong with Howson.'

Nathan was torn between overpowering curiosity and a natural desire not to compromise his professional integrity, loyalty and trust. His personal and intellectual curiosity won the day.

'Okay, but I'm warning you, Ben, if you tell me anything that I think should be passed on, I'll require your absolute promise that Lord Harris will be informed.'

'You have my assurance, Nathan. You know you can trust me on that score.'

'I have no doubt of that,' responded Nathan.

'Okay. Well, it'll not surprise you that I know the identity of the fellow in the picture.'

'And why are you so interested in this?'

'Nathan, you are one of the few at Cranford who have a brain. You surely cannot be entirely impressed with the Head Man.'

'I'll keep my own counsel with respect to my views of the HM,' replied Nathan, somewhat severely.

'Okay, but what would you say if I told you that the man in the picture is linked to the Head?'

Fine proceeded to give Worsthorne a full account of the story of Howson's adoptive father's youthful activities and those of his real father, as well as his links with the Afro-Caribbean in the photograph.

'Well, I'm not entirely surprised about his familial history,' said Nathan. 'As you know, my politics are somewhat diametrically opposed to those of Howson. The Heads of major public schools are not usually admirers of Che Guevara and Lenin. On the other hand, this is a bit steep. I doubt whether the Governors would be entirely chuffed with your discoveries about either his family history or his association with this druggie.'

'I can't say any more at this stage, but if Howson finds out that I am on to all this, I assure you that I could be in grave danger.'

'Well, I've made you a promise, Ben, and, of course, I shall keep it, however, we'll need to decide where this information should go.'

'I am considering my next steps about all this but I wanted you to be in the picture. I trust your discretion in the meantime. See you soon.'

With this, Benjamin turned on his heels and made his way back over to his car.

A combination of the extraordinary information he had just been told and the fresh air had a sobering effect on Nathan Worsthorne and he was now starting to feel somewhat weary. On his way home, he turned the information over and over in his mind. The thought of impending problems for certainly the Head and possibly the school made him seriously anxious.

Chapter Forty Five
FINE'S LAST RESORT
'Every time a newspaper dies, the country moves a little closer to authoritarianism.'
R. Kluger

Benjamin Fine had taken *The Times* newspaper for as long as he could remember; in fact, he had started reading it when he was a schoolboy in the 1960s. As he grew into adulthood, his day would not be complete without a daily dip into its pages, the highlight of the week, of course, being the bumper edition, entitled *The Sunday Times*, complete with its assortment of magazines, around which Benjamin's weekend revolved. He was aware of other journals available and one such he had heard about was the *News of the World*, a newspaper light in the latest news of the world, but heavy in the world of 'celebrity' and the associated private lives of those who lived in the fast lane. He was also aware that this paper was always on the lookout for scandals surrounding figures of public standing: judges, doctors, MPs, head teachers.... Of course, the higher they were, the further they had to fall and the fact that teachers' responsibilities were primarily interlinked with children made pedagogues even more vulnerable and more interesting to a tabloid editor, particularly one as well known as Dr Joseph Howson.

As he arrived at his local *9 till 9*, on a November Sunday morning, his newsagent handed him his *Times*, at which point Benjamin asked also for a copy of the *News of the World*, much to the surprise of the person standing behind the counter.

Once home, Benjamin poured himself a cup of coffee, grilled two slices of toast and sat at his breakfast bar, scouring the pages of his new purchase:

'MY HELL WITH SEX-MAD VICAR' .... 'BIG BROTHER BABE SPILLS BEANS' ... 'OFF HER HEAD, IN MY BED.... BRITAIN'S HOTTEST SHOWBIZ REPORTER REVEALS ALL'.... and so it went on, page after page of intrusive journalism. As he reached page 36 there, at the bottom, was an advert:

"Do you know a scandal we should investigate? Text... email... or call..."

Benjamin placed the paper on the table and dwelled upon the consequences of proceeding. He mulled over, once again, the chances of D.I. Latham and the police at Harleybury bringing Howson to justice. His pal, Martin Trench, had lost his enthusiasm and was now otherwise engaged. So this seemed, he reckoned, the only way remaining of calling his nemesis to account, even if the latter could not be connected to Mary Anne and Kenny's disappearance. On the other hand, if he made this call to the *News of the World*, Cranford College's reputation would be damaged irreparably. What would Sarah think? What would his ex-colleagues make of it? How would the parents and pupils react? They'd be shocked, of course, by the details, but they'd also be aware of the source of the story: too many staff knew of his personal antipathy towards Howson, and Sarah would know for certain who was behind the exposé. It would certainly open a can of worms... an enormous can at that. Most importantly in Ben's thoughts was the damage which would be done, not only to the present school community, but also to every pupil who had ever passed through Cranford, one of England's grandest public schools. Was he acting principally for moral reasons or out of spiteful revenge? He was certainly aware that, in bringing down Howson, he could well do irreparable damage to Cranford College simultaneously. As for himself, he knew the name of Benjamin Fine would likely be remembered for generations to come as the person who ruined Joseph Howson and, thereby, damaged Cranford College.

He finished his breakfast and picked up the phone and dialled the number in bold black print on the page. He felt that if he mulled over the pros and cons for too long, he would lose his nerve.

'Hello, news desk,' came the introduction.

'My name is Benjamin Fine and I am a teacher, recently retired, from Cranford College, near Harleybury in Surrey.'

'How can I help, Sir?'

'I have some interesting facts to tell you about the Headmaster of the College,' said Fine nervously.

'Just a moment, Sir, I'll put you through to a colleague.'

The line went seemingly dead for nearly a minute and Fine presumed that the journalist to whom he was about to speak was being apprised of the subject matter. On re-connection, Fine gave the listening ear precise details of all that had happened, beginning with his own departure from Cranford, about Howson's family background and about his trysts with a call girl, who was now missing. He explained that he had informed the police of everything and that they were highly unlikely to proceed. As requested, he spoke slowly, affording the journalist at the other end of the line enough time to record the main details onto his computer.

It was all music to the journalist's ears, particularly about the visits of a call girl to see the Headmaster *on school premises*. The icing on the proverbial cake was the discovery of drugs at the lodge, for which the Head had accepted responsibility.

'We'll have to check all this out, of course, before we go to print. One allegation we print as fact, which turns out to be erroneous, could cost this paper a lot of money. We have contacts in most of the country's police stations, who speak to us incognito, as 'official sources', so it won't be difficult collating all the actual facts. I don't doubt for a moment that all the info you've given me is correct, it's just, well, we *have* to double check. I'm sure you understand.'

'Quite so,' said Fine, will you use my name in this?'

'That is for you to decide, Sir, all I can say is it makes the story a lot more powerful if we include a picture of the source of the story and attribute a name.'

'I'll think about it,' answered Fine nervously.

After swapping contact details, both men hung up, one ecstatic about the story which, if accurate, he knew would sell thousands, perhaps millions, of copies, the other somewhat saddened that he was about to drag the majestic, the esteemed, the renowned Cranford College into the seedy world of sleaze. But then again, Fine convinced himself, he had tried all other avenues.

It was the following day that Fine received a call back from the journalist.

'Mr Fine, it's Mark Jennings at the *News of the World* features desk. Look, we've been in touch with a regular police contact at Harleybury, on an unofficial basis, and he's confirmed all that you've alleged. One thing we cannot do in our story is in any way imply that Howson had anything to do with those two's disappearance. I think you knew that anyway. Look, I'll need to send one of my team down to see you. He can then get a sense of the area; I don't know whether you've got access to the school?'

'I'm afraid I'm *persona non grata* at Cranford. I wouldn't be able to take anyone over there without my having to answer a score of questions. The only way you're going to get a feel for the place is to write to the school as a prospective parent, take along one of your female colleagues to act as your wife, and you'll be given a free guided tour.'

'That's a great idea, I'll put it to my editor,' replied Mark excitedly.

On the following Monday, two investigative journalists arrived at Benjamin Fine's home at the edge of Harleybury. Fine had already informed them that he was prepared to put his name to the article, so a camera was brought and various photographs were taken of the retired schoolmaster in his home. They asked him various questions about the school: where the lodge was, where Howson lived, the location of his study and of Fine's boarding house. He gave them a detailed map of the various locations which would be of interest to them. Half an hour later a taxi arrived, as arranged, to take both 'parents' up to the school. They did have one problem and that was the fact that they were without their offspring, so an excuse had been prepared that their son was ill and was at home, being looked after by his grandparents. They also had to decide where he was at school at present and a junior school, local to one of the journalists in Camden Town, was decided upon.

They enjoyed an informative tour of the school, guided by two sixth-form pupils, who saw nothing strange in their visitors wanting to take lots of photographs, although the couple were the first parents to insist upon seeing the gardener's lodge: an excuse was given about its interesting architecture.

The culmination of the tour was an interview with the Director of Studies, the prospective Housemaster and finally a brief chat with the Head. Even the two hardened journalists were nervous about the prospect of having a supposed relaxed chat with Dr Joseph Howson. Sarah, the Head's secretary, showed them in and a smiling Howson invited them both to sit down.

'Why have you set your sights on this school?'

'Isn't it one of the finest in the land?'

'And one of the most expensive,' retorted Howson. 'Would it be impolite for me to ask if you are sure you'd be able to meet the annual fees, plus the unseen extras. Normally we reckon it costs £27,000 per annum per pupil. What we try to do is to encourage parents to look ahead for three years up to GCSE and a further two to A levels; that's in excess of £130,000 out of taxed income.'

'I am confident, Dr Howson, that we have in no way made a mistake coming here today.'

'Presumably you'd like to return with your son before you commit yourselves,' said Howson.

'Quite,' was the reply. 'We shall be back in touch within the next couple of days, Doctor.'

Both 'parents' smiled nervously. And so it was that, just before lunch, two journalists from Britain's most famous gossip tabloid took their leave from the hallowed portals of Cranford College, to return to London to prepare their double-page spread for the following Sunday's edition. Life could never be quite the same again at one of the country's most successful public schools.

Chapter Forty Six
HOWSON CAUGHT OFFGUARD
*'We have no more right to happiness without deserving it
than earning money without deserving it.'*
G.B. Shaw

Dr Joseph Howson was just about to go into a monthly assessment meeting, which took place in the Common Room and involved the entire body of teaching staff. The purpose of these meetings was to pinpoint individual pupils' academic progress or, in the case of most of those mentioned, complete lack of progress. Howson found these meetings pretty tedious at the best of times, feeling that they could have been efficiently completed in half the time, as certain verbose members of staff felt they had to make constant, long-winded contributions, so unnecessarily elongating matters. They simply seemed to enjoy the sound of their own voice. Howson had lost count of the number of times he had to use that well-worn phrase, 'right, well, moving on...' It was uttered so regularly that the Head sometimes felt he was part of a *Vicar of Dibley* council meeting.

As he descended the staircase from his study at 5.55p.m on the Tuesday evening he heard his secretary's desk telephone ring. Usually, of course, Sarah would be there to answer it, but she left each evening at 5.30p.m. Uncharacteristically, he went back up the staircase, unlocked his study door and made his way into Sarah's office, adjacent to his own, to pick up the receiver.

'Headmaster of Cranford College speaking,' he blurted out, somewhat impatiently.

'Good evening, my name is Mark Jennings and I am a reporter for the *News of the World.*'

Howson had to place his left hand on the desk to steady himself.

'Why are you ringing me?' he faltered.

'I would like to talk to you about certain allegations which have been made about you. Allegations which we feel would be in the public interest to print in our newspaper next Sunday.'

Howson felt as though he had been hit by a sledgehammer.

'Look, I am on my way to an important meeting. Could we not meet to talk about whatever has come your way? I am sure you have not been apprised accurately.'

'I would be happy to meet you. Shall I come down to you or would you prefer to come here?'

'I'll ring you in an hour. What is your contact number?' asked a trembling Howson.

Jennings furnished him with both his office landline and his mobile number.

Howson hung up and sat for a moment at his secretary's desk. Just when he thought he had re-found his life, another bombshell had come his way. Had Murko or Jason told someone of the killings? If they had, and an allegation came his way, he was done for. Had the drugs' business leaked? This was the moment he had secretly dreaded, although he had managed to push it to the back of his mind. He *had* to carry on as best he could and pretend all was normal. He got up and made his way down to the Common Room.

Subsequent events were a blur to him – as best as he might, he was unable to concentrate on anything at all. The meeting came and went; he hardly said a word; after the meeting finished he had to endure the usual members of staff who engaged him in dreary conversations about matters he had little interest in – usually he feigned some interest (it was always the same three or four who collared him whenever they found themselves in the same room as him) – but on this occasion he was abrupt and took his leave almost mid-sentence as Janet Witney droned on about some examination re-sits.

He returned to his study and he'd hardly sat down when there was a knock on the door. It was his deputy, Nathan Worsthorne, still reeling somewhat from the information that Ben Fine had recently told him about his boss.

'Are you all right, Headmaster? You seemed unusually distracted during the staff meeting, somewhat quiet.'

'Oh, you know how it is, Nathan, the travails of being a Headmaster. I wish we could just get on in these meetings, instead of going round in endless circles. Drives me up the wall,' complained Howson.

'I sometimes think these assessment meetings are a comparative waste of time. I'm sure we could achieve our objective far more efficiently. Shall I look into it?'

Howson did not answer because he hadn't heard the question. He was gazing out of the window, the journalist's words resonating in his head, **'I would like to talk to you about certain allegations... public interest'.**

'Headmaster?'

'Yes?'

'Do you think I should look into this?'

'Sorry, what was it you said?'

'The assessment meetings – finding an alternative.'

'Oh, yes, good idea.'

Howson attempted to show interest but was aware he was failing badly.

'If you'll excuse me, Nathan, I have some urgent business to attend to.'

'Certainly, Headmaster.'

Worsthorne withdrew, leaving Howson sitting disconsolately at his desk. As soon as the Deputy had closed the door, the Head took out his mobile and dialled the journalist's landline at his office.'

'Newsroom,' came the answer.

'Could you put me through to Mr Mark Jennings, please?'

'Just one moment.'

'Mark Jennings, hello.'

'This is Joseph Howson; we spoke earlier about some information that has come your way. I don't suppose you could give me some idea as to what all this is about?'

'I'd prefer to speak to you person-to-person, if that's possible. I can drive down to you, if it suits.'

A rendezvous time and midway venue for the following day were settled and Howson decided there was nothing more he could do until then. He had to try and be as normal as possible, in spite of the fact that his head was in turmoil. The most difficult test for him was going to be convincing his beloved wife that everything was fair and well. He knew that she could read him like a book; dissembling his true state of mind in front of her was not going to be easy.

Joseph endeavoured to be something like his usual self at dinner, but he found it extremely difficult focusing on mundane news of his son's day at nursery when there was every good chance his wife would take him away for good the following week. There was no doubt in Howson's mind that sharing a house with an adulterous husband was something his wife had not considered when she took her marriage vows eighteen years previously. Then again, perhaps the *News of the World* was unaware of his relationship with Mary Anne. As Joseph floated into another of his reveries, which he had been doing ever since he'd put down the telephone receiver in his study just before 6p.m that evening, his son approached him for his customary goodnight kiss. Usually the non-tactile dad gave him a quick peck on the cheek, occasionally followed by a paternal tap on the head. Marie-Christine was surprised that this evening he was treated to an enveloping hug, which lasted for nearly ten seconds.

As she went to the kitchen to load the dishwasher, her husband repaired to the lounge, picking up his daily newspaper en route. As he attempted to focus on the lead story, something about banning the consumption of alcohol in the streets, Joseph Howson's mind tracked back to what Tony Harris had said to him at their last dinner together –**'if the press get hold of all this, boy, you're history'.**

Joseph found it particularly difficult to sleep that night – not an uncommon thing to happen to a Headmaster. Marie-Christine was used to her husband getting up in the middle of the night and creeping downstairs to watch *The News Channel.* That night he could barely understand what was being said, he half expected his own school's name would appear on the screen: "**CRANFORD COLLEGE HEAD IN DRUGS' SCANDAL**" – "**PUBLIC SCHOOL HEAD CONFIRMS NAZI CONNECTION**". "**HEAD CONSORTS WITH PROSTITUTE**".

He knew that the headlines in the Sunday paper would be as salacious as possible, leaving little to the imagination. As he sat in front of the television, cup of coffee in hand, he shuddered at the thought of the embarrassment it would all cause to the school, the school he had built up into the well-oiled centre of learning it had become. As the moonlight filtered in through the half-open lounge curtains, Joseph finally drifted off to sleep; he didn't even notice his wife enter the room and sit down next to him, putting her head on his shoulder, whispering:

'Je t'adore, mon chéri. Je t'adorerai pour toujours.'

Chapter Forty Seven
CAKES AND DIRTY LINEN
'We only really face up to ourselves when we are afraid.'
T. Bernhard

It was agreed that Joseph Howson and Mark Jennings would meet at a hotel on the Harleybury by-pass at 4p.m. When he appeared, Jennings was not, in Howson's mind, the image of a tabloid investigative reporter: he was tall, athletically built, well dressed and sported a healthy mane of dark hair, which belied his years – Howson took him to be mid-forties.

Afternoon tea was ordered although, such was the turmoil in Howson's stomach, he had little enthusiasm for either the plate of sandwiches or the selection of cakes on offer. It was a strange feeling that here was the man who could well be instrumental in ruining his career and possibly his marriage, sitting opposite him, tucking into sandwiches with the crusts cut off. After a period of small talk, Jennings put to Howson what his informant had alleged. He asked him to listen to all the allegations and he would then have an opportunity to respond.

'You don't mind if I record our conversation, do you?' Jennings asked.

'Go ahead,' was Howson's curt, nervous response.

'Our story...' (Howson noticed the journalistic speak, not "the allegations" but "our story") '... is in three sections. I'll start with the first, which appertains to your being questioned at Harleybury, Police Station on 27 July 2002, and your accepting responsibility for a wrap of heroin found on the school premises.'

He paused, waiting for the Head to respond. Howson nodded in confirmation – what else could he do?

'The second strand is to do with your family background.'

Jennings proceeded to give an account of all the information that Trench, Frost and Fine had managed to unearth, without mentioning the names of his sources.

'Have you anything in response to what has been alleged?'

'You seem to know far more about my parents than I do. What's more, I fail to see how the publication of any of my family affairs is in the public interest, as you say. Isn't all of this just a means of selling copies? Don't, please, try and suggest to me that there is some sort of moral high ground at work here.'

Jennings proceeded as if Howson had not said a word.

'The third strand is to do with a prostitute. We would very much like to have checked out details with the person concerned but, unfortunately, no one seems able to locate her, or her boyfriend for that matter. Perhaps this is just as well for you. What we do know for sure is that she paid a number of visits to school premises and we have it on good authority that she was seeing you. You paid money to an agency, *Paradise Babes*, who hire out women for sex.'

This part of the 'story' struck Howson like a bolt out of the blue: so, people were aware of his having consorted with a prostitute – but how could they? The police can't have divulged the information and he, himself, had been so careful to cover his tracks. Howson paused: he was kidding himself, he mused, he brought her to the bloody school; is that being careful? He had been deluding himself to think so. So, he was going to have to pay for his stupidity – denial was a waste of time. The press wouldn't dare to make a direct accusation without firm evidence. If he were to deny the liaison, it would provoke even more headlines. Best to hold your hands up and drift into obscurity. Denial could even prompt further snooping and, after all, there was so much more to unearth.

'We did meet on a couple of occasions,' said Howson.

'At least three that we know about. I have the actual dates and times,' interrupted Jennings.

'I see. I wasn't aware it was as many as that,' answered Howson guardedly. 'Look, I'm sorry about all this, I appreciate it was foolish but, under the circumstances, my wife was pregnant and then she suffered badly from PND; I sought sexual solace elsewhere. I only ever used this one girl, who seemed clean, respectable, intelligent. I'm not going to deny that we had sex, but we did spend a lot of time talking, laughing and generally enjoying each other's company.'

'Why did you stop seeing her?'

'I felt she was becoming emotionally involved and there is only one woman in the world who I've ever loved.'

'We're not going to flay you alive, Doctor Howson, we're just going to present the facts. You've been very cooperative and I can tell you this will have a bearing on our final copy.'

Suddenly Howson fell to his knees in front of the reporter, inciting puzzled glances from a number of guests, also taking afternoon tea:

'Please, I beg you, I entreat you, I beseech you, don't do this to me, please, please, please; Howson's cheeks were already wet with tears.

'Please, please, I beg, I beg.' Howson held out a hand to touch the reporter's.

'I think it prudent you sit back in your chair, Doctor.'

A pathetic-looking Howson dragged himself back into the elegant armchair.

'I'm afraid it is no longer within my own gift to decide whether this story is published or not. This is for the Editor to decide. I'm sorry.'

With this, Jennings stood up, dropped a £20 note on the table to cover the refreshments, and said goodbye.

One man drove north, back up into London, the other returning to, for now, his school. More tears welling up in his eyes as he made his way along the Farnham bypass, Howson realised that the time had come to telephone both Anthony Harris and Sir Marcus Silver. But did he have the courage to do so? Wouldn't it be better to suffer one final humiliation as the news broke on the following Sunday?

In a way the anxiety which had taken hold of Howson's central nervous system had relaxed slightly since the interview. In some ways when you harbour dreaded secrets – hasn't everyone some dark secrets – it can be a relief that you no longer have the responsibility of guarding them. Howson felt sure that this temporary reprieve in his mood would not last long, as the nation would soon be picking up this week's copy of the *News of Howson's World*.

Chapter Forty Eight
A DEBT IS PAID
*'The fall from grace is steep and swift, and when you land,
it does not make a sound, because you are alone.'*
C. Williams

Turmoil, utter turmoil, flooded Howson's mind. In spite of his initial intentions, he had not yet told anyone of the impending story; for the first time in his life he had neither the courage nor the strength. He went into Wednesday morning's school assembly and, as the Captain of Rugby was giving the pupils and staff a résumé of that week's results, from the stage on high, Howson gazed at the assembled throng, realising that this could be his last ever appearance in front of the school community. He pondered that for some in front of him the next time they would see his face would be in a newspaper (if you can stretch the definition of newspaper), probably alongside the visage of a high-class prostitute.

When all the results had been read out, Howson came centre stage and delivered to the pupils an unprepared, without reference, speech about how fortunate they all were to be members of the Cranford community; in term time, he said, it was that community which was their family. He told them repeatedly how fortunate, how privileged, they all were to attend such a superb educational establishment and that it would be disappointing and such a waste of their parents' money and, more importantly, their own time, if they were not to take full advantage, on a daily basis, of what there was on offer at Cranford. He finished by telling the school how privileged he had been to have spent over two years as Headmaster and that "there was nowhere else he would rather have been."

As he turned on his heels to leave, a couple of members of staff, standing next to each other in the body of the hall, agreed that they were half expecting their leader to finish his rousing oration by informing them all he was departing from Cranford there and then.

Wednesday passed and the Head did everything in his power to act as normally and as rationally as he was able. On occasions, he was left alone in his study and he would be unable to prevent the tears from once more rolling down his cheeks. The emotional pain was excruciating. Sarah would ring through to inform him his next appointment was due and he would make his way to the lavatory, where he'd wipe his eyes, wash his face and return to his study desk. As the day drew to a close and all meetings had been concluded, he took out some paper and, once again, began to write.

He continued to carry out his duties and such was his *tour de force* acting performance, no one realised that their Head was engulfed in a sea of deep anxiety, fear, turmoil and depression. He realised that the life as he knew it, and had known it throughout his unalloyed glorious existence, was now only very temporary – that its walls were soon to come tumbling down, like those of the Twin Towers after that devilish attack. He could envisage nothing left standing – all that he had built up would be reduced to an unadulterated *tabula rasa*. All he could see in front of him was blackness: he searched for a faint light – perhaps Marie-Christine would forgive him, but would he be able to live with her, engulfed as he was by utter shame? He had arranged the murder of two human beings and, even if it were to remain undetected, he was still going to have to bear that dark secret for the rest of his life.

As Wednesday moved into Thursday he avoided his wife's gaze as much as possible as he carried out his familial role. She knew that he was upset but she had realised early in their marriage that if Joseph wanted to discuss something that was troubling him then he would do so. There was little point delving into areas about which he felt uncomfortable. Best to leave alone, she thought.

Thursday was a busy teaching day for the Head and, paradoxically, on that particular Thursday he managed to deliver a series of lessons, outstanding in their delivery, in their content and in their effectiveness. It was as if Joseph Howson knew that this was probably – almost certainly – the very last time that he would stand in front of a class and he wanted to savour every second. Teaching had taken a battering for over twenty years, mainly due to society's almost obsessive indulgence with regard to the adolescent viewpoint, and one of the offshoots of this shift in the former adult-child relationship had been the ever-increasing difficulty for teachers to enjoy their profession, one of the oldest in the world. It had been the deterioration in children's attitude towards, and natural respect for, authority figures that had led to fewer good university graduates choosing the classroom as an environment in which to earn their living. Howson knew at first-hand how difficult it was to find inspiring, hardworking teachers. If only they had the opportunity to spend a few days at schools like Cranford, and could pursue their chosen profession uninterrupted and unthreatened, indeed appreciated, then they would realise that educating young minds was still a very rewarding job, probably *the* most rewarding.

His final class left at 2.35p.m and the pupils made their way back to the house to prepare themselves for the afternoon's games programme. Howson had been teaching Latin to the Lower Sixth form, the Classics Department nestling in the School Tower Block. How extraordinary that a whole classroom block, five minutes previously a hive of activity, could so quickly metamorphose into a building so still, so tranquil... as he stood at the window looking out over the enormous parade ground, Howson could hear only the whistle of the west wind as it made its way across southern Britain and then onto mainland Europe. The campus housed about a thousand people in all. At that moment, the Head felt that he was the only person there... he could neither see nor hear anyone... all he could recognise was a voice from inside his head telling him... 'it is no use, you have to put the school first' ... 'you mustn't wait' ... he must do what this voice was telling him ... now was not the time for cowardice, for indecision. Howson knew he had no choice – he may be outstandingly intelligent and handsome, but these qualities meant nothing if the accompanying soul was corrupt.

I'm so worried, so depressed, my brain hurts. How the hell did I get into this situation? How? How? I had it all and I've screwed up so badly that I've managed to chuck it all away – everything. Was that clever? Of course not; so it just goes to show that your dick will control your brain in an open contest. Fuck it. I bet it was that Benjamin bloody Fine who's screwed me. Who else could be so cunning, so vengeful? Well, come Sunday, he'll be delighted he's got what he wanted. No way can I be around when that article comes out - the acute embarrassment of it all. I'd rather die. People often use this expression but I mean it for real. I'm left with *Hobson's choice* – if I'm here, I'll experience a living death; the alternative is the real thing. Shit. I'm on my own, there's no way out of this one.

It seems a long way down. That pupil walking on the terrace below looks so tiny. It reminds me of my visits with M-C to The Eiffel Tower and looking down from the first floor – *le premier étage* - at the hustle and bustle of the tourists at ground level. As I now look out at the scene below – the parade ground, the sports' fields sloping down to the river beyond – instead of being inspired by the beauty of the prospect, as I usually am, on this occasion I can't prevent myself from reflecting on the dire situation into which my greed and sexual drive have led me. It's entirely my fault that I've got into this desperate situation, they were my choices all along the way. No one else is to blame.

I can feel the final remnants of my energy ebbing away. This is it. These are my final moments on earth. I have to end it all because I can't stand the mental pain any longer....this is worse than any physical pain I have ever endured, even worse than when I dislocated my kneecap playing rugby at uni and that was horrendous. What I'm feeling now is worse, far worse.... I feel so distressed, it's like I've been thrown into a deep, dark pit. For once in my life, I desperately want mum and dad with me. Now I realise how much I love them. Will they forgive me?

I always wondered what profound depression feels like. That word 'depression', which is bandied about so readily these days every time someone feels unhappy. This is depression, alright, what I'm experiencing now. I've been on earth a mere forty-three years, sixteen years longer than Bolan, three years longer than Lennon, I suppose, but, anyway, how desperately sad, not only for me but for Marie-Christine and for Karl. How will M-C ever be able to explain to him what happened to his dad? Will she hide all photos of me? Will there be embarrassed glances every time my name comes up in conversation in front of him? Will her new husband – such a beautiful woman will surely find someone else to share her life – ever mention me? Will what I've done haunt her for the rest of her life? Will Karl conceal the identity of his real father, just like I've done? Bugger it. I'm crying again.

I bet Cranford'll refuse to hang my portrait in the main hall, alongside all the other previous Heads – they'll be too embarrassed. I expect the pupils will joke that *my* portrait is the 'little running green man' above the fire exit door. That'll be a source of merriment for generations, no doubt.

I've got to stop feeling sorry for myself. I'm still fucking crying, so that must stop. I mustn't think of my wife and child, not now, because it's too late. I should've been thinking of them instead of fucking Mary Anne and that other girl, what was her name? Chantelle. My family's better off without me; Cranford, on which I've brought ignominy and shame, in the general scheme of things is better off without me; the world is better off without me.

I can't stop these tears – my eyes are so wet I can't focus properly. Bugger.

I've proven myself to be capable of being a vicious, ruthless, calculating, selfish cheat. I may, on the face of it, have been the golden boy all through my life, but you can't conceal a flawed character for ever. You can fool some of the people some of the time but the truth will always emerge, sooner or later. I've been telling pupils this since I started teaching. I have acquired a PhD, maybe, I've even been privileged to study at the best university in the world, was once the youngest Head in the land and have been blessed with very good looks, but it all counts for nothing if inside there is no soul and I fucking well sold mine, just like Dorian Gray. Was I born evil or am I one of those people who have the capacity, depending on the circumstance, of being evil? In my case, I've appeared to the world as handsome, debonair, charming but this picture was inversely proportionate to the inexorably growing unsightliness of my inner being. In truth, I've ended up as ugly as that portrait in Dorian Gray's attic.

I know what people are going to say – 'it was his choice to throw it all away, to throw himself away, he's better off dead, the world is better off without him.' 'We never really trusted him – he seemed too good to be true: smarmy I'd call him.' 'If you were in his 'camp', you were OK but cross him at your peril.' 'He was just an egoistic, cunning, cruel, privileged bully.' 'He wanted his cake and to eat it, he wanted everything on his own terms, and more.' 'I hate people like that, born to wealth and privilege and abusing it.' 'What a bastard to have betrayed his wife and kids like that – has he no respect for anyone?' 'Pervert.' 'Murderer.' 'Nazi offspring, what do you expect?'

I can't stand this torture any longer. I'm confused, thoroughly depressed and bloody frightened.

I cannot be around to face the music. I cannot face the Sunday exposé. I'm too weak. I'm too sensitive. The time has come. This is it. I must end it all. Now! Now, for fuck's sake! Now!

After removing his teaching gown and placing it, characteristically neatly, over the back of the teacher's chair in Classics Classroom 2, the broken man proceeded to open the fourth floor window, took a deep breath, tears having now saturated his face and, without

368

hesitation, jumped headlong onto the concrete below, his skull spattering into myriad pieces as it hit the ground full on. And that's where the body and the accompanying pieces lay for fully two minutes before a couple of boys emerged from the east side of the parade ground, both in smart house sports' kit, both carrying squash racquets. They were unsure, at a distance of some eighty metres, what it was lying there at the foot of the tower... as they approached they recognised the shape of a slumped man... as they got closer still, they perceived pieces of something they couldn't recognise, which were scattered at a radius of up to thirty feet. Neither of them picked up any of the remnants of their former Headmaster's brain but both soon realised there had been a terrible accident and went to find Matron.

The Epilogue
A TALE OF TWO CHURCHILLS

'Sometimes one has to wait until the evening to see how glorious the day has been.'
Sophocles

Matron Pat Crowe was at the scene within minutes and she immediately used her mobile telephone to summon Deputy Headmaster, Nathan Worsthorne. The latter made immediate arrangements for the area to be cordoned off, having already dialled 999 from his office.

Before long, the disruption to the tranquillity of Cranford was compounded by the sound of police and ambulance sirens. Worsthorne sent for a number of senior colleagues and asked them to organise an immediate assembly of the entire school community, no matter what they were wearing, in the chapel. Meanwhile, he put in a call to the Chairman of Governors. Harris turned out to be engaged in court. His secretary was persuaded to get an urgent note to him and, within fifteen minutes, she had called back to say that the Judge had adjourned the court proceedings and would arrive at the school within the hour.

Within that time the media circus had arrived, including photographers and a couple of local television crews. The housemasters ensured that the pupils assembled in silence, although it was impossible to prevent some of the younger pupils from sobbing, as rumours of the full horror of their headmaster's death permeated the community.

Within an hour of Joseph Howson's skull making contact with the concrete main school terrace, Marie-Christine was being comforted by a member of the ambulance crew back at Cranford House.

Meanwhile, Worsthorne entered the chapel he rarely attended, composed himself and began to address the whole community:

'Ladies and gentlemen, it would be superfluous of me to underline the depth of the tragedy which has engulfed the school this afternoon. I would like you all to try your best to compose yourselves. At this moment our thoughts and prayers,' (he found that word difficult to enunciate) 'must be with Mrs Howson and her family. I must remind you that Cranford has been in existence for well over a century. On account of the tragedy that has befallen us, precise details about how it happened we are still unsure, please understand that the world's spotlight will be upon us for some time. We must conduct ourselves with dignity and remind ourselves that we will recover from what has happened today. I cannot expect you not to discuss today's events amongst yourselves. For those of you who feel particularly upset, please talk to your housemaster or to whichever member of staff you wish. Let us for now have a few moments of silent contemplation and prayer.'

It was a masterful performance by the atheistic classicist, who managed to rise to the occasion with the professionalism for which he was known.

After a couple of minutes, Worsthorne publicly asked the school's Chaplain if he would come forward and address those assembled. The Reverend David Haversham was clearly in a state of shock and it took him a few moments to arrive at the pulpit. Worsthorne whispered to him, suggesting that he simply lead the community in an appropriate prayer and to keep his words brief and simple.

Haversham spoke in a faltering voice:

'This is the first time in my career as a Chaplain when I have had to speak to a full congregation without preparation. Like all of you, I am in a state of complete and utter shock about the death of our leader, Doctor Howson. I can only pray for the Lord to show his mercy and loving kindness to his soul and to provide his love and support to Marie-Christine Howson and to Karl, her son.'

The Chaplain then paused and seemed close to tears. He then echoed Worsthorne's theme, saying:

'We must show the world that we can withstand today's terrible event. May the peace of the Lord be with you and remain with you for evermore. Amen.'

To conclude, Haversham, in an emotional voice, said:

'Let us say the Lord's Prayer together.'

He led the throng, the prayer being delivered quietly and slowly. Haversham glanced at Worsthorne to indicate that he had finished. The latter returned to the rostrum.

'Thank you, Reverend Haversham.' Tight with emotion, he then addressed the assembled community once again:

'When you are dismissed, you are all to return to your classes or to the games field. There will be no exeats today. I must ask all of you not to engage in discussion with anyone whom you do not know or recognise. Of course, many of you will want to contact your parents but I ask you to wait until a letter is sent out to all later today, when we have a clearer understanding of what happened to Doctor Howson. Would the staff and prefects all actively assist pupils to return to their duties as quickly as possible? Housemasters, please remain behind for a few moments.'

The school pupils exited in unaccustomed silence, save the sounds of sniffling and sobbing.

He paused for a short while before addressing the Senior House Staff (the modern nomenclature for those who run a boarding house):

'Gentlemen, in accordance with my standing instructions, I have taken immediate charge of the school. I will be in touch with Lord Justice Harris, who is due to arrive any moment now, for further guidance. Meanwhile, I do not think I need to underline the need for vigilance on your part and I know that you will all do your best to get us through the next twenty-four hours or so without any breakdown of good order. I am sorry but there is no further time now for discussion about how it came to pass that Joseph fell to his death; we will have to await the coroner's report sometime tomorrow. Please, I implore you all, to keep speculation within the community to a minimum.'

The housemasters, all being experienced old hands, nodded and expressed assent and support, then filed out of the chapel.

As Worsthorne emerged through the main chapel door into the bright sunshine, he was compelled to run a gauntlet of journalists and photographers, and he kept repeating to them that he was not able to comment, that he had no knowledge of the circumstances surrounding Joseph Howson's death and that, as far as the school was concerned, it was 'as far as is possible, in the short term, business as usual'. He announced into a camera lens that he had called the Chairman of Governors, Lord Harris, regarding the school making an official statement to the media, and his arrival was keenly awaited.

It was not long before Harris' chauffeured Rolls appeared. Worsthorne was waiting, as were the journalists and photographers, at the top of the drive in front of the main entrance doors. As Lord Harris emerged from the rear door of his car, there were numerous camera flashes. Harris' first words were an aside to Worsthorne:

'Any idea of the circumstances? An accident or suicide?' he whispered.

'None of us knows but it looks like he threw himself out of one of the tower windows.' Worsthorne pointed across to the main classroom building.

'I'll deal with the hacks for the time being. Thanks for your prompt response to the crisis.' Harris was an old hand at handling the press and he had no difficulty in rising to this occasion.

The entire corps was assembled in a circle, with an air of a pack of rottweilers about to pounce on its prey. Harris raised his right hand and asked for their attention and said that he would make an immediate statement. There was total silence as he began.

'Ladies and gentlemen, there has been a tragedy today for the family of our distinguished Headmaster, Doctor Joseph Howson, and also for Cranford College. My first thoughts must be with his family and I wish to offer my deepest condolences to Marie-Christine and her son, Karl, and hope that time will enable them to come to terms with what has happened. As for the school, Cranford is a great British institution, which has been in existence for over 100 years. Given time we will come to terms with today's tragedy and carry on offering our pupils a first-class education, to which Doctor Howson devoted the last two and a bit years of his professional life. I entreat you all to take these facts into consideration when you produce your copy for tomorrow morning's papers. I have nothing further to say at this point but there will, of course, be a press conference in due course when we know precisely how Doctor Howson's tragic death came to pass. Thank you for your attention.'

As usual, there was a flurry of questions thrown Harris' way, which he chose to ignore. He walked purposefully into the main school door, Worsthorne at his side.

It wasn't long before speculation was rife. By the following morning a myriad details of Joseph Howson's private life were in the public domain. Needless to state, the police had immediately leaked details of their interviews with Howson and one tabloid included references to his involvement with a **'drugged-up hooker, who had disappeared in suspicious circumstances'**. The press on these occasions has scant regard for the feelings of family and friends, being all too aware that the more salacious the story, the more copies will be sold. In the grounds of Cranford College there seemed to be more media employees than pupils.

Nathan Worsthorne joined the Board of Governors to discuss the best way forward.

Lord Harris, from the Chair, opened proceedings:

'There is so much disruption, which is likely to continue for some time, that I feel it prudent that we suspend term forthwith. I suggest a week's break for those pupils who live in Britain. We can make arrangements for the foreign students to remain in situ.'

There was general agreement that it would be fruitless to attempt to carry on as normal. A short break seemed to be the optimum way forward.

Harris continued: 'I have just finished a lengthy interview with DI Latham, from Harleybury Police Station, and I'm afraid Joseph had gotten himself involved with a number of unsavoury characters. The full, precise nature of the events leading up to his death have been written in a letter, which Joseph asked to be handed to his wife, following his death, so I can confirm there is no doubt that he threw himself out of an upper window yesterday afternoon.'

At this point Sir Marcus Silver, sitting to Lord Harris' right, started to sniffle audibly.

Harris paused for a short while, as Sir Marcus regained his composure.

'One individual, in particular, seemed to be at the centre of most of his woes, a young prostitute. It seems she visited Joseph here at the school, at the lodge house, on a number of occasions. Unfortunately, she subsequently resorted to blackmail, prompted by her boyfriend, a drug addict, who, some of you will remember, briefly interrupted our procession from the Carol Service last year.'

Most of the Governors remembered the strange incident all too well.

'The girl and her boyfriend have now disappeared from the face of the earth, as they say, and, although he has no proof, D.I. Latham suspects that Joseph may have been, in some way, involved in their disappearance. I daresay we shall be learning more about this in due course.'

Harris slowly poured himself a glass of water amidst stunned silence. The eminent Judge had conducted many harrowing court trials during his illustrious career but he could never remember overseeing such an emotionally charged gathering as that morning in the Cranford College Conference Room.

'Another area of much disquiet is Joseph's familial background and you may not be aware that Ben Fine has been pursuing a relentless campaign behind the scenes since he left Cranford a year ago, in a bid to shed light on, as he describes it, 'the real Joseph Howson'. He uncovered details about Joseph's biological and adoptive fathers' Nazi involvement, in itself not an insurmountable difficulty for us to have managed as a school. However, his dogged detective work subsequently led to other areas being uncovered which were of more concern. We must not be critical of Ben for his unalloyed determination to reveal the truth.'

Total incredulity was etched on the faces of all assembled. After a lengthy pause, Harris continued:

'I have another rendezvous with the press corps shortly, but, before doing so, I am going via the Common Room, to address the staff. Gentlemen, if I could ask you all to remain on the premises for the time being, as I think we will need to re-convene before the end of the day. Now, if you will excuse me for the moment.'

Harris rose to his feet, looked at each member of the Board sitting either side of the long conference table, nodded and proceeded to make his way across the quad to the Common Room, where all seventy members of staff were waiting. The Worst was at the door to greet him.

'Please sit down,' Harris said to the assembled staff, as he entered. Even though the Worst had set a chair for him, Harris preferred to stand to make his address.

He began:

'This has been an extremely difficult twenty-four hours for Cranford College and I fear it is going to get worse before it gets better. There are a number of details surrounding Joseph Howson's death, which are still to be revealed. Some of them will be hard to take, difficult to comprehend and some downright shocking. I, myself, am not fully aware of all that had been going on behind the scenes in Joseph's life during recent years, suffice to say he ended up a very troubled and unhappy man. I, and only I, will be in a position to furnish you with the truth in the coming days, so please be sceptical about much of what you read in the daily papers. In any event, gentlemen, now is the time for total unity, we must speak with one voice, we must put the century-old reputation of Cranford College at the forefront of our hearts and minds. Our duty is to the re-establishment of Cranford as Britain's premier public school. This disaster will either destroy this unparalleled educational establishment or it will make it stronger, more closely-knit. We cannot afford any weak links, we cannot tolerate so much as a word out of place. We must all do our duty and be loyal to the brand that is Cranford. I am certain I can rely on each and every one of you. Thank you. I must now face the press, who are awaiting my presence in Big School.'

With the Worst at his side, Harris swiftly made his way the short distance down the Geography corridor to the awaiting corps of press. As soon as he entered the Hall, there were more camera flashes.

The first question was from a television news reporter:

'Was your Lordship aware of Dr Howson's background?'

The Judge, who had long experience of the folly of being less than frank with the modern media, responded, 'I knew nothing to Dr Howson's personal discredit. I was aware of the nature of his adoptive background.'

'Did you know that his adoptive father, Michael Howson had links with the Nazis and, furthermore, had been a suspect in the slaying of a Jewish shopkeeper in 1936?'

'I was informed of these facts very recently.'

'Why didn't you act upon the information regarding the shopkeeper?'

'This referred to an incident which took place a quarter of a century before Dr Howson's birth. Dr Howson had assured me that he had been unaware of the accusation. I did not feel that this information could possibly affect Dr Howson's suitability as Head of Cranford.'

'Would you have appointed him if you had known about this at the time and had you been aware that Dr Howson's real father reached the rank of Grüppenführer in the Nazi Party and was possibly linked to the death of a Jewish financier?'

'These incidents happened many years prior to Dr Howson's birth. How can anyone hold him in any way responsible for, what actually are, unproven allegations? I cannot speculate on the viewpoint which would have been taken by the Governors. Dr Howson had an immaculate professional record and his application was considered to be far and away the most impressive of the one hundred plus we had received for the post. I was made aware by Dr Howson's knowledge of the details of his family background. I questioned him thoroughly and had no reason to disbelieve him when he told that he knew little about his birth family. I saw no reason to doubt him.'

'Did you know about his fascist leanings?'

'I reject that he had fascist leanings.'

'Were you not, at least, concerned about his political views?'

'I was aware that Dr Howson was hardly a Marxist,' (undercurrent of laughter) 'but then I don't think you would be likely to find too many Heads of independent schools with strong socialist leanings. This is a world away from being a fascist.'

'What do you think about the rumours that Dr Howson may have consorted with a prostitute?'

'I cannot comment on this. I have been made aware within the last twenty-four hours that an allegation of this kind has been made. It is obvious that Dr Howson has made errors of judgement and I am sure that you will all enjoy selling many newspapers with all the salacious revelations you are uncovering; suffice to say, as far as I am aware, none of the community here had any knowledge of such an allegation until today.'

'You must be aware that a former employee, Benjamin Fine, has been the person largely responsible for unearthing most of the facts. Do you feel that he has done the right thing?'

'Mr Fine has been right to bring any matters about which he had grave concerns into the public forum. I do not wish to speculate further.'

'Am I right in saying that Mr Fine was forced out of the school by Dr Howson?'

'Mr Fine resigned of his own volition.'

'Was he not removed from an internal position of seniority?'

'I do believe that there was a problem, which was dealt with by Dr Howson. The Governors were not involved.'

'Do you think that, in the light of what has been revealed, Mr Fine should be invited back to Cranford?'

'As for Mr Fine's position, I repeat, I am unable to make any comment at this stage. You must understand that I would be exceeding my powers as Chairman of Governors to comment at this point. There will be an extraordinary meeting of the Governing Body to discuss all relevant matters as soon as we are all aware of the full facts.'

'Do you think that Cranford will be irreparably damaged by all this?'

'I admit that this is, I believe, the worst thing that has happened in Cranford's history, worse even than the pupil revolt in 1894 over an alleged excess of beating by the then Headmaster, the Reverend William Saunders. However, Cranford is not responsible for the private life of Dr Howson. I am still proud to be Chairman of the School Governors and I have every confidence in the staff and pupils. A school community comprises many people, in our case well over 1,000. I believe that the parents will judge the school on its results in and out of the classroom and not on the tragedy of Dr Howson as an individual. I must emphasise that since Dr Howson took over the helm, this school has enjoyed hitherto unalloyed success and is currently top of the National League Tables; indeed, we are enjoying an extremely successful time in all areas of school life – please give Dr Howson credit for these outstanding achievements.'

'You are now without an appointed Headmaster. What do you propose to do about this?'

'The school has a very capable and experienced Deputy Headmaster, who has temporarily taken charge.'

'Am I correct in saying that Mr Worsthorne is known to be an atheist with left wing sympathies?'

'It goes to show that we do not choose our staff on the basis of political and religious orientation, but on that of their abilities.'

'But Cranford is a Church of England foundation. Do you not have a problem with Mr Worsthorne on this matter?'

The Judge's composure was remarkable, given the rapid fire of awkward questions.

'I cannot deny that we have an emergency and that we have to do what is best for the school immediately. The current situation involves temporary measures. The Governors met with me just minutes ago and will be meeting again as soon as possible to determine the way forward. In any event, the post of Headmaster of Cranford will be advertised as soon as is practicable. Meanwhile, I have full confidence in Mr Worsthorne and his staff.'

'What about Dr Howson's widow? Will she be forced to move out of the Head's house?'

'I am sure that the Governors will treat Mrs Howson with respect, kindness and consideration.'

The Judge concluded that he didn't really feel he could add much more at this stage and that he would take one more question and then attend to the school's urgent business.

'You have already indicated that you are aware that the public will be very interested in all the revelations unfolding. Do you think that it will affect your ability to recruit new pupils next year?'

'I think that the parents of potential pupils are sufficiently discerning not to be unduly influenced by these events. This experience, if anything, will make us all stronger and I have full confidence that Cranford will continue to go from strength to strength in the classroom, on the field and in its extra curricular provision.'

With that, there was a chorus of 'thank you' and even the hardened press corps muttered how impressed they were with his Lordship's composure and the quality and detail of his responses. As for Worsthorne, he was very relieved that the Chairman had put himself into the firing line, as he was certain he himself could not have performed as well. In any case, he believed that it was better for general confidence that Cranford was represented by the distinguished public figure of the Lord Justice than a hitherto unknown schoolmaster. Without appearing obsequious, Worsthorne congratulated the Judge on the manner in which he had fielded the press onslaught. The Judge smiled, retorting:

'Well, I was simply doing my job. I have had to face these sorts of hounds on so many occasions!'

With that, the Judge indicated that he would have a private talk with Worsthorne later that day but, in the meantime, needed to speak to Marie-Christine.

Marie-Christine was at home with her son, a nurse and her closest friend at the school, the wife of one of the housemasters. The Judge was anxious to reassure Marie-Christine that there would be no hurry for her to vacate Cranford House and that the Governors would continue to contribute generously towards her finances. It was Mrs Minns, Marie-Christine's personal assistant and close friend, who met the Judge as he made his way up the front drive leading to Cranford House. She informed him that Marie-Christine had asked to be left alone and that her parents were already on their way over to England. She added that Marie-Christine and Karl would be returning to France at the earliest opportunity. She asked the Judge if he would wait for a moment.

Minutes later she re-emerged from the house and handed him a piece of paper. 'Marie-Christine thinks that you ought to read this.'

My dearest Marie,

I am so, so sorry. What a mess I have made of things. I cannot find the words to express my sense of guilt and sorrow for what I have done to you and to Karl, whom I love more than life itself.

When I had choices, I made the ones which I thought best suited me. When temptation reared its ugly head, I succumbed. I thought, everyone thought, that I was strong, but, as events have proved, I am not. The last year has exposed the real man. My spoon may have been made of silver but I dipped it in acid. Part of me has been stripped bare and what has been uncovered is a tableau of weakness, of selfishness, of arrogance, of recklessness and of ruthlessness.

I had two human beings murdered because they had become a threat to my reputation, to my career and, most importantly, to my family life. Details of what happened are written in a diary, which I have placed in the bottom drawer of my study desk, hidden under a file. On the enclosing envelope is written:
"To be opened in the event of my death"
All I cared about is what was important to me, my good name, my family, yes, my family and my reputation – these things are everything to me and if it entailed ending other people's lives to protect my interests, then I acted accordingly.

The girl I had killed was a prostitute, whom I had used purely and simply for selfish sexual gratification, no more, no less. She eventually discovered who I really was and, prompted by her boyfriend, (an appalling specimen of humanity if ever there was one, whom I also had killed), they both proceeded to blackmail me.

My love, these have been dark days. I acted as normally as I could in front of you and Karl (a veritable tour-de-force, I'm sure you'll agree) but it was nigh on impossible, at times, to maintain the pretence, such was the anxiety inside. I know you had an inkling all was not well; you always know, don't you? My school went from strength to strength as my state of mind commensurately deteriorated. I had no choice – it was either the blackmailers or I to win this particular battle; they would never have left me alone. Joseph Howson always wins, as you well know!

You know that I am not all evil. You know that I would do anything for you and for Karl. That is why I am about to do what will have been done by the time you read this. I could not bear being alive without you and Karl. You are the only woman I have loved and you have borne me the most beautiful child on the earth and I thank you for this with all my heart. Quite simply, I could not bear having to spend the rest of my days knowing you and my beloved son were no longer part of my existence. I prefer to die for this reason alone.

As for my background, I did not choose it. Was it a crime to have been in awe of the father I never knew? I was brought up that way. I never knew about dad Michael's crimes, nor did I know about the bad things my real father did: I was told only about the service he did for the fatherland and his bravery in refusing to be taken alive by the enemies of that fatherland.

As for Cranford, I loved my job and loved the school. As you know, I worked hard to fulfil the promises I had given to Lord Harris, Sir Marcus and the Governors. The mistake I made was bowing to sexual temptation, for which I am to pay the ultimate price.

Once again, I am faced with no choice. I cannot face staying alive and losing everything I have worked so hard for. I must join my real father. Give my love to mum and dad and say sorry. Also, tell your parents they have the most beautiful daughter in the world. Lastly, when he is old enough, tell Karl how much I loved him, more than life itself, just the way I feel about his mother.

Please don't think too badly of me, chérie, and, once again, I am so, so sorry. Thanks for all the good times together and now try and forget about me and move on with your life.

I love you,
Joseph X.

Harris stared at the letter and was obliged to catch a tear before it left his eye.

'Excuse me, Sir, but Marie-Christine asked if you would be kind enough to hand the letter on to the appropriate authorities. She would like it returned to her in due course.'

The Judge made his way back across to the main school complex, in order to arrange for the letter to be taken down to D.I. Latham and to call a follow-up meeting with the Governors. Within the hour all had reconvened. Harris proceeded to divulge the contents of the letter amidst a deathly hush.

'If I could prevail upon you all to be discreet for the time being, until I have had the opportunity to inform the staff of the contents of the letter. The question of the 'succession' will have to be dealt with very urgently and, to this end, I have sent for Nathan Worsthorne. We will be having an informal chat in private.'

Almost on cue, there was a knock on the Conference Room door.

'Excuse me, Gentlemen.'

Harris beckoned the Worst to follow him into an adjoining room.

'Nathan, I am very grateful for all you have done since Joseph's death. You have certainly earned about a year's salary in only a few hours! What do you think we should do about the management situation? Who should we go for as the interim Head?'

Worsthorne's response was immediate:

'Your Lordship, I have tried my best today, in these very traumatic circumstances, but I have never aspired to the office of Headmaster. I will, of course, do whatever is needed but I know that I cannot convincingly preside over Christian services in a Christian chapel, which we claim in our prospectus is at the centre of school life. There are others who I believe are better fitted to hold the reins while the Governors go through the long, drawn-out process of appointing a new permanent Head.'

'I understand your position. I am sure that you are capable of holding the fort, as it were, but if you feel that the Governors should consider alternatives, then I would be very grateful for your advice.'

'Well frankly, you may think that what I have to say is controversial but I shall say it nevertheless. There are two or three possible candidates. In particular, there are the two most senior current housemasters, as well as one housemaster, who recently retired. All of them have experience and have the right 'religious credentials'; however, my concern would be that none of them has very much academic standing and I would doubt if any would command sufficient respect and confidence from some of our older and more able staff. I am going to make a bold and outrageous suggestion. Would you hear me out?'

'Of course. You are the man on the spot. You know the staff. Please go ahead.'

'I am going to recommend that you recall Benjamin Fine. He has the experience, the capability and, frankly, I believe that he is the person most likely to restore public confidence in the school. He knows this place inside out. What's more, he would've been a Headmaster years ago if he hadn't devoted himself so single-mindedly to this school.'

'Nevertheless, Fine has no experience of any responsibility above running a House. Also, am I not right in saying that he was removed from his position as Housemaster for unprofessional conduct?'

'Fine is a Balliol Scholar, a man of penetrating intellect, enormous integrity and as adaptable and capable a chap as I have ever come across. He is also of Jewish origin and his appointment would make a clear statement of Cranford's distance from the values rumoured to be espoused by the late Dr Howson. With respect to the Jeremy Major incident, I must tell you, Tony, that I have never been entirely happy about that. The boy who complained was not of good character and, furthermore, against my advice and that of other senior colleagues, he was made a house prefect.'

386

'Is that so? Well perhaps you could urgently investigate the circumstances and provide me with a report on this as soon as possible?'

'Will do,' said Worsthorne, scribbling a note in his pocket book in his usual organised manner.

'One other thing, Nathan, Fine is a bachelor. That is not ideal these days. The Governors would want to appoint a married man.'

'I agree, but I have a feeling that Benjamin is not going to remain a bachelor for long. As you must be aware, he is very friendly with Sarah, the HM's secretary, who has handed in her resignation for undisclosed reasons, although now we can be sure that it was due to information she had obtained from Benjamin about Joseph. I have heard on the grapevine that the two will be announcing their engagement in the near future.'

Harris smiled. 'Another consideration is whether Fine can be relied upon to be a safe pair of hands. After all, his activities have in some way brought the school into disrepute.'

'Fine was at Cranford for almost a third of a century. He has a reputation for professionalism and discretion. It would be an understatement to say that Dr Howson treated him unfairly. After all, Fine wanted to clear his name. He felt that to do that he had to discredit Howson. You could argue that he has the strength of character and single-minded determination that we need now. I don't think a safe pair of hands is the answer. We need someone for the wider school community to rally around. I think he would be honoured to be asked and I have no doubt that he would rise to the occasion and give Cranford his total loyalty. After all, his target was Howson, not Cranford, and he has succeeded.'

'Well, Nathan, I leave it to you to investigate the Jeremy Major incident. If there is anything you can do discreetly to ascertain the likelihood of er... marriage plans, we would be extremely grateful.'

Worsthorne's investigation did not take long. He obtained the young man's statement from the file and lost no time in summoning Major. He asked him to recount his statement against Fine. Major repeated what he had said in his statement but seemed uncomfortable about recounting it.

Worsthorne asked him directly:

'Are you sure that Mr Fine was under the influence of drink at the time?'

'Pretty much so.'

'Did you smell any alcohol on his breath?'

Major was silent for a few moments. 'I couldn't be sure. I can't really remember that clearly.

'Did Mr Fine touch you?'

'Yes, he did'

'Did he touch any part of your body directly?'

'No, Sir, he grabbed hold of my collar.'

'Did he actually hurt you?'

Major remained silent.

'Come on, did he actually cause you any physical discomfort?'

'I was a bit shaken, Sir.'

'You'd been rather rude, hadn't you?

'I suppose I had, Sir.'

'Look, I need you to tell me the full truth. It is very important. If there is anything on your conscience about this matter, don't worry. You won't be in any trouble over it.'

Worsthorne didn't want to put words into the lad's mouth. He was hoping to induce him into making his own admission. He also didn't want to influence him to blame it on Howson, although, by now, Worsthorne had very little doubt that Howson had encouraged Major to elevate the incident into a complaint.

Worsthorne probed further:

'I presume you were frightened to criticise your housemaster to the Headmaster?'

The reply was rapid fire:

'Actually, Sir, I think Dr Howson was quite keen for me to make a complaint. To tell you the truth, I never complained at all. It was Dr Howson who made me describe what happened!'

Worsthorne then produced the official, signed statement from the file and showed it to the boy.

' I don't remember it being headed like that,' complained Major.

'What was it then?'

'Simply a statement of facts.'

'Are you telling me that the heading was not there when you signed it?'

'Positive! There was no heading. It must've been added afterwards.'

Worsthorne had what he wanted. He asked the boy if he would do the honourable thing and be prepared to withdraw his so-called complaint and sign to that effect. He also asked him to confirm in writing that there had been no such heading on the document which he had signed.

'Sorry about all this, Sir,' Major blurted.

'It wasn't your fault; you will remain a house prefect. There will be nothing recorded to your detriment concerning this matter. You can go now. I will prepare a statement for you to agree and sign. Could you come back in about half an hour?'

In effect, it took him only five minutes to prepare a short and simple statement for the young man to sign.

Worsthorne decided to tackle the marriage issue as soon as possible. He telephoned Fine and came straight to the point,

'You must be aware that at the moment your star is rising high in the firmament. I have some very good news: Jeremy Major has retracted his complaint against you. Indeed, it transpires that he had never even complained in the first place.'

'Thank you, Nathan, I knew I could rely upon you to do the right thing.'

'It wasn't my idea. It was Lord Harris'! He is thinking about reinstating you in some way or other. Would you be interested?'

'I miss Cranford, but I would return only if I were fully restored to my position.'

'I think you can rest assured that there would be no question of you returning to a lower position than that. In fact, there is a possibility that you might be asked to take on considerable responsibility. Will you forgive me, but how is Sarah? I understand that the two of you have become quite close.'

'Well, Nathan, I don't at this stage want this bandied about, but Sarah and I will shortly be announcing our engagement to be married.'

'Congratulations. I couldn't think of a lovelier woman. Would you allow me to convey this information to Lord Harris?'

'Why on earth would he be interested?'

'Trust me, it will be of considerable interest to him.'

Events moved swiftly. The local paper announced that Benjamin Fine had been invited to return and act as Headmaster. Within a matter of days, it was also announced that the new acting Headmaster would be marrying Sarah, the school secretary.

Solomon Lazarus and his family were delighted with the news story, which appeared widely in the media. The *Daily Mail* wrote a full account under the sub-heading **AFTERMATH OF CRANFORD: 70 YEAR OLD MURDER MYSTERY SOLVED**. It finished with a quotation from the sole surviving son, Solomon Lazarus, who expressed how pleased he was that his father's killers had been named and that, although one was dead and the other, due to failing health, was unfit to stand trial, his family was extremely grateful to Benjamin Fine and the detective, Trench, who had been responsible for the official resolution of the mystery.

Readers were treated to lurid biographical accounts of the exploits of Howson's real father and the activities of the SS Secret Service. They were also informed of the arrest of two Harleybury men, picked up in central London, who were both "assisting" the police in their enquiries into the disappearance of Mary Anne Marshall and Kenneth Churchill. Many stories about the exploits of Benjamin Fine appeared. One was headed: **THE SCHOLAR WHO CAME IN FROM THE COLD**. Fine's return in glory was compared to the wartime recall of Churchill from retirement, to lead the nation's war effort.

As for Mary Anne's and Kenny's bodies, they were gone forever but the circumstances surrounding their death were fully outlined in Howson's diary.

Stories about Frost's Detective Agency painted Trench as comparable to Philip Marlowe, legendary fictional detective, which afforded the agency more work than they could possibly cope with.

The wedding of Benjamin Fine and Sarah took place in the Cranford chapel the following summer, under the Reverend David Haversham. The Governors had eventually advertised the permanent headship of Cranford and Benjamin had been invited to apply. By the time candidates had been selected for the shortlist, the Governors were so pleased with his interim performance, particularly the raising of staff morale and the restoration of parental confidence, that he was the unanimous choice and was confirmed, in May 2003, as the fifteenth Headmaster of Cranford College.

****

SIMON WARR

Simon Warr, M. A. was educated at the Royal Masonic School for Boys, near Watford, and, on leaving school, after a spell at drama school in London, he went on to university in the capital, reading Modern Languages and Education at Goldsmiths' College.

Most of his professional life has been spent either teaching French and Latin, and producing plays, at the Royal Hospital School, in Ipswich (a secondary Independent School) or broadcasting for BBC Radio Suffolk, where he commentates and reports on sport. He also has a weekly programme on the radio, entitled "The Warrzone", in which he comments unequivocally on issues of the day (this is coupled with a weekly column in the East Anglian Daily Times).

He has enjoyed a varied television career, including appearing on BBC's "Mastermind" with Magnus Magnusson (Magnus mentioned Simon in his autobiography "I've Started, So I'll Finish"), playing the role of Headmaster on Channel 4's successful series "That'll Teach 'Em" and appearing on "Noel's House Party", performing on stage with a famous glam rock band: these are just a few examples.

Passionate and erudite, he is regularly heard proffering his views on both Radio 2 and 5.

He resides either at his house in Suffolk or at his London flat.

www.simonwarr.co.uk

MICHAEL GOLD

Michael Gold was born in 1949 , the son of first generation Jewish immigrants from Russia, Poland and Lithuania. He was educated at Carmel College and Balliol College, Oxford where he was an Open scholar in Natural Science. He has a degree in Physics with Philosophy. His varied career has included flying instructor, airline pilot, public school master teaching Physics, Mathematics, English, Philosophy and Logic. He has been a Boarding School Headmaster, Director of an International Concert Orchestra, Church organist and choirmaster, Bridge Club Owner and Founder/ Director of a Bridge internet Company. He has also published research on Money Laundering. He was a county junior chess champion and a bridge Olympiad Gold medallist. He is also an amateur concert pianist and has participated in many chamber concerts as a virtuoso pianist.

Michael is married to Rosemary, has three adult sons and lives in Tilehurst, Reading.